Sixth Edition

Assessment of Student Achievement

Norman E. Gronlund
University of Illinois

Allyn and Bacon
Boston • London • Toronto • Sydney • Tokyo • Singapore

Series editor: Nancy Forsyth
Series editorial assistant: Cheryl Ouellette
Manufacturing buyer: Suzanne Lareau

Copyright © 1998, 1993, 1988, 1982, 1977, 1968 by Allyn & Bacon
A Viacom Company
Needham Heights, MA 02194

Internet: www.abacon.com
America Online: keyword: College Online

This book was formerly published under the titles *How to Make Achievement Tests
and Assessments, Constructing Achievement Tests,* and *How to Construct Achievement Tests.*

Library of Congress Cataloging-in-Publication Data

Gronlund, Norman Edward,
    Assessment of student achievement / Norman E. Gronlund—6th ed.
        p.   cm.
    Rev. ed. of: How to make achievement tests and assessments. 5th
ed.   c1993.
    Includes bibliographical references and index.
    ISBN 0-205-26858-7
    1. Achievement tests—Design and construction.   2. Examinations—
Design and construction.   I. Gronlund, Norman Edward.   How
to make achievement tests and assessments.   II. Title.
    LB3060.65.G766   1998
    371.26′1—dc21   97-28326
                                                                                    CIP

Printed in the United States of America
10 9 8 7 6   01

To
Marie Ann Gronlund
and
Dave, Derek, and Erik

◢ Contents

▶ Preface

Like earlier editions, this book is a practical guide for assessing the intended learning outcomes of classroom instruction. It is based on the premise that assessment of student achievement plays a vital role in instruction and that its main goal is to improve learning. All other uses are secondary.

The new title, *Assessment of Student Achievement*, Sixth Edition, reflects the shift from major concern with classroom testing to greater emphasis on other types of achievement assessments. The book still stresses the importance of using both classroom tests and performance assessments, however, for a comprehensive assessment of all intended learning outcomes. Each makes a unique and important contribution and, thereby, complement and supplement each other.

In addition to knowing how to prepare and use classroom tests and performance assessments, teachers need to know how to assign grades and how to interpret standardized test scores to students and parents. Each of these topics is covered in a separate chapter. A final chapter on validity and reliability provides a general framework for preparing and using classroom assessments and for evaluating standardized tests. It was placed last, and written as an independent chapter, so that it could be used wherever it best fits the course schedule. An introduction to the basic features of validity and reliability were included in Chapter 2, along with a list of ways for "building in" validity and reliability during the preparation of tests and performance assessments.

This sixth edition of this book includes a number of important changes, including the following:

1. The first chapter was changed from a narrow focus on testing to the broader concept of assessment.
2. A new Chapter 2 was added that describes the various assessment procedures used in teaching and the basic qualities of an effective assessment.
3. The method of item analysis in Chapter 7 was simplified and illustrated for use with classroom tests.
4. The chapter on performance assessment was expanded to include more comprehensive types of assessments and more attention to scoring.

5. An illustration of how to compute composite scores for grading was added to Chapter 9.
6. Chapter 10 was completely rewritten to focus on interpreting standardized test results.
7. In Chapter 11 the description of validity was revised and the consequences of using an assessment was added. A description of the reliability of performance assessments was added to the reliability section.
8. New boxed material was added to some chapters to highlight significant points.
9. A glossary of assessment terms was added.
10. New references were added to the "Additional Reading" lists.

Like earlier editions, this book presents the material in a simple, direct, and understandable manner without slighting basic concepts or sacrificing technical accuracy. Numerous practical examples are provided, and checklists, boxed material, and summaries of main points are used to aid in learning the content. No prior knowledge of measurement or statistics is required to understand the material in the book. In short, it is a practical guide for beginners. More elaborate treatment of many of the topics can be found in the "Additional Reading" list at the end of each chapter.

My appreciation is expressed to the reviewers who made valuable suggestions for revision: Betty Jo Simmons of Longwood College, Paul Nichols of the University of Wisconsin, Milwaukee, and James Terwilliger of the University of Minnesota, Minneapolis; to the authors and publishers referred to in this book; to the Allyn and Bacon editorial staff; to Irene Palmer for her excellent typing; and to my wife, Marie, for her patience and understanding during work on this revision.

N. E. G.

▶ 1

Achievement Assessment and Instruction

Studying this chapter should enable you to[1]

1. Explain why both testing and performance assessment are important in achievement assessment.
2. Write a definition of **achievement assessment.**
3. Describe the relation between instruction and assessment.
4. Distinguish among the various roles of assessment in the instructional process.
5. List the ways that assessments can directly aid learning.

All of us have taken various types of paper-and-pencil tests during our many years of schooling. Some of these were teacher made tests requiring us to select an answer (e.g., true-false, multiple choice, or matching) or to supply an answer (e.g., short answer or essay). Others were standardized tests of aptitude or achievement, primarily using multiple-choice items. The widespread use of paper-and-pencil testing in the schools was due, at least in part, to the

---

[1]Space does not permit using the preferred two-step method of stating intended learning outcomes described in Chapter 3. These statements, however, should provide a focus for your study and for application of the content in each chapter.

efficiency with which they could measure a large number of learning outcomes and the ease of scoring and recording the results.

In recent years there has been a reaction to the heavy emphasis on paper-and-pencil testing. Some critics have contended that there should be more emphasis on the assessment of **authentic,** "real-life" tasks (e.g., solving problems that exist in the real world). Others have contended that paper-and-pencil testing should be replaced, at least in part, by **alternative** types of assessment. Some reactions have been extreme but they highlight the importance of focusing more attention on the actual performance of students. If you want to determine if students can write, have them write something. If you want to determine if students can operate a machine, have them operate the machine. If you want to determine if students can conduct an experiment, have them conduct an experiment. In short, if you want to determine if they can perform a task, have them perform the task. There is little doubt that more emphasis on performance assessment in the schools would improve the assessment of our intended learning outcomes. However, paper-and-pencil testing still has an important role to play, even as we focus more directly on performance-based tasks.

Most types of performance have a knowledge component that is important to the performance. Good writing includes such factors as knowledge of vocabulary, grammar and spelling. These are not well sampled by a writing task because we tend to use only the words we know, use sentence structures that we can punctuate easily, and substitute words we can spell for those we can't spell. Thus, in writing, we can structure it to conceal our weaknesses. A separate test of vocabulary, grammar, and spelling can identify these weaknesses and be used to improve writing skill. Just don't interpret the test results as measures of "writing ability." The tests measure knowledge useful in

---

Commonly Used Assessment Terms

Performance Assessments Assessments requiring students to demonstrate their achievement of understandings and skills by actually performing a task or set of tasks (e.g., writing a story, giving a speech, conducting an experiment, operating a machine).

Alternative Assessments A title for performance assessments that emphasizes that these assessment methods provide an alternative to traditional paper-and-pencil testing.

Authentic Assessments A title for performance assessments that stresses the importance of focusing on the application of understandings and skills to real problems in "real world" contextual settings.

writing but writing ability is determined by assessing the actual writing (**per-formance assessment**). Similarly, in operating machinery, the actual opera-tion of the machine is the ultimate goal, but tests measuring knowledge of how to operate the machine and the safety precautions to follow may be needed before the hands-on performance assessment. Likewise, before con-ducting an experiment, tests can be used to determine how well students know the information needed for a well controlled experiment.

Throughout this book, the emphasis will be on achievement assessment that includes both paper-and-pencil testing and performance assessment. Tests can provide direct measures of many important learning outcomes, ranging from simple to complex, and they can provide needed information for assessing and improving actual performance tasks. Thus, although we should strive for as authentic assessment as we can obtain, within the con-strains of the school setting, both tests and performance-based tasks are needed for a complete assessment of student achievement.

As used in this book, **achievement assessment** is a broad category that includes all of the various methods for determining the extent to which stu-dents are achieving the intended learning outcomes of instruction. Because we are limiting our concern to achievement assessment, the single term *as-sessment* is used throughout the book as a matter of convenience.

RELATION BETWEEN INSTRUCTION AND ASSESSMENT

In preparing for any type of instructional program our main concern is "How can we most effectively bring about student learning?" As we ponder this question, our attention is naturally directed toward the methods and materi-als of instruction. However, at the same time we should also consider the role of assessment in the instructional process. When properly designed and ap-propriately used, assessment procedures can contribute to more effective in-struction and greater student learning.

The close relation between instruction and assessment can be seen in Table 1.1. Both require that we clearly specify the learning outcomes to be achieved by students, and the provisions of well-designed assessments closely parallel the characteristics of effective instruction. This relation high-lights the importance of broadening instructional planning to include assess-ment planning. The typical procedure of limiting instructional planning to the teaching-learning process is inadequate. Effective instruction requires that we expand our concern to a teaching-learning-assessment process, with assessment as a basic part of the instructional program. As with all instruc-tional activities, the main function of assessment is to improve learning and it can contribute to this end in a number of ways.

TABLE 1.1   Relation Between Instruction and Assessment

INSTRUCTION	ASSESSMENT
Instruction is most effective when	**Assessment is most effective when**
1. Directed toward a clearly defined set of intended learning outcomes.	1. Designed to assess a clearly defined set of intended learning outcomes.
2. The methods and materials of instruction are congruent with the outcomes to be achieved.	2. The nature and function of the assessments are congruent with the outcomes to be assessed.
3. The instruction is designed to fit the characteristics and needs of the students.	3. The assessments are designed to fit the relevant student characteristics and are fair to everyone.
4. Instructional decisions are based on information that is meaningful, dependable, and relevant.	4. Assessments provide information that is meaningful, dependable, and relevant.
5. Students are periodically informed concerning their learning progress.	5. Provision is made for giving the students early feedback of assessment results.
6. Remediation is provided for students not achieving the intended learning.	6. Specific learning weaknesses are revealed by the assessment results.
7. Instructional effectiveness is periodically reviewed and the intended learning outcomes and instruction modified as needed.	7. Assessment results provide information useful for evaluating the appropriateness of the objectives, the methods, and the materials of instruction.

ASSESSMENT IN THE INSTRUCTIONAL PROCESS

To be fully integrated with instruction, plans for assessment should be made during the planning for instruction. From the beginning of instruction to the end there are numerous decisions that teachers need to make. Carefully planned assessment procedures can improve the effectiveness of many of these decisions by providing more objective information on which to base judgments. Let us consider some of the decisions teachers need to make at (1) the beginning of instruction, (2) during instruction, and (3) at the end of instruction.

Beginning of Instruction (Placement Assessment)

There are two major questions that teachers need to answer before proceeding with the instruction:

1. To what extent do the students possess the skills and abilities that are needed to begin instruction?

2. To what extent have the students already achieved the intended learning outcomes of the planned instruction?

Information concerning the first question are frequently obtained from *readiness* pretests. These are tests given at the beginning of a course or unit of instruction that cover those prerequisite skills necessary for success in the planned instruction. For example, a test of computational skill might be given at the beginning of an algebra course, or a test of English grammar might be given at the beginning of a German course. Students lacking in prerequisite skills could be given remedial work, or they could be placed in a special section that had lower prerequisites.

The second question is frequently answered by a *placement* pretest covering the intended learning outcomes of the planned instruction. This might very well be the same test that is given at the end of the instruction; preferably it should be another form of it. Here we are interested in determining whether students have already mastered some of the material we plan to include in our instruction. If they have, we might need to modify our teaching plans, encourage some students to skip particular units, and place other students at a more advanced level of instruction. The function of placement assessment is summarized in Figure 1.1.

In addition to the use of pretests, performance-based tasks may also be useful for determining entry skills. In the area of writing, for example, ob-

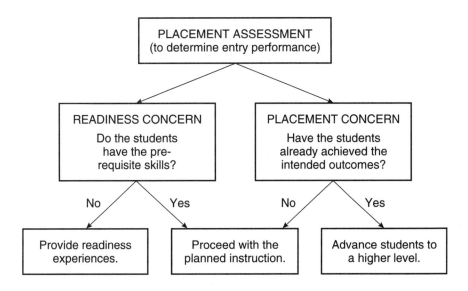

FIGURE 1.1   Simplified Model for the Instructional Role of Placement Assessment

taining writing samples at the beginning of instruction can establish a base for later assessments of progress. This type of preassessment would be especially valuable if portfolios of student work were to be maintained during the instruction.

The contribution that preassessment can make to instruction depends on the nature of the instruction, how well we know students, and how the results are to be used. A pretest in arithmetic may be quite useful at the beginning of an algebra course, whereas a pretest in a course that lacks a clearly defined set of prerequisite skills (e.g., social studies) may be of little value. Similarly, the results of a test of basic skills may be of great value to a new teacher unfamiliar with the students and of less value to an experienced teacher familiar with the students' backgrounds. In addition, preassessment will contribute little to the instructional program unless plans are made to remedy deficiencies, place students in the most beneficial position in the instructional sequence, or use the results as a base for assessing future progress. To be most effective, the use of preassessment should be considered during the instructional planning stage.

During Instruction (Formative and Diagnostic Assessment)

During the instructional program our main concern is with the learning progress being made by students. Questions such as the following must be answered.

1. On which learning tasks are the students progressing satisfactorily? On which ones do they need help?
2. Which students are having such severe learning problems that they need remedial work?

Tests used to monitor student progress during instruction are called *formative* tests. Formative tests are typically designed to measure the extent to which students have mastered the learning outcomes of a rather limited segment of instruction, such as a unit or a textbook chapter. These tests are similar to the quizzes and unit tests that teachers have traditionally used, but they place greater emphasis on (1) measuring all of the intended outcomes of the unit of instruction, and (2) using the results to improve learning (rather than to assign grades). The purpose is to identify the students' learning, successes and failures so that adjustments in instruction and learning can be made. When the majority of students fail a test item, or set of items, the material is typically retaught in a group setting. When a minority of students experience learning failures, alternate methods of study are usually prescribed for each student (for example, reading assignments in a second book, computer instruction, and visual aids). These corrective prescriptions are frequently keyed to each item, or to each set of items designed to measure a separate learning task, so that students can begin immediately after testing to correct their individual learning errors.

Formative assessment using performance-based tasks may involve periodic assessments of a product (e.g., writing sample, drawing) or of a process (e.g., giving a speech, operating a machine) with feedback to students concerning strengths and weaknesses. The aim here, as with formative testing, is to monitor learning progress and to provide corrective prescriptions to improve learning.

When a student's learning problems are so persistent that they cannot be resolved by the corrective prescriptions of formative assessment, a more intensive study of the student's learning difficulties is called for. It is here that *diagnostic* assessment is useful. Diagnostic assessment attempts to answer such questions as the following: Are the students having difficulty in addition because they don't know certain number combinations or because they don't know how to carry? Are the students' difficulties in reading German due to their inadequate knowledge of vocabulary or to their poor grasp of certain elements of grammar? Are the students unable to apply scientific principles to new situations because they don't understand the principles, because their knowledge of particular concepts is weak, or because the new situations are too unfamiliar to them? Thus, diagnostic assessment focuses on the common sources of error encountered by students, so that the learning difficulties can be pinpointed and remedied.

Diagnostic assessment can frequently be aided by the use of diagnostic tests. These tests typically include a relatively large number of test items in each specific area with slight variations from one set of items to the next so that the cause of specific learning errors can be identified. In detecting errors in the addition of whole numbers, for example, we might construct a test that includes a set of items requiring no carrying, a set that requires simple carrying, and one that requires repeated carrying to determine if carrying is the source of the difficulty. Unfortunately, diagnostic tests are difficult to construct in most areas of instruction. Therefore, we must depend more heavily on observation and judgment.

Diagnosing learning problems is a matter of degree. Formative assessment determines whether a student has mastered the learning tasks being taught and, if not, prescribes how to remedy the learning failures. Diagnostic assessment is designed to probe deeper into the causes of learning deficiencies that are left unresolved by formative assessment. Of course, this is not to imply that all learning problems can be overcome by formative and diagnostic assessment. These are simply methods to aid in the identification and diagnosis of specific learning difficulties so that appropriate remedial steps can be taken. Diagnosing and remedying severe learning problems fre-

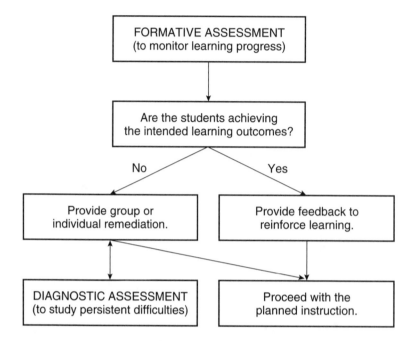

FIGURE 1.2   Simplified Model for the Instructional Role of Formative Assessment

quently requires a wide array of assessment procedures and the services of specially trained personnel. All we are attempting to do here is to show how formative and diagnostic assessment can contribute to improved student learning during instruction. The model presented in Figure 1.2 summarized the process.

End of Instruction (Summative Assessment)

At the end of a course or unit of instruction we are concerned primarily with the extent to which the students have achieved the intended outcomes of the instruction. Questions such as the following must be answered:

1. Which students have mastered the learning tasks to such a degree that they should proceed to the next course or unit of instruction?
2. What grade should be assigned to each student?

Achievement assessment at the end of instruction for the purpose of certifying mastery or assigning grades is called *summative* assessment. This assessment is typically comprehensive in coverage and includes both tests and

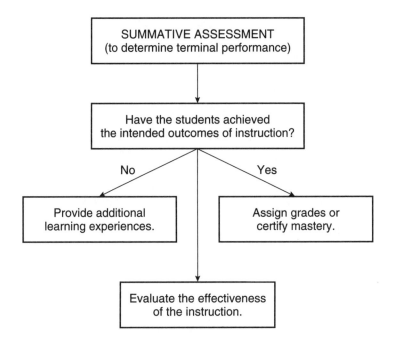

FIGURE 1.3   Simplified Model for the Instructional Role of Summative Assessment

performance assessments. Although the results are used primarily for grading, there should be some feedback to students and they should be used for evaluating the effectiveness of the instruction. See Figure 1.3 for the summative assessment model.

OTHER WAYS ASSESSMENTS CAN AID LEARNING

As noted in the previous section, assessments can aid the teacher in making various instructional decisions having a direct influence on student learning. In addition, assessments can aid student learning in a number of other ways.

Assessments Can Aid Student Motivation

A carefully planned assessment program can have a direct influence on student learning by (1) providing them with short-term goals, (2) clarifying the types of tasks to be learned, and (3) providing feedback concerning their learning progress. Short-term goals are more motivating than telling students

"Some day you will find this knowledge or skill useful." An expected assessment stimulates learning activity and directs it toward the learning tasks to be assessed. Its contribution to learning depends to a large extent on how faithfully our assessments reflect all of the important outcomes of the instruction and how we use the results. For example, if the application of principles is stressed in our assessment as well as in our teaching, we can expect students to direct greater efforts toward learning how to apply principles. Also, if the assessment results are reported to students as soon as possible, this feedback concerning their strengths and weaknesses in the application of principles will further clarify the nature of the task and indicate what changes are needed for effective performance. Thus, properly used assessments can motivate students to work toward the instructional objectives of a course by arousing greater learning activity, by directing it toward the intended learning outcomes, and by providing prompt knowledge of results.

Assessments Can Aid Retention and Transfer of Learning

Because assessments tend to direct students' learning efforts toward the intended outcomes of instruction, they can be used as tools for increasing the retention and transfer of learning. In general, learning outcomes at the understanding, application, and interpretation levels are likely to be retained longer and to have greater transfer value than outcomes at the knowledge level. By including assessments of these more complex learning outcomes, we can direct attention to their importance and provide reinforcing practice in the skills, applications, and interpretations we are attempting to develop. Thus, assessments can be used to supplement and complement our teaching efforts in these areas and thereby increase the likelihood that the learning will be of greater permanent value to the students.

Assessments Can Aid Student Self-Assessment

All instruction should be directed toward helping individuals better understand themselves so that they can make more intelligent decisions. Periodic assessment and feedback of the results can help students gain insight into what they can do well, the misconceptions that need correction, and the degree of skill they have in various areas. Such information provides the students with a more objective basis for assessing their own strengths and weaknesses. Properly used assessments tend to provide evidence of learning progress in such an objective and impartial way that the results can be accepted with little resistance or distortion. This assumes, of course, that the assessments are properly prepared and are being used to improve learning rather than to threaten or label students. In the latter instance, self-assessment is apt to be distorted by the psychological defense mechanisms an individual uses to maintain a positive self-image.

Assessments Can Aid In Evaluating Instructional Effectiveness

Assessment results can be used to evaluate the effectiveness of various aspects of the instructional process. For example, they can help determine the extent to which the instructional objectives were realistic, whether the methods and materials of instruction were appropriate, and how well the learning experiences were sequenced. When the majority of the students do poorly on an assessment, it may be the fault of the students but the difficulty is more likely to be found in the instruction. The teacher may be striving for learning outcomes that are unattainable by the students, may be using inappropriate materials, or may be using ineffective methods for bringing about the desired changes. An analysis of the students' responses and a class discussion of the results should provide clues to the source of the instructional difficulty so that corrective steps can be taken.

SUMMARY OF POINTS

1. In recent years there has been a reaction to the heavy emphasis on paper-and-pencil testing with a plea for more realistic performance assessment.
2. A well-balanced assessment program should include both testing and performance assessment, with each used where most appropriate.
3. *Achievement assessment* is a general category that includes a broad range of methods for determining the extent to which students are achieving intended learning outcomes.
4. Instruction is more effective when well-designed assessments are an integral part of the instructional process.
5. Assessment procedures can be used for measuring entry performance (placement assessment), monitoring learning progress (formative and diagnostic assessment), or measuring end of instruction achievement (summative assessments).
6. Achievement assessments can contribute to student motivation, the retention and transfer of learning, student self-evaluation skills, and an evaluation of instructional effectiveness.

ADDITIONAL READING

Airasian, P. W., *Classroom Assessment,* 3rd ed. (New York: McGraw-Hill, 1997). See Chapter 3, "Assessment for Instructional Planning," for a general discussion of the purpose and procedures of instructional planning.

Bloom, B. S., Madaus, G. T., and Hastings, J. T., *Evaluation to Improve Learning* (New York: McGraw-Hill, 1981). Chapters 4, 5, and 6 provide a comprehensive treatment of summative, diagnostic, and formative evaluation.

Linn, R. L., and Gronlund, N. E., *Measurement and Assessment in Teaching*, 7th ed. (Englewood Cliffs, NJ: Prentice-Hall, 1995). See Chapter 1, "The Role of Measurement and Assessment in Teaching," for a more extensive treatment of the material covered in this chapter.

McMillan, J. H., *Classroom Assessment* (Boston: Allyn & Bacon, 1997). See Chapter 1, "The Role of Assessment in Teaching," for descriptions of procedures and trends in classroom assessment and a list of assessment standards for teachers.

Stiggins, R. J., *Student-Centered Classroom Assessment* (Columbus, OH: Merrill, 1994). See Chapter 3, "Understanding the Critical Roles of Assessment," for discussions of how assessments are used in making instructional decisions and promoting student learning.

▶ 2

Nature of Student Assessment

Studying this chapter should enable you to

1. Describe a situation where both testing and performance assessment are needed and indicate why.
2. Describe the major types of assessment methods and give an example of each.
3. Distinguish between tests and performance assessments in terms of realism of tasks, complexity of tasks, assessment time needed, and judgment in scoring.
4. List the guidelines for effective student assessment.
5. Describe the meaning of validity and reliability and the role they play in preparing assessment procedures.
6. Distinguish between norm-referenced and criterion-referenced assessments.

As noted in the first chapter, *assessment* is used as a broad category that includes all of the various methods used to determine the extent to which students are achieving the intended learning outcomes of instruction. This includes both testing and performance assessments. To assess a student's driving ability, for example, an **objective test** is used to measure knowledge of how to drive and follow the rules of the road, and driving over a prescribed course (performance assessment) is used to determine skill in driving the automobile. The test on rules of the road covers a much larger sample of driving rules than are likely to be encountered in the driving performance, but skill in driving can only be determined by sitting behind the wheel and driving. Both are important. The knowledge test tells how well the student knows what to do and the performance assessment tells how skillfully the student can do it.

Teachers have tended to favor selection-type tests (i.e., multiple choice, true-false, matching) because many questions can be asked in a relatively short time, they are easy to administer and score, and the results can be expressed in numbers that are easily recorded, compared, and reported to others. Unfortunately, teachers have also limited selection-type tests almost entirely to knowledge of facts and terms. Various studies have shown that between 80 and 90 percent of teacher-made tests focus on knowledge outcomes. There is little doubt that this overemphasis on selection-type tests and simple knowledge outcomes have led to the movement toward assessment techniques that measure more complex learning outcomes in realistic settings. The fact that paper-and-pencil tests can be designed to measure a wide array of complex learning outcomes has frequently been overlooked in the movement toward performance assessment. It is our contention that education is best served by using both paper-and-pencil testing and the assessment of actual performance, with both focusing on more complex learning tasks than typically has been the case in the past.

MAJOR TYPES OF ASSESSMENT METHODS

Assessment methods vary widely but they can be summarized in four major categories as shown in Table 2.1. Selected-response tests require the student to choose the correct or best answer, as in multiple-choice, true-false, and matching tests. Supply response tests require students to respond with a word, short phrase, or complete essay answer. Restricted performance assessments are concerned with the performance of a limited task that is highly structured, such as writing a brief paragraph on a given topic, selecting laboratory equipment, measuring humidity, or locating information with a computer. Extended performance assessments involve more comprehensive and less structured performance tasks, such as writing a short story, conducting a laboratory experiment, predicting weather, or using a computer to solve a problem. Besides requiring more extended performances, the assessment typically requires students to integrate and apply knowledge and skills to performance tasks in a realistic setting. If there is a product involved (e.g., a short story) students may also be expected to review and revise the product before submitting it, to add greater realism to the task.

These major types of assessment can be further clarified by reviewing

TABLE 2.1   Summary Comparison of Assessment Methods

TESTING		PERFORMANCE ASSESSMENT	
SELECTED RESPONSE	**SUPPLY RESPONSE**	**RESTRICTED PERFORMANCE**	**EXTENDED PERFORMANCE**
LOW ◄—— REALISM OF TASKS ——► HIGH			
LOW ◄—— COMPLEXITY OF TASKS ——► HIGH			
LOW ◄—— ASSESSMENT TIME NEEDED ——► HIGH			
LOW ◄—— JUDGMENT IN SCORING ——► HIGH			

some of the characteristics that are typical of each. These have been summarized in Table 2.1.

Realism of Tasks

By realism of assessment tasks, we mean the extent to which they simulate performance in the real world. Traditional selection-type tests are low in realism because they involve selecting a response from a given set of possible answers. The response is limited to the listed alternatives and such highly structured problems seldom occur in the real world. The extended performance assessment is high in realism because it attempts to simulate performance in the real world. Assessing how well a student can drive an automobile, operate a machine, give a speech, or apply knowledge and understanding to a real-life problem (e.g., how to protect the environment) requires comprehensive sets of responses that approximate those occurring in the real world. In between these extremes are the supply-type tests (e.g., short answer and essay) and the restricted response performance assessments that provide a moderate amount of structure but greater freedom of response and thus more realistic type problems than the selection-type tests.

In addition to the movement to increase realism in assessment by moving toward extended performance assessment, there has also been a trend toward making traditional paper-and-pencil tests more authentic (i.e., have greater realism). This has resulted in the designing of tests to measure more complex learning outcomes and in the use of problems and procedures more like those in the real world. In a math problem, for example, students may be given more facts than are needed to solve the problem to see if they can select the facts needed to solve it. In solving a science problem, students might be given the freedom to select the procedure for solving the problem and be asked to justify the procedure used. In some cases this involves a shift from selection-type items to supply-type items but in others it may be a combination of the two items types (e.g., explain why the selected answer was chosen).

Complexity of Tasks

Selected-response items tend to be low in the complexity of the problem presented and in the nature of the expected response. Although items can be designed to measure understanding and thinking skills, they typically present a single, limited problem and require choice of the correct or best answer. Extended performance problems, on the other hand, typically involve multiple learning outcome, the integration of ideas and skills from a variety of sources, the availability of various possible solutions and the need for multiple criteria for evaluating the results (e.g., preparing a plan for reducing drug traffic in the United States). Similarly, performance of a hands-on nature involves complex movement patterns that are guided by the integration of information and specific skills from various learning experiences (e.g., playing a musical instrument, operating a machine, repairing electronic equipment). As with the realism category, supply-type tests fall in between the two extremes. Essay tests, for example, can be designed to measure the ability to select, integrate, and express ideas, but the tasks are usually more limited and structured than in performance assessments.

Assessment Time Needed

A large number of selected-response items can be administered to a group of students in a relatively short time and the results can be quickly scored, by hand or by machine. This efficiency has no doubt been a major factor in their widespread use. Performance assessments tend to be extremely time consuming. Some tasks may require days or even weeks to complete (e.g., conduct an experimental study) and others may require assessing students one at a time (e.g., giving a speech, operating a machine). In most cases, evaluating the process or product of the performance is also difficult and time consuming. Supply-response tests, like the essay test, require more time to score than selected-response tests but less than that of performance assessments.

The greater amount of time needed for performance assessment may result in loss of content coverage because of the limited number of assessment problems that can be included in the instructional program. This raises a question concerning the extent to which the assessment results are generalizable to other comparable tasks. We can present "real world" problems to students but problems are frequently unique to a particular contextual setting and the real world changes. Thus, transfer of learning is a key consideration in performance assessment. We can justify the greater time needed only if the assessment is an integral part of instruction and transferable learning outcomes are emphasized (e.g., reasoning, critical thinking, psychomotor skills).

Judgment in Scoring

The amount of judgment involved in scoring varies widely. Each selected-response item is marked right or wrong so the scoring is completely objective (i.e., different scorers will arrive at the same score). The essay test provides more freedom of response and this introduces greater subjectivity into the scoring. Different scorers can and do arrive at different scores as they weight elements of the answer differently (e.g., completeness, organization, clarity of writing, and the like) and introduce other personal biases into their judgments. As the tasks become more comprehensive and complex, as in performance assessment, the demands on teacher judgment become even greater. Complex performance tasks that involve the integration of various types of information and skill and may have multiple solutions make it difficult, and in many cases undesirable, to have model answers as might be used with essay testing. With performance assessment we are most likely to have to depend on identification of the **criteria** of a quality performance and then apply the criteria by means of a **rating scale** or set of **scoring rubrics.** Each of these steps is based on subjective judgment.

A review of these categories makes clear that each assessment method has its strengths and weaknesses. When we use selected-response tests, we can obtain a comprehensive coverage of a content domain, and can administer, score, and interpret it easily, but we sacrifice realism and some types of complexity. When we use extended performance assessment, we can obtain a high degree of realism and increase the complexity of the tasks we can assess, but the time needed for assessment is frequently excessive and the evaluation of the performance is highly judgmental. A useful rule would be to use the most efficient method as long as it is appropriate for assessing the intended learning outcomes, but don't neglect complex learning outcomes just because the assessment methods are time consuming and the results are difficult to score or judge.

GUIDELINES FOR EFFECTIVE STUDENT ASSESSMENT

The main purpose of a classroom assessment program is to improve student learning. This is most likely to result if assessment is closely integrated with instruction and is guided by a basic set of conditions. The following guidelines provide a general framework for using student assessment effectively.

1. *Effective assessment requires a clear conception of all intended learning outcomes.* During both instructional and assessment planning, we need to ask ourselves—What are the intended learning outcomes of the instruction? What types of knowledge, understanding, application, and performance skills are we willing to accept as evidence that the instruction has been successful? Here, there is always the danger of focusing too narrowly on knowledge outcomes because they are easy to identify, state, and measure. Unless we include the more complex learning outcomes at this stage, they are likely to be neglected during assessment. We need to specify all intended learning outcomes in terms of student performance and make plans to assess them all.

2. *Effective assessment requires that a variety of assessment procedures be used.* The vast array of possible learning outcomes in any particular area of instruction means that various types of assessment procedures must be considered when planning for assessment. Selected-response tests may be used for some learning outcomes and essay tests for others, where ability to express ideas is important. In assessing performance skills, where we must depend largely on judgment, rating scales or checklists may be needed.

In assessing the more complex learning outcomes, a combination of methods may be most suitable. Solving a complex problem, for example, may involve gathering information from diverse sources, analyzing it, integrating it, writing out a suggested solution, and making an oral presentation to a group. Similarly, locating and correcting a malfunction in a machine may involve reading a technical manual, identifying machine sounds, selecting proper tools, testing machine parts, and making the needed repairs. In addition to correcting the malfunction, speed of performance, following the proper sequence of steps, and similar factors may be an important part of the assessment. In evaluating performance skills, multiple assessment is likely to be the rule rather than the exception.

3. *Effective assessment requires that the instructional relevance of the procedures be considered.* Instructionally relevant assessment means that the intended outcomes of instruction, the domain of learning tasks, and the assessment procedures will all be in close agreement, as shown in Figure 2.1. It also means that plans for using the assessment results in the instructional program must be considered. Will the classroom test be sufficiently diagnostic to provide for remedial action? Can the assessment of a complex performance skill be designed as an on-going activity so that it can contribute directly to the instruction? These and similar questions are needed to obtain maximum integration of instruction and assessment. Remember, the main purpose of both instruction and assessment is to improve student learning. With a well-designed assessment program, assessment activities may become barely distinguishable from instructional activities.

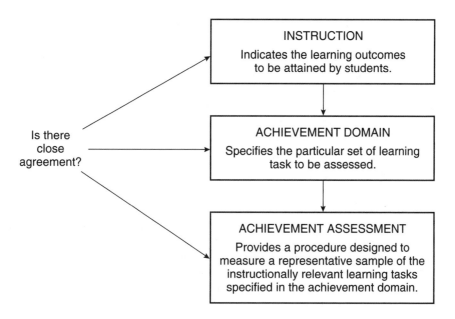

FIGURE 2.1   **Sequence in Preparing Instructionally Relevant Assessment**

4. *Effective assessment requires an adequate sample of student performance.* Assessment is always a matter of sampling. Our instruction typically covers numerous knowledge and skill outcomes, but because of the limited time available for assessment and other constraints, we can only measure or judge a limited sample of student performance in any particular area. In preparing a classroom test, for example, there may be 100 terms that the students should know but we only have room for 20 terms in our test. Thus, we must select a representative sample from the 100 words because we want to be able to generalize from performance on the 20 terms as to how well students know the 100 terms. If our sample is adequate, we can estimate that 18 correct answers on the 20 terms indicates that a student knows about 90 percent of the 100 terms (with allowance for a margin of error, of course).

Sampling is also a problem in performance assessment. In assessing driving skill, for example, it would be impossible to include all possible driving problems in a brief driving test so we must settle for a representative sample of them. It is interesting to note that, for licensing purposes, some states are now including driving on the expressway to obtain a more adequate sample of driving skill.

In the assessment of performance skills in the classroom there are typically two problems of sampling. In a writing project, for example, we might ask (1) does the project include a representative sample of the writing skills we are stressing in our teaching? and (2) does performance on this project represent what writing performance would be like on other similar projects? Because extended performance assessment (e.g., giving a speech, conducting an experiment, applying math to a real world problem) is so time consuming and context bound, the adequacy of sampling is always an important concern in planning the assessment.

5. *Effective assessment requires that the procedures be fair to everyone.* An assessment program that makes the intended learning outcomes clear to students, that uses assessment procedures which are instructionally relevant and that adequately sample student performance, and that uses assessment results to improve learning goes a long way toward creating an atmosphere of fairness. In addition, however, special efforts must be made to eliminate irrelevant sources of difficulty and bias of various types. Student performance may be inadequate because the directions were ambiguous, the reading level was inappropriate, or the performance called for knowledge or skills that were not intended as parts of the assessment task. Similarly, including racial or gender stereotypes in the assessment material may distort the results and create a feeling of unfairness. Fairness requires care in preparing and using assessment procedures, clearly communicating our intentions to students, and using the results to improve learning.

6. *Effective assessment requires the specifications of criteria for judging successful performance.* In the past, success was typically determined by comparing a student's performance to that of others (norm-referenced interpretation). If performance surpassed that of others it was considered excellent performance. If performance was lower than that of others it was considered poor performance. Although this method of judging success has its merits and is useful in certain situations, it is not satisfactory as a measure of how well students are learning the intended outcomes of instruction. For this purpose we need **criteria** that describe what students can do when they perform successfully (e.g., type 40 words per minute with no more than two errors).

Establishing performance criteria is difficult in many areas but if the intended learning outcomes are clearly stated in performance terms, the criteria for success can be more easily established. In assessing vocabulary, for example, we can describe success in terms of how well students can define each term and use it in a sentence, how well they can distinguish between similar terms, and how well they can use the terms in a writing project. Effective laboratory performance can be described in terms of the selection and manipulation of equipment, the accuracy of measurements, the procedures followed, and the written description and interpretation of results. By specifying success in performance terms, we can describe what students are achieving and how well. The degree of success can be expressed by separate scores, by scoring rubrics that describe degrees of effectiveness, by rating scales, or by whatever means is most useful for describing student performance.

Students should have a clear notion of what is expected of them and clearly specified criteria of successful performance can be used to clarify the learning tasks. In some cases, students may participate in defining the desired performance. In planning for oral reports, for example, a discussion of criteria and listing them on the board will cause students to focus on the criteria of a good oral report and help them improve their performance. This is one way that instruction and assessment can be blended together to the benefit of students.

7. *Effective assessment requires feedback to students that emphasizes strengths of performance and weaknesses to be corrected.* Feedback of assessment results to students is an essential factor in any assessment program. To be most effective, feedback must meet the following criteria.

A. Should be given immediately following or during the assessment.
B. Should be detailed and understandable to students.
C. Should focus on successful elements of the performance and the errors to be corrected.
D. Should provide remedial suggestions for correcting errors.
E. Should be positive and provide a guide for improving both performance and self assessment.

In performance assessment, our immediate goal is to improve performance. But if we are to develop self-learners, who will continue to improve performance on their own, then we need to also help them develop self-assessment skills. Thus, feedback must focus on both performance skills and self-assessment skills. For example, we not only suggest how to modify performance but also how to check on the effect of the modifications on performance and ways to determine future improvement. A final question concerning feedback might be, Will this feedback to students make them more dependent on the teacher or will it contribute to more independent learning? The most desirable choice is obvious and is illustrated in Figure 2.2.

8. *Effective assessment must be supported by a comprehensive grading and reporting system.* All too frequently teachers have used various types of assessment procedures and then assigned grades on the basis of scores on an objective test. Instead, we need to have the grading and reporting system reflect the emphasis in our assessments. If half of our learning outcomes are assessed by tests and half by performance assessments, and a single grade is used, the two types of assessment should receive equal weight in the grade. With the re-

FIGURE 2.2   Role of Assessment Feedback

cent emphasis on performance assessment, more elaborate grading and re-- porting systems are needed to describe student performance adequately. Reports based on the intended learning outcomes and portfolios of student work are becoming increasingly important for reporting learning progress to students, parents, and others. These more elaborate reports are in harmony with the more elaborate assessment procedures being used.

Because letter grades are still required for some purposes (e.g., college admission), it may be necessary to use both letter grades and a more elaborate report. In any event, the grading and reporting procedures should reflect and support the assessment procedures, be made clear to students at the beginning of instruction, and provide for periodic feedback to students concerning their learning progress.

VALIDITY AND RELIABILITY IN ASSESSMENT PLANNING

Two of the most important characteristics of a well-designed assessment procedure are **validity** and **reliability.** These characteristics are of primary concern during assessment planning and most of the suggestions in this book are directed toward preparing assessments that provide for valid and reliable interpretation of results.

Validity refers to the appropriateness and meaningfulness of the inferences we make from assessment results for some intended use. For example, if we give a vocabulary test, we would like to be able to interpret the scores as a representative sample of the terms we have been teaching. If we do a good job of (1) clearly defining the domain of vocabulary items to be measured, (2) carefully prepare the test specifications, and (3) construct a representative sample of relevant test items, our interpretations from the results are likely to be valid. We are now able to infer that high scores represent good knowledge of the vocabulary that has been taught. Note that it is the inference that is important. If we infer that high scores indicate good writing ability or good verbal ability, we are generalizing beyond the limited assessment domain being tested and the validity of our inference is in doubt, without further evidence. Thus, it is not the test scores that are valid or invalid but the inferences we make from them.

Performance assessments are typically viewed as providing more valid inferences concerning learning than traditional paper-and-pencil tests because they focus more directly on the types of performance tasks we are teaching. If we want to determine if students can read, we have them read something. If we want to determine if students can give a speech, we have them give a speech. If we want to determine if students can operate a computer, we have them operate a computer. In each case the task has the appearance of being valid (i.e., we have good *face* validity). However, it is not as simple as it seems. In performance assessment, the problem of defining the assessment domain, of specifying how the performance will be judged, and of obtaining a representative sample of performance tasks poses special problems. For example, there are many different types of reading, many different types of speeches, and many different types of problems to be solved on the computer. Each requires its own specifications and scoring rubrics, and because of the time consuming nature of performance assessment, the sampling tends to be limited. This restricts the extent to which we can infer that performance on one assessment task is generalizable to performance on other assessment tasks in the same area.

With both tests and performance assessments we need to make plans and follow procedures that are most likely to yield valid inferences concerning learning. This involves selecting appropriate procedures, preparing them carefully, applying them effectively, and then interpreting the results within the limits of the particular achievement domain being assessed. In using the results we are also, of course, concerned about the consequences of the assessment. Did its use contribute to increased student learning, as intended? This is a legitimate validity-related question because our main purpose in assessing student achievement is to improve learning.

Reliability refers to the *consistency* of assessment results. For example, if a student earns a score of 60 on a test, we would like to be able to say that 60 accurately represents the student's test performance. Thus, if we tested the student at a different time or with a different sample of equivalent items, we would expect to obtain a similar score. Similarly, if a student receives a high rating on a writing project, we would like to say that it represents the student's writing skill and that if others rated the project the results would be similar. This consistency of results would indicate that they are relatively free from errors and thus we can rely on them (i.e., they have "rely-ability").

We cannot, of course, expect assessment results to be perfectly consistent over different occasions or over different samples of the same achievement domain. Such factors as ambiguities, variations in samples, fluctuations in motivation and attention, and luck can introduce errors that cause assessment results to vary. Likewise, in judging performance tasks, the personal biases of the rater can introduce error into the results. An important goal in assessment is to keep these various types of errors to a minimum so that our results are as reliable as possible.

In addition to being important in its own right, reliability is necessary to obtain valid inferences from assessment results. After all, if an individual's test score fluctuated widely on a given sample of items, we could not expect to draw valid inferences concerning the student's achievement. Similarly, if ratings varied widely on a student's writing project, valid inferences could not be made concerning writing skill. Thus, *reliability provides the consistency of results that makes valid inferences possible.* Of course, the consistency of results is just one important requirement for valid inferences. We could be consistently assessing the wrong thing, using inappropriate procedures, or generalizing beyond the achievement domain being assessed. Thus, reliability is a necessary, but not a sufficient, condition for making valid inferences.

Both the validity and reliability of assessment results can be provided for during the preparation of assessment procedures. When we clearly specify the intended learning outcomes, define the achievement domain to be assessed, and select a relevant and representative set of assessment tasks, we are providing for valid inferences concerning learning. When we include an adequate number of tasks in our assessment and we use procedures that are free from ambiguity, irrelevant sources of difficulty, unintended clues, and other factors that might distort the results, we are providing for both reliability and validity. In fact, most of the suggestions for constructing achievement tests and preparing performance assessments are directed toward improving the reliability of the assessment results and the validity of the interpretations we make from them.

A more elaborate discussion of validity and reliability and methods for determining them is presented in Chapter 11. Although high quality assessments can be made without a detailed study of validity and reliability, understanding the basic concepts involved can contribute to improved skill in preparing assessment procedures, making appropriate interpretations of the results, and using the results effectively.

Some of the most important features that enhance the validity and reliability of assessment results are presented in Table 2.2. This table makes clear that concern about validity and reliability takes place in the early stages of as-

TABLE 2.2   Desirable Features for Enhancing the Validity and Reliability of Assessment Results

DESIRED FEATURES	PROCEDURES TO FOLLOW
1. Clearly specified set of learning outcomes.	1. State intended learning outcomes in performance terms.
2. Representative sample of a clearly defined domain of learning tasks.	2. Prepare a description of the achievement domain to be assessed and the sample of tasks to be used.
3. Tasks that are relevant to the learning outcomes to be measured.	3. Match assessment tasks to the specified performance stated in the learning outcomes.
4. Tasks that are at the proper level of difficulty.	4. Match assessment task difficulty to the learning task, the students' abilities, and the use to be made of the results.
5. Tasks that function effectively in distinguishing between achievers and nonachievers.	5. Follow general guidelines and specific rules for preparing assessment procedures and be alert for factors that distort the results.
6. Sufficient number of tasks to measure an adequate sample of achievement, provide dependable results, and allow for a meaningful interpretation of the results.	6. Where the students' age or available assessment time limit the number of tasks, make tentative interpretations, assess more frequently, and verify the results with other evidence.
7. Procedures that contribute to efficient preparation and use.	7. Write clear directions and arrange procedures for ease of administration, scoring or judging, and interpretation.

sessment planning and preparation, not after the assessment results have been obtained. The procedures listed in Table 2.2 will be described in more detail in the chapters on preparing tests and performance-based assessments. Here, we are simply emphasizing their importance in obtaining valid and reliable interpretations of assessment results and the need for early assessment planning to "build in" the desired features.

NORM-REFERENCED AND CRITERION-REFERENCED ASSESSMENT

An achievement assessment can be used to provide (1) a relative ranking of students or (2) a description of the learning tasks a student can and cannot perform. Results of the first type are interpreted in terms of each student's relative standing among other students (for example, "He is third highest in a class of 35 students"). This method of interpreting student performance is called **norm-referenced interpretation.** Results of the second type are expressed in terms of the specific knowledge and skills each student can demonstrate (e.g., "She can identify the parts of a microscope and demonstrate its use"). This method of interpreting assessment results is called **criterion-referenced interpretation.** Both methods of describing assessment

---

Terms Similar to Criterion-Referenced Interpretation

Domain-Referenced Interpretation	Assessment results are interpreted in terms of a relevant and clearly defined set related tasks (called a *domain*). Meaning is similar to criterion-referenced interpretation but is less used, even though it is a more descriptive term.
Content-Referenced Interpretation	Essentially the same meaning as domain-referenced interpretation when the content domain is broadly defined to include tasks representing both content and process (i.e., reactions to the content). This term is declining in use and being replaced by criterion-referenced interpretation.
Objective-Referenced Interpretation	Assessment results are interpreted in terms of each specific objective that a set of test items represents. This is frequently called *criterion-referenced interpretation* but the more limited designation is preferable where interpretation is limited to each separate objective.

---

results are useful. The first tells how an individual's performance compares with that of others. The second tells in specific performance terms what an individual can do without reference to the performance of others.

Strictly speaking, the terms *norm referenced* and *criterion referenced* refer only to the method of interpreting the results. Thus, both types of interpretation could be applied to the same assessment. For example, we might say, "Joan surpassed 90 percent of the students (norm-referenced interpretation) by correctly completing 20 of the 25 chemical equations" (criterion-referenced interpretation). The two types of interpretation are likely to be most meaningful, however, when the assessment is designed specifically for the type of interpretation to be made. In general, norm-referenced interpretation is facilitated by a wide spread of scores so that reliable discriminations can be made among students at various levels of achievement. Criterion-referenced interpretation is facilitated by assessment tasks that provide a detailed description of student performance. In testing, this means a larger number of test items per task. In performance assessment, this means performance tasks that make clear what parts of the task a person can and cannot do.

Although norm-referenced and criterion-referenced interpretations apply to all types of achievement assessments, the differences can be most clearly indicated when applied to testing. A summary of some common characteristics of tests specifically designed for each type of interpretation is presented in Table 2.3. It must be kept in mind, however, that these are primarily matters of emphasis. For example, norm-referenced tests are typically, but not exclusively, used for surveying achievement over a broad range of learning outcomes. By the same token, criterion-referenced tests are typically, but not exclusively, used for **mastery testing.** A review of the characteristics of each testing approach in Table 2.3 will reveal the differences that exist when each test is constructed to serve its principal use. It is not uncommon, however, to view the two test types as the ends of a continuum rather than as discrete categories, and to combine the best features of each in constructing achievement tests.

For most instructional purposes, criterion-referenced assessments are to be favored. We can best help students improve learning by determining what tasks they can and cannot perform. Thus, the classroom assessment program should be based on instruments and procedures that provide for this type of interpretation. Norm-referenced interpretation is most useful when we are concerned about the relative ranking of students, as in the selection and classification of students (e.g., advance placement, grouping, giving awards, and relative grading).

Most of the discussions of procedures for constructing tests and making performance assessment will apply to all types of tests and assessments. Where there are significant differences due to the type of interpretation to be made, these will be noted.

**TABLE 2.3   Summary Comparison of Two Basic Approaches
to Achievement Testing**

	NORM-REFERENCED TESTING	CRITERION-REFERENCED TESTING
Principal Use Major Emphasis	Survey testing. Measures individual differences in achievement.	Mastery testing. Describes tasks students can perform.
Interpretation of Results	Compares performance to that of other individuals.	Compares performance to a clearly specified achievement domain.
Content Coverage	Typically covers a broad area of achievement.	Typically focuses on a limited set of learning tasks.
Nature of Test Plan	Table of specifications is commonly used.	Detailed domain specifications are favored.
Item Selection Procedures	Items are selected that provide maximum discrimination among individuals (to obtain a reliable ranking). Easy items are typically eliminated from the test.	Includes all items needed to adequately describe performance. No attempt is made to alter item difficulty or to eliminate easy items to increase the spread of scores.
Performance Standards	Level of performance is determined by *relative* position in some known group (e.g., ranks fifth in a group of 20).	Level of performance is commonly determined by *absolute* standards (e.g., demonstrates mastery by defining 90 percent of the technical terms).

SUMMARY OF POINTS

1. Student assessment needs to be expanded to include the assessment of more complex learning outcomes than has been the case in the past.
2. Assessment methods vary widely but they can be classified as selected-response tests, supply-response tests, restricted-response performance assessments, or extended-response performance assessments.
3. Selected-response tests (e.g., multiple-choice tests) are lowest in realism and complexity of the tasks assessed, but require little time to administer and can be scored quickly and objectively.
4. Supply-response tests (e.g., essay tests) are higher in realism and the complexity of tasks they can measure (e.g., ability to originate, integrate, and

express ideas) than selected-response tests, but they are more time consuming to use and more difficult to score.

5. Performance assessments, both restricted response and extended response, can be designed with high degrees of realism (i.e., like "real world" problems) that focus on highly complex learning tasks, but they require large amounts of time to use and the scoring is judgmental and highly subjective.

6. A sound assessment policy would be, to use the most efficient method available for assessing each intended learning outcome as long as it is appropriate, but don't neglect complex learning outcomes just because the assessment methods are more time consuming to use and more difficult to score or judge.

7. Effective assessment requires a clear conception of all intended learning outcomes, a variety of assessment procedures that are relevant to the instruction, an adequate sample of tasks, procedures that are fair to everyone, criteria for judging success, timely and detailed feedback to students, and a grading and reporting system that is in harmony with the assessment program.

8. Validity and reliability are the two most important characteristics of any assessment method and must be considered during the planning and preparation of assessment procedures.

9. Valid and reliable interpretations of assessment results require clearly defined intended learning outcomes, a representative sample of instructionally relevant tasks, a sound scoring system, and freedom from irrelevant factors that introduce error.

10. Assessment results can be interpreted by comparing a student's performance to that of others (norm-referenced) or by describing the student's performance on a clearly defined set of tasks (criterion-referenced).

11. Criterion-referenced interpretation is especially important for instructional uses of assessment results but norm-referenced interpretation may be needed for selection and classification decisions.

12. In some cases both criterion-referenced and norm-referenced interpretation may be used with the same assessment.

ADDITIONAL READING

McMillan, N. H., *Classroom Assessment* (Boston: Allyn & Bacon, 1997). See Chapter 3, "Establishing High Quality Classroom Assessments," for a description of the various factors involved and suggestions for enhancing validity, reliability, and fairness.

Popham, W. J., *Classroom Assessment* (Boston: Allyn & Bacon, 1995). See Chapter 1, "What do Teachers Need to Know About Assessment?" for a general overview of the role of assessment in teaching.

Rothman, R., *Measuring Up: Standards, Assessment, and School Reform* (San Francisco, CA: Jossey-Bass, 1995). Describes and illustrates radical changes in classroom assessment programs and the reactions of teachers, administrators, and the community to them.

Stiggins, R. J., *Student Centered Classroom Assessment* (Columbus, OH: Merrill, 1994). See Part 2, "Understanding Assessment Methods," for the use of selected response tests, essay tests, performance assessments, and personal communication in classroom assessment.

Wiggins, G. P., *Assessing Student Performance* (San Francisco, CA: Jossey-Bass, 1993). Makes a strong case against the widespread use of tests and for the use of authentic assessment. A main theme throughout is that "student assessment should improve performance, not just monitor or audit it." Provides a basic philosophy of assessment and a general framework for assessment reform.

Planning the Achievement Test

Studying this chapter should enable you to

1. List the steps to follow in preparing an achievement test.
2. State instructional objectives as intended learning outcomes and define them in performance terms.
3. Prepare a set of specifications for a test.
4. Describe the relative merits of selection and supply types items.
5. Match test items to the specific learning outcomes they measure.
6. Describe the factors to consider when preparing items for a test.

Preparing an **achievement test** involves the following steps:

1. Identifying and defining the intended learning outcomes to be measured.
2. Preparing test specifications.
3. Constructing relevant test items.
4. Reviewing and editing the items.
5. Arranging the items in the test.
6. Preparing directions.

The first three steps will be considered in Chapters 3–6 and the last three steps will be considered in Chapter 7, after we have described the procedures for writing the various types of items that are typically used in achievement tests.

IDENTIFYING AND DEFINING THE INTENDED LEARNING OUTCOMES

The learning outcomes measured by a test should faithfully reflect the objectives of instruction. This requires the identification of those instructional objectives to be measured by the test and then clearly stating them in performance terms. There are various guides that are helpful in focusing attention beyond the knowledge level (that tends to be overused by teachers). One useful guide is the cognitive domain of the *Taxonomy of Educational Objectives*. This is an older guide but one that was carefully developed by a group of educators. It contains a range of types of learning outcomes to consider when planning a test. Another guide that is similar to the Taxonomy but is much simpler and easy to use is the Quellmalz Framework. Both guides make clear the wide range of learning outcomes that are to be considered when writing instructional objectives.

Cognitive Domain of the Taxonomy

Learning outcomes in the cognitive domain are divided into two major classes: (1) knowledge and (2) intellectual abilities and skills. These are further subdivided into six main areas as follows:

Knowledge

1.00 KNOWLEDGE (Remembering previously learned material)
   1.10 Knowledge of specifics
      1.11 Knowledge of terms
      1.12 Knowledge of specific facts
   1.20 Knowledge of ways and means of dealing with specifics
      1.21 Knowledge of conventions
      1.22 Knowledge of trends and sequences
      1.23 Knowledge of classifications and categories
      1.24 Knowledge of criteria
      1.25 Knowledge of methodology
   1.30 Knowledge of the universals and abstractions in a field
      1.31 Knowledge of principles and generalizations
      1.32 Knowledge of theories and structures

Intellectual Abilities and Skills

2.00 COMPREHENSION (grasping the meaning of material)
   2.10 Translation (converting from one form to another)
   2.20 Interpretation (explaining or summarizing material)
   2.30 Extrapolation (extending the meaning beyond the data)
3.00 APPLICATION (using information in concrete situations)

4.00 ANALYSIS (breaking down material into its parts)

  4.10 Analysis of elements (identifying the parts)

  4.20 Analysis of relationships (identifying the relationship)

  4.30 Analysis of organizational principles (identifying the organization)

5.00 SYNTHESIS (putting parts together into a whole)

  5.10 Production of a unique communication

  5.20 Production of a plan or proposed set of operations

  5.30 Derivation of a set of abstract relations

6.00 EVALUATION (judging the value of a thing for a given purpose using definite criteria)

  6.10 Judgments in terms of internal evidence

  6.20 Judgments in terms of external criteria[1]

As can be seen in this outline the outcomes are arranged in order of increasing complexity. They begin with the relatively simple recall of factual information, proceed to the lowest level of understanding (comprehension), and then advance through the increasingly complex levels of application, analysis, synthesis, and evaluation. The subdivisions within each area are also listed in order of increasing complexity. This scheme for classifying student behavior is thus hierarchical; that is, the more complex behaviors include the simpler behaviors listed in the lower categories.

    The cognitive domain of the taxonomy is especially useful in planning the achievement test. It focuses on a comprehensive and apparently complete list of mental processes to be considered when identifying learning outcomes, it provides a standard vocabulary for describing and classifying learning outcomes, and it serves as a guide for stating learning outcomes in terms of specific student performance.

    Although the cognitive domain of the taxonomy provides a valuable guide for identifying learning outcomes, not all of the areas listed under this domain will be covered in a particular test or even in a particular course. Moreover, the classification scheme is neutral concerning the relative importance of the learning outcomes listed. Thus, it is the instructor who must decide which learning outcomes will guide their teaching and testing, and how much emphasis each outcome will receive. The taxonomy serves merely as a convenient checklist of outcomes that prevents relevant areas of student performance from being overlooked during the planning of an achievement test. A more elaborate description of the Bloom taxonomy, along with lists of illustrative instructional objectives and descriptive verbs can be found in Gronlund (1995).

---

[1]Reprinted from Benjamin S. Bloom, ed., and others, *Taxonomy of Educational Objectives: Cognitive Domain* (New York: David McKay Co., Inc., 1956), pp. 201–207. Reprinted with permission of the publisher.

The Quellmalz Framework

The Quellmalz Framework is presented in Table 3.1. It represents a kind of modified version of the Bloom taxonomy, that teachers find easier to use. The descriptions within each category are followed by an indication of how the categories relate to the Bloom taxonomy. Quellmalz found that these categories were also common to various other frameworks that she reviewed.

Stating the General Learning Outcomes

The learning outcomes to be measured by a test are most useful in test construction when they are stated as a *terminal performance* that is *observable*. That is, they should clearly indicate the student performance to be demonstrated at the end of the learning experience. The following list of learning outcomes for a unit in the planning of an achievement test illustrates this type of statement. It should be noted that these statements include only objectives that can be tested and that they are stated as *general outcomes*. Before being used for

TABLE 3.1   The Quellmalz Framework for the Cognitive Domain

QUELLMALZ LEVELS AND BRIEF DESCRIPTIONS		BLOOM'S CATEGORIES	GENERALIZED OUTCOMES TO ILLUSTRATE LEVELS
RECALL	Verbatim recalling or paraphrasing of basic information	Knowledge	Knows specific facts.
		Comprehension	Understands principles.
ANALYSIS	Reasoning based on component parts and their relationships	Analysis	Analyzes organizational structure and describes part-whole relationships.
COMPARISON	Reasoning based on similarities and differences	Analysis	Explains the similarities and differences between two events.
INFERENCE	Reasoning both deductively and inductively	Application	Applies principles to new situations.
		Synthesis	Generalizes from given facts.
EVALUATION	Making value judgments based on definite criteria	Synthesis	Judges the organization structure of written material.
		Evaluation	Judges the quality of a research plan.

Adapted from E. S. Quellmalz, "Developing Reasoning Skills" (pp. 86–105) in J. R. Baron and R. J. Sternberg (Eds.) *Teaching Thinking Skills: Theory and Practice* (New York: Freeman, 1987).

test construction, each one would need to be further defined in terms of specific learning outcomes.

At the end of this unit in achievement test planning the student will demonstrate that he or she:

1. Knows the meaning of common terms.
2. Knows specific facts about test planning.
3. Knows the basic procedures for planning an achievement test.
4. Comprehends the relevant principles of testing.
5. Applies the principles in test planning.

These statements of general learning outcomes have been deliberately kept free of specific course content so that with only slight modification they can be used with various units of study. As we shall see later, the test specifications provide a means of relating intended outcomes to specific subject matter topics.

This list of general outcomes could, of course, be expanded by making the statements more specific, and in some cases it may be desirable to do so. The number of general learning outcomes to use is somewhat arbitrary, but somewhere between 5 and 15 items provide a list that is both useful and manageable. Typically, a shorter list is satisfactory for a unit of study, while a more comprehensive list is needed for summative testing at the end of a course.

Defining the General Outcomes in Specific Terms

When a satisfactory list of general learning outcomes has been identified and clearly stated, the next step is to list the specific types of student performance that are to be accepted as evidence that the outcomes have been achieved. For example, what specific types of performance will show that a student "knows the meaning of common terms" or "comprehends the relevant principles of testing"? For these two areas the specific learning outcomes may be listed as follows:

1. Knows the meaning of common terms.
   1.1 Identifies the correct definitions of terms.
   1.2 Identifies the meaning of terms when used in context.
   1.3 Distinguishes between terms on basis of meaning.
   1.4 Selects the most appropriate terms when describing testing procedures.

4. Comprehends the relevant principles of testing.
   4.1 Describes each principle in his or her own words.
   4.2 Matches a specific example to each principle.

4.3 Explains the relevance of each principle to the major steps in test planning.

4.4 Predicts the most probable effect of violating each of the principles.

4.5 Formulates a test plan that is in harmony with the principles.

Note that the terms used to describe the specific learning outcomes indicate student performance that can be demonstrated to an outside observer. That is, they are *observable* responses that can be called forth by test items. The key terms are listed below to emphasize what is meant by defining learning outcomes in *specific performance terms*.

Identifies	Matches
Distinguishes between	Explains
Selects	Predicts
Describes	Formulates

Action verbs such as these indicate precisely what the student is able to do to demonstrate achievement. Such vague and indefinite terms as "learns," "sees," "realizes," and "is familiar with" should be avoided, since they do not clearly indicate the terminal performance to be measured.

Sample action verbs for stating specific learning outcomes at each level of the cognitive domain of the taxonomy are presented in Table 3.2. Although

TABLE 3.2   Illustrative Action Verbs for Defining Objectives in the Cognitive Domain of the Taxonomy

TAXONOMY CATEGORIES	SAMPLE VERBS FOR STATING SPECIFIC LEARNING OUTCOMES
Knowledge	Identifies, names, defines, describes, lists, matches, selects, outlines
Comprehension	Classifies, explains, summarizes, converts, predicts, distinguishes between
Application	Demonstrates, computes, solves, modifies, arranges, operates, relates
Analysis	Differentiates, diagrams, estimates, separates, infers, orders, subdivides
Synthesis	Combines, creates, formulates, designs, composes, constructs, rearranges, revises
Evaluation	Judges, criticizes, compares, justifies, concludes, discriminates, supports.

certain action verbs may be used at several different levels (e.g., "identifies"), the table provides a useful guide for defining intended outcomes in performance terms. For more comprehensive lists of action verbs, see Linn and Gronlund (1995) listed at the end of this chapter.

In defining the general learning outcomes in specific performance terms, it is typically impossible to list all of the relevant types of performance. The proportion that need be listed depends to a large extent on the nature of the test. In planning a test that is to be used to *describe* which learning tasks a student has mastered (criterion-referenced test), we should like as comprehensive a list as possible. For a test that is used to *rank* students in order of achievement (norm-referenced test), however, it is usually satisfactory to include a sufficient number of specific types of performance to clarify what the typical student is like who has achieved the intended outcomes.

PREPARING THE TEST SPECIFICATIONS

The writing of test items should be guided by a carefully prepared set of test specifications. The function of the specifications is to describe the achievement domain being measured and to provide guidelines for obtaining a representative sample of test tasks. Although the nature and detail of test specifications can be expected to vary considerably, here we shall describe two of the more commonly recommended procedures. In the construction of norm-referenced achievement tests, one of the most widely used devices has been a two-way chart called a *table of specifications.*

Building a Table of Specifications

Preparing a table of specifications involves (1) selecting the learning outcomes to be tested, (2) outlining the subject matter, and (3) making a two-way chart. The two-way chart describes the sample of items to be included in the test.

Selecting the Learning Outcomes to Be Tested. The learning outcomes for a particular course will depend on the specific nature of the course, the objectives attained in previous courses, the philosophy of the school, the special needs of the students, and a host of other local factors that have a bearing on the instructional program. Despite the variation from course to course, most lists of instructional objectives will include learning outcomes in the following areas: (1) knowledge, (2) intellectual abilities and skills, (3) general skills (laboratory, performance, communication, work-study), and (4) attitudes, interests, and appreciations. It is in the first two areas covered by the cognitive domain of the taxonomy that achievement testing is most useful. Learning outcomes in the other areas are typically evaluated by rating scales, check-lists, anecdotal records, inventories, and similar nontest evaluation proce-dures. Thus, the first step is to separate from the list of learning outcomes those that are testable by paper-and-pencil tests. The selected list of learning outcomes should, of course, be defined in specific terms, as described in the previous section. Clarifying the specific types of performance to be called forth by the test will aid in constructing test terms that are most relevant to the intended learning outcomes.

Outlining the Subject Matter.   The stated learning outcomes specify how students are expected to react to the subject matter of a course. Although it is possible to include both the student performance and the specific subject mat-ter the student is to react toward in the same statement, it is usually desirable to list them separately. The reason for this is that the student can react in the same way to many different areas of subject matter, and he can react in many different ways to the same area of subject matter. For example, when we state that a student can "define a term in her own words," "recall a specific fact," or "identify an example of a principle," these types of performance can be ap-plied to almost any area of subject matter. Similarly, in studying the taxon-omy of educational objectives we may expect students merely to recall the categories in it, or we could require them to explain the principles on which it is organized, to summarize its usefulness in test planning, to classify a given set of learning outcomes with it, or to use it in the actual construction of a test. Since particular types of student performance can overlap a variety of subject matter areas, and vice versa, it is more convenient to list each as-pect of performance and subject matter separately and then to relate them in the table of specifications.

The content of a course may be outlined in detail for teaching purposes, but for test planning only the major categories need be listed. The following outline of subject matter topics based on a unit on achievement testing illus-trates sufficient detail for the test plan.

A. Role of testing in the instructional process
    1. Instructional decisions and test types
    2. Influence of tests on learning and instruction
B. Principles of achievement testing
    1. Relation to instructional objectives
    2. Representative sampling
    3. Relevance of items to outcomes
    4. Relevance of test to use of results
    5. Reliability of results
    6. Improvement of learning

    C. Norm-referenced versus criterion-referenced testing
    D. Planning the test
        1. Determining the purpose of the test
        2. Identifying the intended learning outcomes
        3. Preparing the test specifications
        4. Constructing relevant test items

Making the Two-Way Chart.   When the learning outcomes have been selected and clearly defined and the course content outlined, the two-way chart should be prepared. This is called a **table of specifications**. It relates outcomes to content and indicates the relative weight to be given to each of the various areas. As noted earlier, the purpose of the table is to provide assurance that the test will measure a representative sample of the learning outcomes and the subject matter topics to be measured.

An example of a table of specifications for a norm-referenced summative test on a unit on achievement testing is given in Table 3.3. Note that only the general learning outcomes and the major subject matter categories have been included. A more detailed table may be desirable for test purposes, but this is sufficient for illustration.

The numbers in each cell of the table indicate the number of test items to be devoted to that area. For example, 15 items in the test will measure knowledge of terms; 4 of them pertain to the "role of tests" in instruction," 4 to "principles of testing," 4 to "norm referenced versus criterion referenced," and 3 to "planning the test." The number of items assigned to each cell is determined by the weight given to each learning outcome and each subject matter area.

A number of factors will enter into assigning relative weights to each learning outcome and each content area. How important is each area in the total learning experience? How much time was devoted to each area during instruction? Which outcomes have the greater retention and transfer value? What relative importance do curriculum specialists assign to each area? These and similar criteria must be considered. In the final analysis, however, the weights assigned in the table should faithfully reflect the emphasis given during instruction. In Table 3.3, for example, it is assumed that twice as much emphasis was given to "planning the test" (20 items) as was given to "norm referenced versus criterion referenced" (10 items). Similarly, it is assumed that knowledge outcomes were given approximately two-thirds of the emphasis during instruction (40 items) and that comprehension and application outcomes were each given approximately one-sixth of the total emphasis (10 items each).

In summary, preparing a table of specifications includes the following steps:

TABLE 3.3 Table of Specifications for a Summative Test on a Unit for Achievement Testing

OUTCOMES / CONTENT	KNOWS			COMPREHENDS PRINCIPLES	APPLIES PRINCIPLES	TOTAL NUMBER OF ITEMS
	TERMS	FACTS	PROCEDURES			
Role of Tests in Instruction	4	4		2		10
Principles of Testing	4	3	2	6	5	20
Norm Referenced versus Criterion Referenced	4	3	3			10
Planning the Test	3	5	5	2	5	20
Total Number of Items	15	15	10	10	10	60

1. Identify the learning outcomes and content areas to be measured by the test.
2. Weigh the learning outcomes and content areas in terms of their relative importance.
3. Build the table in accordance with these relative weights by distributing the test items proportionately among the relevant cells of the table.

The resulting two-way table indicates the type of test needed to measure the learning outcomes and course content in a balanced manner. Thus, the table of specifications serves the test maker like a blueprint. It specifies the number and the nature of the items in the test, and it thereby provides a guide for item writing.

Specifications for Formative Tests

Whether a table of specifications is useful in preparing a formative test depends greatly on the nature of the achievement domain being measured. In some cases the test may cover such a limited area that a table of specifications is unnecessary. In constructing a test to measure "knowledge of the categories in the cognitive domain of the taxonomy," for example, a list of specific ways students are to demonstrate their knowledge may provide a sufficient basis for test planning. The specifications could then simply indicate the number of items to be used to measure each specific type of performance as shown in Table 3.4. For some purposes it may be desirable to use a listing like that in Table 3.4 *and* a table of specifications. In any event the test plan should indicate the achievement domain to be measured and the specific nature of the student performance to be accepted as evidence of achievement.

When formative tests are being prepared by more than one person (e.g., for a mastery testing program) more detailed test specifications are desirable.

TABLE 3.4   Specific Knowledge Outcomes to Result from Study of the Cognitive Domain of the *Taxonomy* and the Number of Test Items for Each Intended Outcome

TYPES OF STUDENT PERFORMANCE	NUMBER OF ITEMS
Describes the meaning of each major category.	6
Identifies the hierarchical order of the major categories.	4
Identifies a verb that best fits each main category.	6
States a specific learning outcome for each main subcategory.	10
Distinguishes between given pairs of categories.	4

General Outcome:	Comprehends the meaning of measurement terms.
Specific Outcome:	Identifies an example of each term.
Type of Test:	Multiple choice (10 items).
Item Characteristics:	Each test will consist of a question or incomplete statement followed by four possible answers placed in alphabetical order. The *correct* answer will be an example that best fits the meaning of the term. The *incorrect* alternatives (distracters) will be made plausible by using common student misunderstandings and by matching the correct answer in terms of length, content, and grammatical structure.
Sample Item:	Which of the following is an example of a *performance term*?

                      *A   Defines
                      B   Fears
                      C   Realizes
                      D   Thinks

FIGURE 3.1   Specifications for a Ten-Item Test Measuring One Specific Comprehension Outcome

These specifications should include a description of the test items to be used plus a sample item that illustrates the item characteristics. A brief example of such specifications is shown in Figure 3.1.

CONSIDERATIONS IN CONSTRUCTING RELEVANT TEST ITEMS

The construction of a set of relevant test items is greatly simplified if the intended learning outcomes have been clearly defined and the test specifications carefully prepared. The quality of the test will then depend on how closely the test maker can match the specifications. Here we shall confine our discussion to some of the general specifications in preparing test items. More detailed procedures and rules for item writing will be described in the chapters that follow.

Selecting the Types of Test Items to Use

The items used in achievement tests can be classified as either *selection-type* items or *supply-type* items. The selection-type item presents students with a set of possible responses from which they are to select the most appropriate answer. The supply-type item requires students to create and supply their own answers. These two major categories can be used to classify the most widely used item types as follows.

Selection-Type Items

1. Multiple choice
2. True-false
3. Matching
4. Interpretive exercise

Supply-Type Items

1. Short answer
2. Essay (restricted response)
3. Essay (extended response)

These categories are sometimes referred to as *recognition* and *recall* items. This is a case of mislabeling that confuses the method of responding with the mental reaction needed to make the response. When measuring knowledge of facts, test responses might be limited to either the recognition or recall of the answer. However, when measuring complex learning outcomes with selection-type items, the answer is not achieved through mere recognition of a previously learned answer. It typically involves some use of higher mental processes to arrive at a solution (e.g., verbal or mathematical reasoning) before the correct answer can be selected. Similarly, a short-answer item may require reasoning or problem solving rather than simply recalling and supplying factual information. Essay answers, of course, typically require analysis, synthesis, and evaluation skills in addition to recall. Using the *selection* and *supply* labels makes clear how the responses are made but it does not imply limits on the types of learning outcomes that can be measured with each.

In deciding which item types to use in a test, a guiding principle should be: *Use the item types that provide the most direct measures of student performance specified by the intended learning outcome.* Thus, if you want to determine if students can spell, have them spell from dictation. If you want to determine if students can solve mathematics problems, have them solve problems and supply the answers. If you want to determine if students can write, have them write something. Use selection-type items for supply-type outcomes only if there is a compelling reason for doing so (e.g., electronic scoring) and then take into account, during interpretation of the results, that a less direct measure has been used. In some cases, of course, both types of items are useful in the same area. For example, a writing project may provide the best evidence of writing skill but a selection-type test would provide the most systematic coverage of the elements of grammar needed for effective writing.

There are a number of achievement areas where either selection-type items or supply-type items would measure equally well. In these cases, our choice between them must be based on other item characteristics. The preparation of good selection-type items is difficult and students can get a proportion of answers correct by guessing. However, these disadvantages are offset by the fact that (1) they can be scored quickly and objectively (i.e., scorers agree on the answers), (2) they eliminate bluffing, (3) they eliminate the influence of writing skill, (4) they provide an extensive sample of student performance (because of the large number of items used), and (5) they provide for the identification of specific learning errors. In comparison, supply-type items are easier to construct (although harder than commonly believed) but more difficult to score. The scoring of short-answer items is contaminated by answers of varying degrees of correctness and by adjustments needed for misspellings. The scoring of essay tests is tedious, time consuming, and influenced by bluffing, writing skill, and the shifting of standards during scoring. Another major shortcoming of supply-type items is the limited sample of learning tasks that can be measured. The short-answer item is restricted primarily to measuring knowledge outcomes. Although the essay test is especially suited to measuring complex learning outcomes, its sampling is limited by the relatively few questions that can be included in a test.

A summary comparison of the relative merits of selection-type and supply-type items is presented in Table 3.5. Although this should serve as a guide in selecting the types of items to use in a given test, as noted earlier, the most

TABLE 3.5   Summary of the Relative Merits of Selection-Type Items and Supply-Type Items

| | | SUPPLY-TYPE ITEMS | |
CHARACTERISTIC	SELECTION-TYPE ITEMS	SHORT ANSWER	ESSAY
Measures factural information	Yes	Yes	Yes(*)
Measures understanding	Yes	No(**)	Yes
Measures synthesis	No(**)	No(**)	Yes
Easy to construct	No	Yes	Yes
Samples broadly	Yes	Yes	No
Eliminates bluffing	Yes	No	No
Eliminates writing skill	Yes	No	No
Eliminates blind guessing	No	Yes	Yes
Easy to score	Yes	No	No
Scoring is objective	Yes	No	No
Pinpoints learning errors	Yes	Yes	No
Encourages originality	No	No	Yes

(*)The essay test can measure knowledge of facts, but because of scoring and sampling problems it probably should not be used for this purpose.

(**)These items can be designed to measure limited aspects of these characteristics.

important question to ask is: *Does this item type provide the most direct measure of the intended learning outcome?* If the various item types are equal in this regard, the selection-type items would be favored because of the broad sampling, the objective scoring, and the pinpointing of specific learning errors.

Matching Items to Specific Learning Outcomes

Effective achievement testing requires that a set of test items be constructed that calls forth the performance described in the intended learning outcomes. While we can never be certain of a perfect correspondence between outcome and item, the following examples illustrate how items should be written to measure the specific type of performance stated in the specific learning outcome.

EXAMPLES

Specific Learning Outcome: Defines terms in student's own words.
  Directions: Define each of the following terms in a sentence or two.
  1. Taxonomy
  2. Cognitive
  3. Measurement
  4. Evaluation

Specific Learning Outcome: Identifies procedural steps in planning for a test.
  1. Which one of the following steps should be completed first in planning for an achievement test?[2]
      A. Select the types of test items to use.
      B. Decide on the length of the test.
      *C. Define the intended learning outcomes.
      D. Prepare the test specifications.

Specific Learning Outcome: Identifies the hierarchical order of the categories in the cognitive domain of the taxonomy.
  1. Which one of the following categories in the taxonomy indicates the highest level of learning?
      A. Analysis
      B. Application
      C. Comprehension
      *D. Synthesis

Specific Learning Outcome: Distinguishes between sound and unsound principles of achievement testing.
  Directions: Read each of the following statements. If the statement indicates a sound principle of achievement testing, circle the S; if it indicates an unsound principle, circle the U.

---

[2]The correct answer is indicated throughout this book by an asterisk.

*S   U   **1.** The specific learning outcomes to be tested should be stated in terms of student performance.

S   *U   **2.** Achievement testing should be limited to outcomes that can be measured objectively.

*S   U   **3.** Each achievement test item should measure a clearly defined type of student performance.

Specific Learning Outcome: Identifies examples of properly stated learning outcomes.
   1. Which one of the following learning outcomes is properly stated in performance terms?
      A. Student realizes the importance of tests in teaching.
      B. Student has acquired the basic principles of achievement testing.
      C. Student demonstrates a desire for more experience in test construction.
      *D. Student predicts the most probable effect of violating a test construction principle.

It should be noted in these examples that each specific learning outcome provides a precise definition of the student performance to be measured, and the test item simply provides a task that makes measurement of the specified performance possible.

Improving the Functioning Content of Items

If test items are to call forth the performance described in the intended learning outcomes, great care must be taken in phrasing the items. We need to eliminate all barriers that might prevent a knowledgeable person from responding and all clues that might lead the uninformed to the correct answer. Only those who have achieved the outcome being measured should get the item right. All others (no matter how intelligent) should miss it.

Some of the common *barriers* to be avoided during test preparation are:

Vocabulary that is unnecessarily difficult.

Sentence structure that is unnecessarily complex.

Statements containing ambiguity.

Unclear pictorial materials.

Directions that are vague.

Material reflecting race, ethnic, or sex bias.

Awareness of such barriers during the planning and preparation of the test is the first step in their elimination. Essentially, we can avoid these barriers by (1) writing each test item so that it presents a clearly formulated task, (2) stating the items in simple, clear language, (3) keeping the items free from biased and nonfunctional material, and (4) using a test format and directions that contribute to effective test taking. Much of the material presented later in this book is directed toward constructing tests that prevent extraneous factors from distorting the test results.

Some of the common *clues* to be avoided during test preparation are:

Verbal associations that give away the answer.

Grammatical inconsistencies that eliminate wrong answers.

Specific determiners that make certain answers probable (e.g., sometimes) and others improbable (e.g., always).

Stereotyped or textbook phrasing of correct answers.

Length or location of correct answers.

Material in an item that aids in answering another item.

Just as in controlling extraneous factors that provide barriers to the correct answer, clues such as these can be eliminated by being aware of them and by following sound principles of test construction. Many of the rules for item writing and test preparation in the chapters that follow provide guidelines for this purpose.

Determining the Number of Test Items to Use

The number of items to use should be indicated in the test specifications, as noted earlier, and is modified by a number of practical constraints, such as the following:

1. Age of the students tested
2. Time available for testing
3. Type of test items used
4. Type of interpretation to be made

In the testing of elementary school students, the testing time typically should be no more than 20 or 30 minutes so that proper motivation is maintained. At the high school and college levels, students can be given tests lasting several hours (for example, a final examination), but most tests are limited to a testing time of 40 to 50 minutes because of the length of the typical class period.

In matching the number of items to available testing time, we are faced with the problem of estimating how many items students can complete per minute. Unfortunately there are no simple answers. It depends on the type of test item, the complexity of the learning outcome measured, and the age of the students. As a rule of thumb, high school and college students should be able to answer one multiple-choice item, three short-answer items, or three true-false items per minute when the items are measuring knowledge outcomes. For measuring more complex learning outcomes such as comprehension and application, and for testing younger age groups, more time per item is needed. In estimating the number of items to be used, keep in mind the slower students in the group, for it is desirable to give all students an opportunity to complete the test. Experience in testing a given group of students is frequently the only dependable guide for determining proper test length.

In addition to our concern with total test length, consideration must be given to the number of test items needed for each type of interpretation to be made. This issue is especially crucial in criterion-referenced interpretation, where we want to describe student performance in terms of each intended learning outcome. For this purpose we should use at least 10 items per outcome. Where practical constraints make it necessary to use fewer than 10 items for an intended outcome, only tentative judgments should be made and these should be verified by other means. In some cases it is possible to combine items into larger item clusters for a more meaningful interpretation.

Checklist for Evaluating the Test Plan

1. Is the purpose of the test clear?
2. Have the intended learning outcomes been identified and defined?
3. Are the intended learning outcomes stated in performance (measurable) terms?
4. Have test specifications been prepared that indicate the nature and distribution of items to be included in the test?
5. Does the specified set of items provide a representative sample of the tasks contained in the achievement domain?
6. Are the types of items appropriate for the learning outcomes to be measured?
7. Is the difficulty of the items appropriate for the students to be tested and the nature of the measurement (e.g., mastery or survey)?
8. Is the number of items appropriate for the students to be tested, the time available for testing, and the interpretations to be made?
9. Does the test plan include "built-in" features that contribute to valid and reliable scores?
10. Have plans been made for arranging the items in the test, writing directions, scoring, and using the results (see Chapter 7)?

GENERAL GUIDELINES FOR ITEM WRITING

There are a number of general suggestions that apply to the writing of all item types. These provide a general framework for writing items that function as intended and that contribute to more valid and reliable results.

1. *Select the type of test item that measures the intended learning outcome most directly.* Use a supply-type item if supplying the answer is an important element of the task (e.g., writing). Use a selection-type item if appropriate (e.g., identification) or if both types are equally appropriate.

2. *Write the test item so that the performance it elicits matches the performance in the learning task.* The intended learning outcome specifies the learning task in performance terms and the test task should call forth the same performance.

3. *Write the test item so that the test task is clear and definite.* Keep the reading level low, use simple and direct language, and follow the rules for correct punctuation and grammar.

4. *Write the test item so that it is free from nonfunctional material.* Material not directly relevant to the problem being presented increases the reading load and may detract from the intent of the item. Use extraneous material only where its detection is part of the task (e.g., in math problems).

5. *Write the test item so that irrelevant factors do not prevent an informed student from responding correctly.* Avoid trick questions that might cause a knowledgeable student to focus on the wrong aspect of the task. Use clear, unambiguous statements that maximize the performance to be measured and minimize all other influences. For example, word problems measuring mathematical reasoning should keep reading level and computational demands simple if an uncontaminated measure of reasoning ability is desired.

6. *Write the test item so that irrelevant clues do not enable the uninformed student to respond correctly.* Removing unwanted clues from test items requires alertness during item writing and reviewing the items after setting them aside for a while. The most common clues for each item type will be considered in the following chapters. It is also important to prevent the information given in one item from providing an answer to another item in the test.

7. *Write the test item so that the difficulty level matches the intent of the learning outcome, the age group to be tested, and the use to be made of the results.* When difficulty is altered to obtain a wide spread of test scores, check to be certain that the added difficulty is relevant to the intended learning outcome and that the item is free from sources of irrelevant difficulty (e.g., obscure materials, overly fine discriminations).

8. *Write the test item so that there is no disagreement concerning the answer.* Typically the answer should be one that experts would agree is the correct or best answer. Most problems arise here when students are to provide the best answer (best procedure, best explanation). This involves a matter of judgment and to be defensible the answer must be clearly best and identified as such by experts in the area. Where experts disagree, it may be desirable to ask what a particular authority would consider to be the best method, the best reason, and the like. When attributed to a source, the answer can be judged as correct or incorrect.

9. *Write the test items for enough in advance that they can be later reviewed and modified as needed.* A good time to write test items is shortly after the material has been taught, while the questions and context are still clearly in mind. In any event, reviewing and editing items after they have been set aside for a while can detect flaws that were inadvertently introduced during the original item writing.

10. *Write more test items than called for by the test plan.* This will enable you to discard weak or inappropriate items during item review, and make it easier to match the final set of items to the test specifications.

SUMMARY OF POINTS

1. Test planning should be guided by the nature of the learning tasks to be measured.
2. Test planning should include stating the instructional objectives as intended learning outcomes and defining them in terms of student performance.
3. Test specifications that describe the set of tasks to be measured should be prepared before writing or selecting test items.
4. Test specifications typically consist of a twofold table of specifications, but a more limited set of specifications may be useful for formative testing.
5. The types of test items used in a test should be determined by how directly they measure the intended learning outcomes and how effective they are as measuring instruments.
6. Each test item should provide a task that matches the student performance described in a specific learning outcome.
7. The functioning content of test items can be improved by eliminating irrelevant barriers and unintended clues during item writing.
8. For mastery testing and criterion-referenced interpretation, the difficulty of a test item should match the difficulty of the learning task to be measured.

9. For survey testing and norm-referenced interpretation, item difficulty may be altered to provide a larger spread of scores, but care must be taken not to introduce irrelevant difficulty (e.g., by using obscure material).
10. An achievement test should be short enough to permit all students to attempt all items during the testing time available.
11. A test should contain a sufficient number of test items for each type of interpretation to be made. Interpretations based on fewer than 10 items should be considered highly tentative.
12. Following a general set of guidelines during item writing will result in higher quality items that contribute to the validity and reliability of the test results.

ADDITIONAL READING

Ebel, R. L., and Frisbee, D. A., *Essentials of Educational Measurement*, 5th ed. (Englewood Cliffs, NJ: Prentice-Hall, 1991). See Chapter 7, "Achievement Test Planning," for a discussion of factors to consider when preparing a test plan.

Gronlund, N. E., *How to Write and Use Instructional Objectives*, 5th ed. (Englewood Cliffs, NJ: Prentice-Hall, 1995). Describes how to state objectives as intended learning outcomes and define them in performance terms. Has separate chapters on higher-level thinking skills and performance outcomes, and contains an elaboration of the *Taxonomy or Educational Objectives* with illustrative instructional objectives and action verbs.

Linn, R. L., and Gronlund, N. E., *Measurement and Assessment in Teaching*, 7th ed. (Englewood Cliffs, NJ: Prentice-Hall, 1995). See Chapter 5, "Planning Classroom Tests and Assessments," for a comprehensive treatment of test planning.

Payne, D. A., *Measuring and Evaluating Educational Outcomes* (New York: Macmillan, 1992). See section 2, "Planning for Instrument Development," for descriptions and illustrations of how to specify intended learning outcomes and plan the test.

▶ 4

Writing Selection Items

Multiple Choice

Studying this chapter should enable you to

1. Describe the characteristics of multiple-choice items.
2. Describe the strengths and limitations of multiple-choice items.
3. Distinguish between well-stated and poorly stated multiple-choice items.
4. Identify and correct faults in poorly stated multiple-choice items.
5. Match multiple-choice items to intended learning outcomes.
6. Construct multiple-choice items that are well stated, relevant to important learning outcomes, and free of defects.

Multiple-choice items are the most widely used and highly regarded of the selection-type items. They can be designed to measure a variety of learning outcomes, from simple to complex, and can provide the highest quality items. Because they play such an important role in achievement testing, they will be treated in this chapter in considerable detail. Other selection-type items (true-false, matching, and interpretive exercise) will be described in the following chapter.

NATURE OF MULTIPLE-CHOICE ITEMS

The multiple-choice item consists of a *stem,* which presents a problem situation, and several *alternatives (options* or *choices),* which provide possible solutions to the problem. The stem may be a question or an incomplete statement. The alternatives include the correct answer and several plausible wrong answers called *distracters.* The function of the latter is to distract those students who are uncertain of the answer.

The following items illustrate the question form and the incomplete-statement form of a multiple-choice item.

EXAMPLE

Which one of the following item types is an example of a supply-type test item?
   A. Multiple-choice item.
   B. True-false item.
   C. Matching item.
 *D. Short-answer item.

An example of a supply-type test item is the:
   A. multiple-choice item.
   B. true-false item.
   C. matching item.
 *D. short-answer item.

Although stated differently, both stems pose the same problem. Note, however, that the incomplete statement is more concise. This is typically the case. The question form is easier to write and forces the test maker to pose a clear problem but tends to result in a longer stem. An effective procedure for the beginner is to start with a question and shift to the incomplete statement whenever greater conciseness can be obtained.

The alternatives in the preceding examples contain only one correct answer, and the distracters are clearly incorrect. Another type of multiple-choice item is the *best-answer* form in which the alternatives are all partially correct but one is clearly better than the others. This type is used for more complex achievement, as when the student must select the best reason for an action, the best method for doing something, or the best application of a principle. Thus, whether the correct-answer or best-answer form is used depends on the learning outcomes to be measured.

EXAMPLE

Which item is *best* for measuring computational skill?
   A. Multiple-choice item.
   B. True-false item.
   C. Matching item.
 *D. Short-answer item.

The examples given illustrate the use of four alternatives. Multiple-choice items typically include either three, four, or five choices. The larger number will, of course, reduce the student's chances of obtaining the correct answer by guessing. Theoretically, with five alternatives there is only one chance in five of guessing the answer, whereas with four alternatives there is one chance in four. It is frequently difficult to obtain five plausible choices, however, and items are not improved by adding obviously wrong answers merely to have five alternatives. There is no reason why the items in a given test should all have the same number of alternatives. Some might contain three, some four, and some five, depending on the availability of plausible distracters. This would pose a problem only if the test were to be corrected for guessing—a practice, as we see later, that is not recommended for informal achievement tests.

USES OF MULTIPLE-CHOICE ITEMS

The multiple-choice item can be used to measure knowledge outcomes and various types of complex learning outcomes. The single-item format is probably most widely used for measuring knowledge, comprehension, and application outcomes. The interpretive exercise consisting of a series of multiple-choice items based on introductory material (e.g., paragraph, picture, or graph) is especially useful for measuring analysis, interpretation, and other complex learning outcomes. The interpretive exercise will be described in the following chapter. Here, we confine the discussion to the use of single, independent, multiple-choice items.

Knowledge Items

Knowledge items typically measure the degree to which previously learned material has been remembered. The items focus on the simple recall of information and can be concerned with the measurement of terms, facts, or other specific aspects of knowledge.

EXAMPLES

Outcome: Identifies the meaning of a term.
　Reliability means the same as:
　　*A. consistency.
　　B. relevancy.
　　C. representativeness.
　　D. usefulness.

Outcome: Identifies the order of events.
　What is the first step in constructing an achievement test?

A. Decide on test length.
*B. Identify the intended learning outcomes.
C. Prepare a table of specifications.
D. Select the item types to use.

The wide variety of knowledge outcomes that can be measured with multiple-choice items is best shown by illustrating some of the types of questions that can be asked in various knowledge categories. Sample questions stated as incomplete multiple-choice stems are presented in the accompanying box.

The series of questions shown in the box, of course, provides only a sample of the many possible questions that could be asked. Also, the questions are stated in rather general terms. The stems for multiple-choice items need to be more closely related to the specific learning outcome being measured.

Comprehension Items

Comprehension items typically measure at the lowest level of understanding. They determine whether the students have grasped the meaning of the material without requiring them to apply it. Comprehension can be measured by requiring students to respond in various ways but it is important that the items contain some *novelty*. The following test items illustrate the measurement of common types of learning outcomes at the comprehension level.

EXAMPLES

Outcome: Identifies an example of a term.
   Which one of the following statements contains a *specific determiner?*
      A. America is a continent.
      B. America was discovered in 1492.
      *C. America has some big industries.
      D. America's population is increasing.

Outcome: Interprets the meaning of an idea.
   The statement that "test reliability is a necessary but not a sufficient condition of test validity" means that:
      A. a reliable test will have a certain degree of validity.
      *B. a valid test will have a certain degree of reliability.
      C. a reliable test may be completely invalid and a valid test completely unreliable.

Outcome: Identifies an example of a concept or principle.
   Which of the following is an example of a criterion-referenced interpretation?
      A. Derik earned the highest score in science.
      B. Erik completed his experiment faster than his classmates.
      C. Edna's test score was higher than 50 percent of the class.
      *D. Tricia set up her laboratory equipment in five minutes.

Illustrative Knowledge Questions*

1.11 *Knowledge of Terminology*
What word means the same as _____?
Which statement best defines the term _____?
In this sentence, what is the meaning of the word _____?

1.12 *Knowledge of Specific Facts*
Where would you find _____?
Who first discovered _____?
What is the name of _____?

1.21 *Knowledge of Conventions*
What is the correct form for _____?
Which statement indicates correct usage of _____?
Which of the following rules applies to _____?

1.22 *Knowledge of Trends and Sequences*
Which of the following best describes the trend of _____?
What is the most important cause of _____?
Which of the following indicates the proper order of _____?

1.23 *Knowledge of Classifications and Categories*
What are the main types of _____?
What are the major classifications of _____?
What are the characteristics of _____?

1.24 *Knowledge of Criteria*
Which of the following is a criterion for judging _____?
What is the most important criterion for selecting _____?
What criteria are used to classify _____?

1.25 *Knowledge of Methodology*
What method is used for _____?
What is the best way to _____?
What would be the first step in making _____?

1.31 *Knowledge of Principles and Generalizations*
Which statement best expresses the principle of _____?
Which statement best summarizes the belief that _____?
Which of the following principles best explains _____?

1.32 *Knowledge of Theories and Structures*
Which statement is most consistent with the theory of _____?
Which of the following best describes the structure of _____?
What evidence best supports the theory of _____?

*Based on *Taxonomy of Educational Objectives* (see Chapter 3).

Outcome: Predicts the most probable effect of an action.

What is most likely to happen to the reliability of the scores for a multiple-choice test, where the number of alternatives for each item is changed from three to four?

    A. It will decrease.
    *B. It will increase.
    C. It will stay the same.
    D. There is no basis for making a prediction.

In this last example, the student must recognize that increasing the number of alternatives in the items produces the same effect as lengthening the test.

These examples would, of course, represent measurement at the comprehension level only where the situations were new to the students. If the solutions to these particular problems were encountered during instruction, the items would need to be classified as knowledge outcomes.

Some of the many learning outcomes at the comprehension level that can be measured by multiple-choice items are illustrated by the incomplete questions in the accompanying box.

Illustrative Comprehension and Application Questions

Comprehension Questions

Which of the following is an example of _____?
What is the main thought expressed by _____?
What are the main differences between _____?
What are the common characteristics of _____?
Which of the following is another form of _____?
Which of the following best explains _____?
Which of the following best summarizes _____?
Which of the following best illustrates _____?
What do you predict would happen if _____?
What trend do you predict in _____?

Application Questions

Which of the following methods is best for _____?
What steps should be followed in applying _____?
Which situation would require the use of _____?
Which principle would be best for solving _____?
What procedure is best for improving _____?
What procedure is best for constructing _____?
What procedure is best for correcting _____?
Which of the following is the best plan for _____?
Which of the following provides the proper sequence for _____?
What is the most probable effect of _____?

Application Items

Application items also measure understanding, but typically at a higher level than that of comprehension. Here, the students must demonstrate that they not only grasp the meaning of information but can also apply it to concrete situations that are new to them. Thus, application items determine the extent to which students can transfer their learning and use it effectively in solving new problems. Such items may call for the application of various aspects of knowledge, such as facts, concepts, principles, rules, methods, and theories. Both comprehension and application items are adaptable to practically all areas of subject matter, and they provide the basic means of measuring understanding.

The following examples illustrate the use of multiple-choice items for measuring learning outcomes at the application level.

EXAMPLES

Outcome: Distinguishes between properly and improperly stated outcomes.
   Which one of the following learning outcomes is properly stated in terms of student performance?
      A. Develops an appreciation of the importance of testing.
      ***B.** Explains the purpose of test specifications.
      C. Learns how to write good test items.
      D. Realizes the importance of validity.

Outcome: Improves defective test items.
   Directions: Read the following test item and then indicate the best change to make to improve the item.
   Which one of the following types of learning outcomes is most difficult to evaluate objectively?
      1. A concept.
      2. An application.
      3. An appreciation.
      4. None of the above.

   The best change to make in the previous item would be to:
      A. change the stem to incomplete-statement form.
      B. use letters instead of numbers for each alternative.
      C. remove the indefinite articles "a" and "an" from the alternatives.
      ***D.** replace "none of the above" with "an interpretation."

When writing application items, care must be taken to select problems that the students have not encountered previously and therefore cannot solve on the basis of general knowledge alone. Each item should be so designed that it calls for application of the particular fact, concept, principle, or proce-

---

Multiple-Choice Items

Strengths

1. Learning outcomes from simple to complex can be measured.
2. Highly structured and clear tasks are provided.
3. A broad sample of achievement can be measured.
4. Incorrect alternatives provide diagnostic information.
5. Scores are less influenced by guessing than true-false items.
6. Scoring is easy, objective, and reliable.

Limitations

1. Constructing good items is time consuming.
2. It is frequently difficult to find plausible distractors.
3. This item is ineffective for measuring some types of problem solving and the ability to organize and express ideas.
4. Score can be influenced by reading ability.

---

dure indicated in the intended learning outcome. See the accompanying box for some of the many questions that might be asked at the application level.

RULES FOR WRITING MULTIPLE-CHOICE ITEMS

An effective multiple-choice item presents students with a task that is both important and clearly understood, and one that can be answered correctly by anyone who has achieved the intended learning outcome. Nothing in the content or structure of the item should prevent an informed student from responding correctly. Similarly, nothing in the content or structure of the item should enable an uninformed student to select the correct answer. The following rules for item writing are intended as guides for the preparation of multiple-choice items that function as intended.

1. *Design each item to measure an important learning outcome.* The problem situation around which an item is to be built should be important and should be related to the intended learning outcome to be measured. The items in the previous section illustrate how to match items to intended outcomes. When writing the item, focus on the functioning content of the item and resist the temptation to include irrelevant material or more obscure and less significant content to increase item difficulty. Remember that the purpose of each item is to call forth the type of performance that will help determine the extent to which the intended learning outcomes have been achieved.

Items designed to measure complex achievement must contain some novelty. For example, where a knowledge item might require the identification of a textbook definition of a term, a comprehension item may require the identification of a modified form of it, and an application item may require the identification of an example of its proper use. Both the comprehension and application items would function as intended, however, only if the material was new to the students. Thus, items measuring complex achievement should require students to demonstrate that they have grasped the meaning of the material and can use it in situations that are new to them.

2. Present a single clearly formulated problem in the stem of the item. The task set forth in the stem of the item should be so clear that a student can understand it without reading the alternatives. In fact, a good check on the clarity and completeness of a multiple-choice stem is to cover the alternatives and determine whether it could be answered without the choices. Try this on the two sample items that follow.

EXAMPLE

Poor: A table of specifications:
    A. indicates how a test will be used to improve learning.
    *B.** provides a more balanced sampling of content.
    C. arranges the instructional objectives in order of their importance..
    D. specifies the method of scoring to be used on a test.

Better: What is the main advantage of using a table of specifications when preparing an achievement test?
    A. It reduces the amount of time required.
    *B.** It improves the sampling of content.
    C. It makes the construction of test items easier.
    D. It increases the objectivity of the test.

The first of these examples is no more than a collection of true-false statements with a common stem. The problem presented in the stem of the improved version is clear enough to serve as a supply-type short-answer item. The alternatives simply provide a series of possible answers from which to choose.

Note also in the second version that a *single* problem is presented in the stem. Including more than one problem usually adds to the complexity of the wording and reduces the diagnostic value of the item. When students *fail* such an item, there is no way to determine which of the problems prevented them from responding correctly.

3. *State the stem of the item in simple, clear language.* The problem in the stem of a multiple-choice item should be stated as precisely as possible and should be free of unnecessarily complex wording and sentence structure. Anyone who possesses the knowledge measured by a test item should be able to select the correct answer. Poorly stated item stems frequently introduce sufficient ambiguity to prevent a knowledgeable student from responding correctly. Also, complex sentence structure may make the item a measure more of reading comprehension than of the intended outcome. The first of the two examples that follow is an extreme instance of this problem.

EXAMPLE

Poor: The paucity of plausible, but incorrect, statements that can be related to a central idea poses a problem when constructing which one of the following types of test items?
     A. Short answer.
     B. True-false.
     ***C.** Multiple choice.
     D. Essay.

Better: The lack of plausible, but incorrect, alternatives will cause the greatest difficulty when constructing:
     A. short-answer items.
     B. true-false items.
     ***C.** multiple-choice items.
     D. essay items.

Another common fault in stating multiple-choice items is to load the stem with irrelevant and, thus, nonfunctioning material. This is probably caused by the instructor's desire to continue to teach the students—even while testing them. The following example illustrates the use of an item stem as "another chance to inform students."

EXAMPLE

Poor: Testing can contribute to the instructional program of the school in many important ways. However, the main function of testing in teaching is:

Better: The main function of testing in teaching is:

The first version increases reading time and makes no contribution to the measurement of the specific outcome. Time spent in reading such irrelevant material could be spent more profitably in thinking about the problem presented. But if the purpose of an item is to measure a student's ability to distinguish between relevant and irrelevant material, this rule must, of course, be disregarded.

4. *Put as much of the wording as possible in the stem of the item.* Avoid repeating the same material in each of the alternatives. By moving all of the common content to the stem, it is usually possible to clarify the problem further and to reduce the time the student needs to read the alternatives. Note the improvement in the following item when this rule is followed.

EXAMPLE

Poor: In *objective* testing, the term *objective:*
    A. refers to the method of identifying the learning outcomes.
    B. refers to the method of selecting the test content.
    C. refers to the method of presenting the problem.
    *****D.** refers to the method of scoring the answers.

Better: In *objective* testing, the term *objective* refers to the method of:
    A. identifying the learning outcomes.
    B. selecting the test content.
    C. presenting the problem.
    *****D.** scoring the answers.

In many cases the problem is not simply to move the common words to the stem but to reword the entire item. The following examples illustrate how an item can be improved by revising the stem and shortening the alternatives.

EXAMPLE

Poor: Instructional objectives are most apt to be useful for test-construction purposes when they are stated in such a way that they show:
    A. the course content to be covered during the instructional period.
    *****B.** the kinds of performance students should demonstrate upon reaching the goal.
    C. the things the teacher will do to obtain maximum student learning.
    D. the types of learning activities to be participated in during the course.

Better: Instructional objectives are most useful for test-construction purposes when they are stated in terms of:
    A. course content.
    *****B.** student performance.
    C. teacher behavior.
    D. learning activities.

It is, of course, impossible to streamline all items in this manner, but economy of wording and clarity of expression are important goals to strive for in test construction. Items function better when slim and trim.

5. State the stem of the item in positive form, wherever possible. A positively phrased test item tends to measure more important learning outcomes than a negatively stated item. This is because knowing such things as the *best* method or the *most relevant* argument typically has greater educational significance than knowing the *poorest* method or the *least relevant* argument. The use of negatively stated items stems results all too frequently from the ease with which such items can be constructed rather than from the importance of the learning outcomes measured. The test maker who becomes frustrated by the inability to think of a sufficient number of plausible distracters for an item, as in the first following example, suddenly realizes how simple it would be to construct the second version.

EXAMPLE

Item one: Which one of the following is a category in the taxonomy of the cognitive domain?
*A. Comprehension
B. (*distracter needed*)
C. (*distracter needed*)
D. (*distracter needed*)

Item two: Which one of the following is *not* a category in the taxonomy of the cognitive domain?
A. Comprehension
B. Application
C. Analysis
*D. (*answer needed*)

Note in the second version that the categories of the taxonomy serve as distracters and that all that is needed to complete the item is a correct answer. This could be any term that appears plausible but is *not* one of the categories listed in the taxonomy. Although such items are easily constructed, they are apt to have a low level of difficulty and are likely to measure relatively unimportant learning outcomes. Being able to identify answers that do *not* apply provides no assurance that the student possesses the desired knowledge.

This solution to the lack of sufficient distracters is most likely to occur when the test maker is committed to the use of multiple-choice items only. A more desirable procedure for measuring the "ability to recognize the categories in the taxonomy of the cognitive domain" is to switch to a modified true-false form, as in the following example.

EXAMPLE

Directions: Indicate which of the following are categories in the taxonomy of the cognitive domain, by circling Y for *yes* and N for *no*.

```
*Y   N    Comprehension
 Y   N*   Critical Thinking
 Y   N*   Reasoning
*Y   N    Synthesis
```

In responding to this item, the student must make a separate judgment for each statement—the statement either is or is not one of the categories. Thus, the item calls for the type of performance stated in the learning outcome, yet it avoids the problems of an insufficient number of distracters and of negative phrasing.

6. *Emphasize negative wording whenever it is used in the stem of an item.* In some instances the use of negative wording is basic to the measurement of an important learning outcome. Knowing that you should *not* cross the street against a red light or should *not* mix certain chemicals, for example, is so important that these precepts might be directly taught and directly tested. Any potentially dangerous situation may require a negative emphasis. There are also, of course, less dire circumstances where negative phrasing is useful. Almost any set of rules or procedures places some emphasis on practices to be avoided.

When negative wording is used in the stem of an item, it should be emphasized by being underlined or capitalized and by being placed near the end of the statement.

EXAMPLE

Poor: Which one of the following is not a desirable practice when preparing multiple-choice items?
- **A.** Stating the stem in positive form.
- **B.** Using a stem that could function as a short-answer item.
- **C.** Underlining certain words in the stem for emphasis.
- ***D.** Shortening the stem by lengthening the alternatives.

Better: All of the following are desirable practices when preparing multiple-choice items EXCEPT:
- **A.** stating the stem in positive form.
- **B.** using a stem that could function as a short-answer item.
- **C.** underlining certain words in the stem for emphasis.
- ***D.** shortening the stem by lengthening the alternatives.

The improved version of this item assures that the item's negative aspect will not be overlooked, and it furnishes the student with the proper mind-set just before reading the alternatives.

7. *Make certain that the intended answer is correct or clearly best.* When the correct-answer form of a multiple-choice item is used, there should be only one correct answer and it should be unquestionably correct. With the best-answer form, the intended answer should be one that competent authorities would agree is clearly the best. In the latter case it may also be necessary to include "of the following" in the stem of the item to allow for equally satisfactory answers that have not been included in the item.

EXAMPLE

Poor: What is the best method of selecting course content for test items?

Better: Which one of the following is the best method of selecting course content for test items?

The proper phrasing of the stem of an item can also help avoid equivocal answers when the correct-answer form is used. In fact, an inadequately stated problem frequently makes the intended answer only partially correct or makes more than one alternative suitable.

EXAMPLE

Poor: What is the purpose of classroom testing?

Better: One purpose of classroom testing is:
                   (or)
           The main purpose of classroom testing is:

It is, of course, also necessary to check each of the distracters in the item to make certain that none of them could be defended as the correct answer. This will not only improve the quality of the item but will also prevent a disruptive argument during the discussion of the test results.

8. *Make all alternatives grammatically consistent with the stem of the item and parallel in form.* The correct answer is usually carefully phrased so that it is grammatically consistent with the stem. Where the test maker is apt to slip is in stating the distracters. Unless care is taken to check them against the wording in the stem and in the correct answer, they may be inconsistent in tense, article, or grammatical form. This, of course, could provide a clue to the correct answer, or at least make some of the distracters ineffective.

A general step that can be taken to prevent grammatical inconsistency is to avoid using the articles "a" or "an" at the end of the stem of the item.

EXAMPLE

Poor: The recall of factual information can be measured best with a:
   A. matching item.
   B. multiple-choice item.
   ***C.** short-answer item.
   D. essay question.

Better: The recall of factual information can be measured best with:
   A. matching items.
   B. multiple-choice items.
   ***C.** short-answer items.
   D. essay questions.

The indefinite article "a" in the first version makes the last distracter obviously wrong. By simply changing the alternatives from singular to plural, it is possible to omit the article. In other cases, it may be necessary to add an article ("a," "an," or as appropriate) to each alternative or to rephrase the entire item.

Stating all of the alternatives in parallel form also tends to prevent unnecessary clues from being given to the students. When the grammatical structure of one alternative differs from that of the others, some students may more readily detect that alternative as a correct or an incorrect response.

EXAMPLE

Poor: Why should negative terms be avoided in the stem of a multiple-choice item?
   ***A.** They may be overlooked.
   B. The stem tends to be longer.
   C. The construction of alternatives is more difficult.
   D. The scoring is more difficult.

Better: Why should negative terms be avoided in the stem of a multiple-choice item?
   ***A.** They may be overlooked.
   B. They tend to increase the length of the stem.
   C. They make the construction of alternatives more difficult.
   D. They may increase the difficulty of the scoring.

In the first version some students who lack the knowledge called for are apt to select the correct answer because of the way it is stated. The parallel grammatical structure in the second version removes this clue.

9. *Avoid verbal clues that might enable students to select the correct answer or to eliminate an incorrect alternative.* One of the most common sources of extraneous clues in multiple-choice items is the wording of the item. Some such clues are rather obvious and are easily avoided. Others require the constant attention of the test maker to prevent them from slipping in unnoticed. Let's review some of the verbal clues commonly found in multiple-choice items.

(a) *Similarity of wording in both the stem and the correct answer* is one of the most obvious clues. Key words in the stem may unintentionally be repeated verbatim in the correct answer, a synonym may be used, or the words may simply sound or look alike.

EXAMPLE

Poor: Which one of the following would you consult first to locate research articles on achievement testing?
A. *Journal of Educational Psychology*
B. *Journal of Educational Measurement*
C. *Journal of Consulting Psychology*
*D. *Review of Educational Research*

The word "research" in both the stem and the correct answer is apt to provide a clue to the correct answer to the uninformed but testwise student. Such obvious clues might better be used in both the stem and an *incorrect* answer, in order to lead the uninformed *away* from the correct answer.

(b) *Stating the correct answer in textbook language or stereotyped phraseology* may cause students to select it because it looks better than the other alternatives, or because they vaguely recall having seen it before.

EXAMPLE

Poor: Learning outcomes are most useful in preparing tests when they are:
*A. clearly stated in performance terms.
B. developed cooperatively by teachers and students.
C. prepared after the instruction has ended.
D. stated in general terms.

The pat phrasing of the correct answers is likely to give it away. Even the most poorly prepared student is apt to recognize the often repeated phrase "clearly stated in performance terms," without having the foggiest notion of what it means.

(c) *Stating the correct answer in greater detail* may provide a clue. Also, when the answer is qualified by modifiers that are typically associated with true statements (for example, "sometimes," "may," "usually"), it is more likely to be chosen.

EXAMPLE

Poor: Lack of attention to learning outcomes during test preparation:
  A. will lower the technical quality of the items.
  B. will make the construction of test items more difficult.
  C. will result in the greater use of essay questions.
  *D. may result in a test that is less relevant to the instructional program.

The term "may" is rather obvious in this example, but this type of error is common and appears frequently in a subtler form.

(d) *Including absolute terms in the distracters* enables students to eliminate them as possible answers because such terms ("always," "never," "all," "none," "only,") are commonly associated with false statements. This makes the correct answer obvious, or at least increases the chances that the students who do not know the answer will guess it.

EXAMPLE

Poor: Achievement tests help students improve their learning by:
  A. encouraging them all to study hard.
  *B. informing them of their progress.
  C. giving them all a feeling of success.
  D. preventing any of them from neglecting their assignments.

Such absolutes tend to be used by the inexperienced test maker to assure that the incorrect alternatives are clearly wrong. Unfortunately they are easily recognized by the student as unlikely answers, making them ineffective as distracters.

(e) *Including two responses that are all inclusive* makes it possible to eliminate the other alternatives, since one of the two must obviously be the correct answer.

EXAMPLE

Poor: Which one of the following types of test items measures learning outcomes at the recall level?
  *A. Supply-type items.
  B. Selection-type items.
  C. Matching items.
  D. Multiple-choice items.

Since the first two alternatives include the only two major types of test items, even poorly prepared students are likely to limit their choices to these two. This, of course, gives them a fifty-fifty chance of guessing the correct answer.

(f) *Including two responses that have the same meaning* makes it possible to eliminate them as potential answers. If two alternatives have the same meaning and only one answer is to be selected, it is fairly obvious that both alternatives must be incorrect.

EXAMPLE

Poor: Which one of the following is the most important characteristic achievement-test results?
    A. Consistency
    B. Reliability
    *C. Relevance
    D. Objectivity

In this item both "consistency" and "reliability" can be eliminated because they mean essentially the same thing.

Extraneous clues to the correct answer must be excluded from test items if the items are to function as intended. It is frequently good practice, however, to use such clues to lead the uninformed away from the correct answer. If not overdone, this can contribute to the plausibility of the incorrect alternatives.

10. *Make the distracters plausible and attractive to the uninformed.* The distracters in a multiple-choice item should be so appealing to the students who lack the knowledge called for by the item that they select one of the distracters in preference to the correct answer. This is the ideal, of course, but one toward which the test maker must work continually. The art of constructing good multiple-choice items depends heavily on the development of effective distracters.

You can do a number of things to increase the plausibility and attractiveness of distracters:

    a. Use the common misconceptions or errors of students as distracters.
    b. State the alternatives in the language of the student.
    c. Use "good-sounding" words ("accurate," "important,") in the distracters as well as in the correct answer.
    d. Make the distracters similar to the correct answer in both length and complexity of wording.

e. Use extraneous clues in the distracters, such as stereotyped phrasing, scientific sounding answers, and verbal associations with the stem of the item. But don't overuse these clues to the point where they become ineffective.

f. Make the alternatives homogeneous, but in doing so beware of fine discriminations that are educationally insignificant.

The greater plausibility resulting from the use of more homogenous alternatives can be seen in the improved version of the following item.

EXAMPLE

Poor: Obtaining a dependable ranking of students is of major concern when using:
      *A. norm-referenced summative tests.
      B. behavior descriptions.
      C. checklists.
      D. questionnaires.

Better: Obtaining a dependable ranking of students is of major concern when using:
      *A. norm-referenced summative tests.
      B. teacher-made diagnostic tests.
      C. mastery achievement tests.
      D. criterion-referenced formative tests.

The improved version not only increases the plausibility of the distracters but it also calls for a type of discrimination that is more educationally significant.

11. *Vary the relative length of the correct answer to eliminate length as a clue.* There is a tendency for the correct answer to be longer than the alternatives because of the need to qualify statements to make them unequivocally correct. This, of course, provides a clue to the testwise student. Learning this fact, the inexperienced test maker frequently makes a special effort to avoid ever having the correct answer longer than the other alternatives. This, of course, also provides a clue, and the alert student soon learns to dismiss the longest alternative as a possible answer.

    The relative length of the correct answer can be removed as a clue by varying it in such a manner that no apparent pattern is provided. That is, it should sometimes be longer, sometimes shorter, and sometimes of equal length—but never consistently or predominantly of one relative length. In some cases it is more desirable to make the alternatives approximately equal length by adjusting the distracters rather than the correct answer.

EXAMPLE

Poor: One advantage of multiple-choice items over essay questions is that they:
    A. measure more complex outcomes.
    B. depend more on recall.
    C. require less time to score.
    *****D.** provide for a more extensive sampling of course content.

Better: One advantage of multiple-choice items over essay questions is that they:
    A. provide for the measurement of more complex learning outcomes.
    B. place greater emphasis on the recall of factual information.
    C. require less time for test preparation and scoring.
    *****D.** provide for a more extensive sampling of course content.

Lengthening the distracters, as was done in the improved version, removes length as a clue and increases the plausibility of the distracters, which are now more similar to the correct answer in complexity of wording.

12. *Avoid using the alternative "all of the above," and use "none of the above" with extreme caution.* When test makers are having difficulty in locating a sufficient number of distracters, they frequently resort to the use of "all of the above" or "none of the above" as the final option. These special alternatives are seldom used appropriately and almost always render the item less effective than it would be without them.

The inclusion of "all of the above" as an option makes it possible to answer the item on the basis of partial information. Since students are to select only one answer, they can detect "all of the above" as the correct choice simply by noting that two of the alternatives are correct. They can also detect it as a wrong answer by recognizing that at least one of the alternatives is incorrect; of course, their chance of guessing the correct answer from the remaining choices then increases proportionately. Another difficulty with this option is that some students, recognizing that the first choice is correct, will select it without reading the remaining alternatives.

Obviously the use of "none of the above" is not possible with the best-answer type of multiple-choice item, since the alternatives vary in appropriateness and the criterion of absolute correctness is not applicable. When used as the right answer in a correct-answer type of item, this option may be measuring nothing more than the ability to detect incorrect answers. Recognizing that certain answers are wrong is no guarantee that the student knows what is correct. For example, a student may be able to answer the following item correctly without being able to name the categories in the taxonomy.

EXAMPLE

Poor: Which of the following is a category in the taxonomy of the cognitive
         domain?
         A. Critical Thinking
         B. Scientific Thinking
         C. Reasoning Ability
         *****D.** None of above.

All students need to know to answer this item correctly is that the taxonomy
categories are new and different from those that they have commonly associated with intellectual skills. Items such as this provide rather poor evidence
for judging a student's achievement.

The alternative "none of the above" is probably used more widely with
computational problems that are presented in multiple-choice form. The publishers of standardized achievement tests have resorted to multiple-choice
items for such problems in order to make machine scoring possible, and they
have resorted to the alternative "none of the above" in order to reduce the
likelihood of the student estimating the answer without performing the entire computation. Although this use of "none of the above" may be defensible, there is seldom a need to use multiple-choice items for computational
problems in classroom tests. The supply-type item that requires the student
to solve the problems and record the answers provides the most direct and
useful measure of computational skill. This is another case in which it is desirable to switch from multiple-choice items to another item type in order to
obtain more effective measurement.

13. *Vary the position of the correct answer in a random manner.* The correct
answer should appear in each alternative position about the same number of
times, but its placement should not follow a pattern that may be apparent to
the person taking the test. Students who detect that the correct answer never
appears in the same position more than twice in a row, or that A is the correct answer on every fourth item, are likely to obtain a higher score than their
knowledge would warrant. Such clues can be avoided by random placement
of the correct answer.

The easiest way to randomly assign the position of the correct answer in
a multiple-choice item is to develop a code with the aid of a book: simply
open any book at a random place, look at the right-hand page, and let the last
digit of the page number determine the placement of the correct answer.
Since the right-hand page always ends in an odd number, the code might be
as follows: the digit 1 indicates that the correct answer will be placed in position A, 3 = B, 5 = C, 7 = D, and 9 = E.

Sufficient variation without a discernible pattern might also be obtained by simply placing the responses in alphabetical order, based on the first letter in each, and letting the correct answer fall where it will.

When the alternative responses are numbers, they should always be listed in order of size, preferably in ascending order. This will eliminate the possibility of a clue, such as the correct answer being the only one that is not in numerical order.

14. *Control the difficulty of the item either by varying the problem in the stem or by changing the alternatives.* It is usually preferable to increase item difficulty by increasing the level of knowledge called for by making the problem more complex. However, it is also possible to increase difficulty by making the alternatives more homogeneous. When this is done, care must be taken that the finer discriminations called for are educationally significant and are in harmony with the learning outcomes to be measured.

15. *Make certain each item is independent of the other items in the test.* Occasionally information given in the stem of one item will help the students answer another item. This can be remedied easily by a careful review of the items before they are assembled into a test.

A different type of problem occurs when the correct answer to an item depends on knowing the correct answer to the item preceding it. The student who is unable to answer the first item, of course, has no basis for responding to the second. Such chains of interlocking items should be avoided. Each item should be an independently scorable unit.

16. *Use an efficient item format.* The alternatives should be listed on separate lines, under one another, like the examples in this chapter. This makes the alternatives easy to read and compare. It also contributes to ease of scoring since the letters of the alternatives all appear on the left side of the paper. A copy of the test can be used as a scoring stencil: simply circle the letters of the correct answers on the copy, then place the copy next to the student's paper so that the columns of letters correspond.

The use of letters in front of the alternatives is preferable to the use of numbers, since numerical answers in numbered items may be confusing to the students.

17. *Follow the normal rules of grammar.* If the stem is in question form, begin each alternative with a capital letter and end with a period or other appropriate punctuation mark. Omit the period with numerical answers, however, to avoid confusion with decimal points. When the stem is an incomplete statement, start each alternative with a lower-case letter and end with whatever terminal punctuation mark is appropriate.

18. *Break (or bend) any of these rules if it will improve the effectiveness of the item.* These rules for constructing multiple-choice items are stated rather dogmatically as an aid to the beginner. As experience in item writing is ob-

---

Checklist for Evaluating Multiple-Choice Items

1. Is this type of item appropriate for measuring the intended learning outcome?
2. Does the item task match the learning task to be measured?
3. Does the stem of the item present a single, clearly formulated problem?
4. Is the stem stated in simple, clear language?
5. Is the stem worded so that three is no repetition of material in the alternatives?
6. Is the stem stated in positive form wherever possible?
7. If negative wording is used in the stem, is it emphasized (by underlining or caps)?
8. Is the intended answer correct or clearly best?
9. Are all alternatives grammatically consistent with the stem and parallel in form?
10. Are the alternatives free from verbal clues to the correct answer?
11. Are the distracters plausible and attractive to the uninformed?
12. To eliminate length as a clue, is the relative length of the correct answer varied?
13. Has the alternative "all of the above" been avoided and "none of the above" used only when appropriate?
14. Is the position of the correct answer varied so that there is no detectable pattern?
15. Does the item format and grammar usage provide for efficient test taking?

---

tained, situations are likely to occur where ignoring or modifying a rule may be desirable. In a problem-solving item, for example, it may be useful to include extraneous information in the stem to see if students can select what is needed to solve the problem. Until sufficient experience in item writing is gained, however, following the rules in this chapter will yield test items of fairly good quality.

SUMMARY OF POINTS

1. The multiple-choice item is the most highly regarded and useful selection-type item.
2. The multiple-choice item consists of a stem and a set of alternative answers (options or choices).
3. The multiple-choice item can be designed to measure various intended learning outcomes, ranging from simple to complex.
4. Knowledge items typically measure the simple remembering of material.
5. Comprehension items measure the extent to which students have grasped the meaning of material.

6. Application items measure whether students can use information in concrete situations.
7. Items designed to measure achievement beyond the knowledge level must contain some novelty.
8. The stem of a multiple-choice item should present a single, clearly formulated problem that is related to an important learning outcome.
9. The intended answer should be correct or clearly best, as agreed upon by authorities.
10. The distracters (incorrect alternatives) should be plausible enough to lead the uninformed away from the correct answer.
11. The items should be written in simple, clear language that is free of nonfunctioning content.
12. The items should be free of irrelevant sources of difficulty (e.g., ambiguity) that might prevent an informed examinee from answering correctly.
13. The items should be free of irrelevant clues (e.g., verbal associations) that might enable an uninformed examinee to answer correctly.
14. The item format should provide for efficient responding and follow the normal rules of grammar.
15. The rules of item writing provide a framework for preparing effective multiple-choice items, but experience in item writing may result in modifications to fit particular situations.

ADDITIONAL READING

Bloom, B. S., Madaus, G. F., and Hastings, J. T., *Evaluation to Improve Learning* (New York: McGraw-Hill, 1981). See Chapter 8, "Evaluation Techniques for Knowledge and Comprehension Objectives," and Chapter 9, "Evaluation Techniques for Application and Analysis Objectives," for numerous examples of multiple-choice items designed to measure various learning outcomes.

Haladyna, T. H., *Writing Test Items to Evaluate Higher Order Thinking* (Boston: Allyn & Bacon, 1997). See Chapter 4, "Multiple-Choice Formats," for descriptions and examples of how to measure complex learning outcomes with multiple-choice items.

Linn, R. L., and Gronlund, N. E., *Measurement and Assessment in Teaching,* 7th ed. (Englewood Cliffs, NJ: Prentice-Hall, 1995). See Chapter 7, "Constructing Objective Test Items: Multiple-Choice Forms," for illustrative test items representing various content areas, learning outcomes, and grade levels.

Payne, D. A., *Measuring and Evaluating Educational Outcomes* (New York; Macmillan, 1992). See Chapter 7, "Constructing Multiple-Choice and Matching Achievement Test Items," for illustrative items using graphic materials and suggestions for measuring problem solving and thinking skills.

Writing Selection Items

True-False, Matching, and Interpretive Exercise

Studying this chapter should enable you to

1. Describe the characteristics of each item type.
2. Describe the strengths and limitations of each item type.
3. Distinguish between well-stated and poorly stated items of each type.
4. Identify and correct faults in poorly stated items of each type.
5. Match each item type to intended learning outcomes.
6. Construct items of each type that are well-stated, relevant to important learning outcomes, and free of defects.

The multiple-choice item provides the most generally useful format for measuring achievement at various levels of learning. Thus, when selection-type items are to be used, an effective procedure is to start each item as a multiple-choice item and switch to another item type only when the learning outcome and content make it desirable to do so. For example, (1) when there are only two possible alternatives, a shift can be made to a true-false item; (2) when there are a number of similar factors to be related, a shift can be made to a matching item; and (3) when the items are to measure analysis, interpretation, and other complex outcomes, a shift can be made to the interpretive exercise. This procedure makes it possible to use the special strengths of the multiple-choice item and to use the other selection-type items more appropriately.

TRUE-FALSE ITEMS

True-false items are typically used to measure the ability to identify whether statements of fact are correct. The basic format is simply a declarative statement that the student must judge as true or false. There are modifications of this basic form in which the student must respond "yes" or "no," "agree" or "disagree," "right" or "wrong," "fact" or "opinion," and the like. Such variations are usually given the more general name of *alternative-response* items. In any event, this item type is characterized by the fact that only two responses are possible.

EXAMPLE

T   *F   True-false items are classified as a supply-type item.

In some cases the student is asked to judge each statement as true or false, and then to change the false statements so that they are true. When this is done, a portion of each statement is underlined to indicate the part that can be changed. In the example given, for instance, the words "supply-type" would be underlined. The key parts of true statements, of course, must also be underlined.

Another variation is the cluster-type true-false format. In this case, a series of items is based on a common stem.

EXAMPLE

Which of the following terms indicate observable student performance? Circle Y for yes and N for no.

*Y	N	1. Explains
*Y	N	2. Identifies
Y	*N	3. Learns
*Y	N	4. Predicts
Y	*N	5. Realizes

This item format is especially useful for replacing multiple-choice items that have more than one correct answer. Such items are impossible to score satisfactorily. This is avoided with the cluster-type item because it makes each alternative a separate scoring unit of one point. In our example, the student must record whether each term does or does not indicate observable student performance. Thus, this set of items provides an even better measure of

---

True-False Items

Strengths

1. The item is useful for outcomes where there are only two possible alternatives (e.g., fact or opinion, valid or invalid).
2. Less demand is placed on reading ability than in multiple-choice items.
3. A relatively large number of items can be answered in a typical testing period.
4. Complex outcomes can be measured when used with interpretive exercises.
5. Scoring is easy, objective, and reliable.

Limitations

1. It is difficult to write items beyond the knowledge level that are free from ambiguity.
2. Making an item false provides no evidence that the student knows what is correct.
3. No diagnostic information is provided by the incorrect answers.
4. Scores are more influenced by guessing than with any other item type.

---

the "ability to distinguish between performance and nonperformance terms" than would the single answer multiple-choice item. This is a good illustration of the procedure discussed earlier—that is, starting with multiple-choice items and switching to other item types when more effective measurement will result.

Despite the limitations of the true-false item, there are situations where it should be used. Whenever there are only two possible responses, the true-false item, or some adaptation of it, is likely to provide the most effective measure. Situations of this type include a simple "yes" or "no" response in classifying objects, determining whether a rule does or does not apply, distinguishing fact from opinion, and indicating whether arguments are relevant or irrelevant. As we indicated earlier, the best procedure is to use the true-false, or alternative-response, item only when this item type is more appropriate than the multiple-choice form.

Rules for Writing True-False Items

The purpose of a true-false item, as with all item types, is to distinguish between those who have and those who have not achieved the intended learning outcome. Achievers should be able to select the correct alternative without difficulty, while nonachievers should find the incorrect alternative at least as attractive as the correct one. The rules for writing true-false items are directed toward this end.

1. *Include only one central idea in each statement.* The main point of the item should be in a prominent position in the statement. The true-false decision should not depend on some subordinate point or trivial detail. The use of several ideas in each statement should generally be avoided because these tend to be confusing and the answer is more apt to be influenced by reading ability than the intended outcome.

EXAMPLE

Poor: T   *F   The true-false item, which is favored by test experts, is also called an alternative-response item.

Better: *T   F   The true-false item is also called an alternative-response item.

The "poor" example must be marked false because test experts do not favor the true-false item. Such subordinate points are easily overlooked when reading the item. If the point is important, it should be included as the main idea in a separate item.

2. *Keep the statement short and use simple vocabulary and sentence structure.* A short, simple statement will increase the likelihood that the point of the item is clear. All students should be able to grasp what the statement is saying. Passing or failing the item should depend solely on whether a student has achieved the necessary knowledge.

EXAMPLE

Poor: *T   F   The true-false item is more subject to guessing but it should be used in place of a multiple-choice item, if well constructed, when there is a dearth of distracters that are plausible.

Better: *T   F   The true-false item should be used in place of a multiple-choice item when only two alternatives are possible.

Long, involved statements like the "poor" version tend to contaminate the achievement measure with a measure of reading comprehension. A basic rule of item writing is to focus on the intended function of the item and remove all irrelevant influences.

3. *Word the statement so precisely that it can unequivocally be judged true or false.* True statements should be true under all circumstances and yet free of qualifiers ("may," "possible," and so on), which might provide clues. This requires the use of precise words and the avoidance of such vague terms as

"seldom," "frequently," and "often." The same care, of course, must also be given to false statements so that their falsity is not too readily apparent from differences in wording. At first glance, this seems like a simple rule to follow but it causes frequent problems.

EXAMPLE

Poor: T   *F   Lengthening a test will increase its reliability.

Better: *T   F   Lengthening a test by adding items like those in the test will increase its reliability.

The "poor" version of this item must be marked false because it is not true under all conditions. For example, if items are added to the test that all students fail, reliability would not be changed. However, the "poor" version would not be a good item to use in a test because it requires students to mark a very important principle of measurement false. We could say "usually will increase" but the qualifier would encourage those who are uninformed to mark it true and they would receive an unearned point. The "better" version has no such "giveaway" to the answer. In fact, an uninformed student might think that adding similar items to a test of low reliability could not possibly increase reliability—but it does. This example illustrates the great care needed in phrasing statements so that they are unequivocally true but do not contain "giveaways" to the answer.

4. *Use negative statements sparingly and avoid double negatives.* The "no" and/or "not" in negative statements are frequently overlooked and they are read as positive statements. Thus, negative statements should be used only when the learning outcome requires it (e.g., in avoiding a harmful practice), and then the negative words should be emphasized by underlining or by use of capital letters.
Statements including double negatives tend to be so confusing that they should be restated in positive form.

EXAMPLE

Poor: *T   F   Correction-for-guessing is *not* a practice that should *never* be used in testing.

Better: *T   F   Correction-for-guessing is a practice that should sometimes be used in testing.

The double negatives in the "poor" version introduce sufficient ambiguity to cause the item to be a measure of reading comprehension. The "better" version clearly states the same idea in positive form.

5. *Statements of opinion should be attributed to some source unless used to distinguish facts from opinion.* A statement of opinion is not true or false by itself, and it is poor instructional practice to have students respond to it as if it were a factual statement. Obviously, the only way students could mark such an item correctly would be to agree with the opinion of the item writer. It is much more defensible to attribute the item to some source, such as an individual or organization. It then becomes a measure of how well the student knows the beliefs or values of that individual or organization.

EXAMPLE

Poor: T   F   Testing should play a major role in the teaching-learning process.

Better: *T   F   Gronlund believes that testing should play a major role in the teaching-learning process.

In some cases, it is useful to use a series of opinion statements that pertain to the same individual or organization. This permits a more comprehensive measure of how well the student understands a belief or value system.

EXAMPLE

Would the author of your textbook agree or disagree with the following statements? Circle A for agree, D for disagree.

*A   D   1. The first step in achievement testing is to state the intended learning outcomes in performance terms.

A   *D   2. True-false tests are superior to multiple-choice tests for measuring achievement.

Using about 10 items like those listed here would provide a fairly good indication of the students' grasp of the author's point of view. Items like this are useful for measuring how well students understand a textbook without requiring them to agree with the opinions expressed. It is desirable, of course, to select opinion statements that are shared by many experts in the area.

Another valuable use of opinion statements is to ask students to distinguish between statements of fact and statements of opinion. This is an important outcome in its own right and is a basic part of critical thinking.

EXAMPLE

Read each of the following statements and circle F if it is a *fact* and circle O if it is an *opinion*.

*F	O	**1.** The true-false item is a selection-type item.
F	*O	**2.** The true-false item is difficult to construct.
F	*O	**3.** The true-false item encourages student guessing.
*F	O	**4.** The true-false item can be scored objectively.

In addition to illustrating the use of opinion statements in test items, the last two examples illustrate variations from the typical true-false format. These are more logically called *alternative-response* items.

6. *When cause-effect relationships are being measured, use only true propositions.* The true-false item can be used to measure the "ability to identify cause-effect relationships" and this is an important aspect of understanding. When used for this purpose, both propositions should be true and only the relationship judged true or false.

EXAMPLE

Poor:	T	*F	True-false items are classified as objective items	*because*	students must supply the answer.
Better:	T	*F	True-false items are classified as objective items	*because*	there are only two possible answers.

The "poor" version is false because of the second part of the statement. With true-false items, students must *select* the answer rather than *supply* it. However, some students may mark this item false because they think the first part of the statement is incorrect. Thus, they receive one point because they *do not know* that true-false items are classified as objective items. Obviously, an item does not function as intended if misinformation can result in the correct answer. The problem with the "poor" version is that all three elements are permitted to vary (part one, part two, and the relationship between them) and it is impossible to tell what part the student is responding to when the item is marked false. In the "better" version both parts of the statement are true and the students must simply decide if the second part explains why the first part is true. In this case it does not, so it is marked false. Typically, a series of items like this is preceded by directions that make clear that only the relationship between the two parts of each statement is to be judged true or false.

7. *Avoid extraneous clues to the answer.* There are a number of *specific determiners* that provide verbal clues to the truth or falsity of an item. Statements that include such absolutes as "always," "never," "all," "none," and "only" tend to be false; statements with qualifiers such as "usually," "may," and "sometimes" tend to be true. Either these verbal clues must be eliminated from the statements, or their use must be balanced between true items and false items.

EXAMPLE

Poor: T   *F   A statement of opinion should never be used in a true-false item.

Poor: *T   F   A statement of opinion may be used in a true-false item.

Better: *T   F   A statement of opinion, by itself, cannot be marked true or false.

The length and complexity of the statement might also provide a clue. True statements tend to be longer and more complex than false ones because of their need for qualifiers. Thus, a special effort should be made to equalize true and false statements in these respects.

A tendency to use a disproportionate number of true statements, or false statements, might also be detected and used as a clue. Having approximately, but not exactly, an equal number of each seems to be the best solution. When assembling the test, it is, of course, also necessary to avoid placing the correct answers in some discernible pattern (for instance, T, F, T, F). Random placement will eliminate this possible clue.

8. Base items on introductory material to measure more complex learning outcomes. True-false or alternative-response items are frequently used in interpreting written materials, tables, graphs, maps, or pictures. The use of introductory material makes it possible to measure various types of complex learning outcomes. These item types will be illustrated in the section on interpretive exercises later in this chapter.

Checklist for Evaluating True-False Items

1. Is this type of item appropriate for measuring the intended learning outcome?
2. Does the item task match the learning task to be measured?
3. Does each statement contain one central idea?
4. Can each statement be unequivocally judged true or false?
5. Are the statements brief and stated in simple, clear language?
6. Are negative statements used sparingly and double negatives avoided?
7. Are statements of opinion attributed to some source?
8. Are the statements free of clues to the answer (e.g., verbal clues, length)?
9. Is there approximately an even number of true and false statements?
10. When arranged in the test, are the true and false items put in random order?

MATCHING ITEMS

The matching item is simply a variation of the multiple-choice form. A good practice is to switch to the matching format only when it becomes apparent that the same alternatives are being repeated in several multiple-choice items.

EXAMPLE

Which test item is *least* useful for educational diagnosis?
  A. Multiple-choice item.
  *B. True-false item.
  C. Short-answer item.

Which test item measures the greatest variety of learning outcomes?
  *A. Multiple-choice item.
  B. True-false item.
  C. Short-answer item.

Which test item is difficult to score objectively?
  A. Multiple-choice item.
  B. True-false item.
  *C. Short-answer item.

Which test item provides the highest score by guessing?
  A. Multiple-choice item.
  *B. True-false item.
  C. Short-answer item.

Matching Items

Strengths

1. A compact and efficient form is provided where the same set of responses fit a series of item stems (i.e., premises).
2. Reading and response time is short.
3. This item type is easily constructed if converted from multiple-choice items having a common set of alternatives.
4. Scoring is easy, objective, and reliable.

Limitations

1. This item type is largely restricted to simple knowledge outcomes based on association.
2. It is difficult to construct items that contain a sufficient number of homogeneous responses.
3. Susceptibility to irrelevant clues is greater than in other item types.

By switching to a matching format, we can eliminate the repetition of the alternative answers and present the same items in a more compact form. The matching format consists of a series of stems, called *premises,* and a series of alternative answers, called *responses.* These are arranged in columns with directions that set the rules for matching. The following example illustrates how our multiple-choice items can be converted to matching form.

EXAMPLE

Directions: Column A contains a list of characteristics of test items. On the line to the left of each statement, write the letter of the test item in Column B that best fits the statement. Each response in Column B may be used once, more than once, or not at all.

Column A

(B)   **1.** Least useful for educational diagnosis.
(A)   **2.** Measures greatest variety of learning outcomes.
(C)   **3.** Most difficult to score objectively.
(B)   **4.** Provides the highest score by guessing.

Column B

A. Multiple-choice item.
B. True-false item.
C. Short-answer item.

The conversion to matching item illustrated here is probably the most defensible use of this item type. All too frequently, matching items consist of a disparate collection of premises, each of which has only one or two plausible answers. This can be avoided by starting with multiple-choice items and switching to the matching format only when it provides a more compact and efficient means of measuring the same achievement. In our example, we could have also expanded the item by adding other similar premises and responses.

Rules for Writing Matching Items

A good matching item should function the same as a series of multiple-choice items. As each premise is considered, all of the responses should serve as plausible alternatives. The rules for item writing are directed toward this end.

1. *Include only homogeneous material in each matching item.* In our earlier example of a matching item, we included *only* types of test items and their characteristics. Similarly, an item might include *only* authors and their works, inventors and their inventions, scientists and their discoveries, or historical events and their dates. This homogeneity is necessary if all responses are to serve as plausible alternatives (see earlier example).

2. *Keep the lists of items short and place the brief responses on the right.* A short list of items (say less than 10) will save reading time, make it easier for the student to locate the answer, and increase the likelihood that the responses will be homogeneous and plausible. Placing the brief responses on the right also saves reading time.

3. *Use a larger, or smaller, number of responses than premises, and permit the responses to be used more than once.* Both an uneven match and the possibility of using each response more than once reduces the guessing factor. As we noted earlier, proper use of the matching form requires that *all responses be plausible alternatives for each premise.* This, of course, dictates that each response be eligible for use more than once.

4. *Place the responses in alphabetical or numerical order.* This will make selection of the responses easier and avoid possible clues due to placement.

5. *Specify in the directions the basis for matching, and indicate that each response may be used once, more than once, or not at all.* This will clarify the task for all students and prevent any misunderstanding. Take care, however, not to make the directions too long and involved. The previous example illustrates adequate detail for directions.

6. *Put all of the matching item on the same page.* This will prevent the distraction of flipping pages back and forth, and prevent students from overlooking responses on another page.

Checklist for Evaluating Matching Items

1. Is this type of item appropriate for measuring the intended learning outcome?
2. Does the item task match the learning task to be measured?
3. Does each matching item contain only homogeneous material?
4. Are the lists of items short with the brief responses on the right?
5. Is an uneven match provided by making the list of responses longer or shorter than the list of premises?
6. Are the responses in alphabetical or numerical order?
7. Do the directions clearly state the basis for matching and that each response can be used once, more than once, or not at all?
8. Does the complete matching item appear on the same page?

THE INTERPRETIVE EXERCISE

Complex learning outcomes can frequently be more effectively measured by basing a series of test items on a common selection of introductory material. This may be a paragraph, a table, a chart, a graph, a map, or a picture. The test items that follow the introductory material may be designed to call forth any type of intellectual ability or skill that can be measured objectively. This type of exercise is commonly called an *interpretive exercise* and both multiple-choice items and alternative-response items are widely used to measure interpretation of the introductory material.

The following example illustrates the use of multiple-choice items. Note that this item type makes it possible to measure a variety of learning outcomes with the same selection of introductory material. In this particular case, item 1 measures the *ability to recognize unstated assumptions,* item 2 the *ability to identify the meaning of a term,* and item 3 the *ability to identify relationships.*

EXAMPLE

Directions: Read the following comments a teacher made about testing. Then answer the questions that follow by circling the letter of the best answer.

"Students go to school to learn, not to take tests. In addition, tests cannot be used to indicate a student's absolute level of learning. All tests can do is rank students in order of achievement, and this relative ranking is influenced by guessing, bluffing, and the subjective opinions of the teacher doing the scoring. The teacher-learning process would benefit if we did away with tests and depended on student self-evaluation."

1. Which one of the following unstated assumptions is this teacher making?
    A. Students go to school to learn.
    B. Teachers use essay tests primarily.
    *C. Tests make no contribution to learning.
    D. Tests do not indicate a student's absolute level of learning.

2. Which one of the following types of tests is this teacher primarily talking about?
    A. Diagnostic test.
    B. Formative test.
    C. Pretest.
    *D. Summative test.

3. Which one of the following propositions is most essential to the final conclusion?
    *A. Effective self-evaluation does not require the use of tests.
    B. Tests place students in rank order only.
    C. Tests scores are influenced by factors other than achievement.
    D. Students do not go to school to take tests.

The next example uses a modified version of the alternative-response form. This is frequently called a *key-type* item because a common set of alternatives is used in responding to each question. Note that the key-type item is devoted entirely to the measurement of one learning outcome. In this example the item measures the *ability to recognize warranted and unwarranted inferences*.

EXAMPLE

Directions: Paragraph A contains a description of the testing practices of Mr. Smith, a high school teacher. Read the description and each of the statements that follow it. Mark each statement to indicate the type of INFERENCE that can be drawn about it from the material in the paragraph. Place the appropriate letter in front of each statement using the following KEY:

   T—if the statement may be INFERRED as TRUE.
   F—if the statement may be INFERRED as UNTRUE.
   N—if NO INFERENCE may be drawn about it from the paragraph.

Paragraph A

Approximately one week before a test is to be given Mr. Smith carefully goes through the textbook and constructs multiple-choice items based on the material in the book. He always uses the exact wording of the textbook for the correct answer so that there will be no question concerning its correctness. He is careful to include some test items from each chapter. After the test is given, he lists the scores from high to low on the blackboard and tells each student his or her score. He does not return the test papers to the students, but he offers to answer any questions they might have about the test. He puts the items from each test into a test file, which he is building for future use.

Statements on Paragraph A

(T)   **1.** Mr. Smith's tests measure a limited range of learning outcomes.
(F)   **2.** Some of Mr. Smith's test items measure at the understanding level.
(N)   **3.** Mr. Smith's tests measure a balanced sample of subject matter.
(N)   **4.** Mr. Smith uses the type of test item that is best for his purpose.
(T)   **5.** Students can determine where they rank in the distribution of scores on Mr. Smith's tests.
(F)   **6.** Mr. Smith's testing practices are likely to motivate students to overcome their weaknesses.

Key-type items are fairly easy to develop and can be directly related to specific learning outcomes. The key categories can, of course, be reused by simply changing the introductory material and the statements. Thus, they provide a standard framework for test preparation. Other common key categories include the following: (1) the argument is relevant, irrelevant, or neither; (2) the statement is supported by the evidence, refuted by the evidence,

---

Interpretive Exercises

Strengths

1. An efficient means of measuring the interpretation of printed information in various forms (e.g., written, charts, graphs, maps, pictures) is provided.
2. More meaningful complex learning outcomes can be measured than with the single-item format.
3. The use of introductory material provides a common basis for responding.
4. Scoring is easy, objective, and reliable.

Limitations

1. It is difficult to construct effective items.
2. Written material is highly dependent on reading skill.
3. This item type is highly subject to extraneous clues.
4. It is ineffective in measuring the ability to originate, organize, and express ideas.

---

or neither; (3) the assumption is necessary or unnecessary; and (4) the conclusion is valid, invalid, or its validity cannot be determined. Although such standard key categories should not be applied in a perfunctory manner, they can provide guidelines to simplify the construction of the interpretive exercise.

Rules for Constructing Interpretive Exercises

The effectiveness of interpretive exercises, such as those illustrated earlier, depends on the care with which the introductory material is selected and the skill with which the dependent items are prepared. The following rules provide guidelines for preparing high quality exercises of this type.

1. *Select introductory material that is relevant to the learning outcomes to be measured.* The introductory material may take many forms: written material, table, chart, graph, map, picture, or cartoon. In some cases the interpretation of the introductory material is an important learning outcome in its own right, as in the "interpretation of a weather map" or "the interpretation of a line graph." Here the nature of the introductory material is clearly prescribed by the intended outcome. In other cases, however, the introductory material simply provides the means for measuring other important outcomes. The "ability to distinguish between valid and invalid conclusions," for

example, may be measured with different types of introductory material. In this instance we should select the type of material that provides the most direct measure of the learning outcome, is familiar to the examinees, and places the least demand on reading ability. For young children this means pictorial materials should typically be favored.

2. *Select introductory material that is new to the examinees.* Although the form of the material should be familiar to the examinees, the specific content used in an exercise should be new to them. Thus, if they are asked to identify relationships shown in a graph, the type of graph should be familiar but the specific data in the graph must be new. If the data were the same as that presented in the classroom or described in the textbook, the exercise would measure nothing more than the simple recall of information. To measure complex outcomes, some novelty is necessary. How much depends on the specific nature of the intended outcome.

In some cases it is possible to locate introductory material that is new to the examinees by reviewing sources that are not readily available to them. Then it is simply a matter of adapting the material for testing purposes. In other cases it is necessary to prepare completely new material (i.e., write a paragraph, construct a graph, make a map, or draw a picture). In either case further revision will probably be needed when the dependent test items are being prepared. The process is essentially a circular one, with the writing of items requiring some changes in the introductory material and changes there providing ideas for new items. In carrying out this process of adapting and revising the material, be careful not to introduce so much novelty that the exercise no longer provides a valid measure of the intended learning outcome.

3. *Keep the introductory material brief and readable.* It is inefficient for both the test maker and the test taker to use extended introductory material and only one or two test items. If the introductory material is in written form, excessively long selections will also create problems for individuals with inadequate reading skills. Ideally it should be a brief, concise selection that contains enough ideas for several relevant test items. Material of this type can frequently be obtained from summaries, digests, and other condensed forms of written material. In some cases pictures or diagrams may provide the most concise summary of the material. As noted earlier we should always favor the type of material that places the least demand on reading ability.

4. *Construct test items that call forth the type of performance specified in the learning outcome.* To adequately measure the intended interpretation of the introductory material requires careful phrasing of the questions and special attention to two important cautions. First, *the answer to an item should not be given directly in the material* since some mental process beyond "recognition of a stated fact" is required in measures of intellectual skills. Second, *it should not be possible to answer the question without the introductory material.* If an item can be answered on the basis of general knowledge, it is not measuring the ability to interpret the material in the exercise. A good check on this type of error is to cover the introductory material and attempt to answer the questions without it.

5. *Follow the rules of effective item writing that pertain to the type of objective item used.* All of the rules for constructing the various types of objective test items discussed in the last two chapters are applicable to the construction of items used in interpretive exercises. Even greater care must be taken to avoid extraneous clues, however, since items in interpretive exercises seem especially prone to such clues and they tend to be more difficult to detect in these items. If the introductory material includes illustrations, for example, special attention should be directed to such things as the size, shape, and position of objects as possible extraneous clues. These are frequently overlooked by the test maker who is concentrating on the intricacies of the mental response required, but not by the unprepared student who is frantically searching for any solution to the problem.

The greatest help in constructing interpretive exercises is to review a wide range of sample exercises that use different types of introductory material and different forms of dependent test items. For locating illustrative exercises, see the list of references at the end of the chapter.

Checklist for Evaluating Interpretive Exercises

1. Is this type of exercise appropriate for measuring the intended learning outcome?
2. Is the introductory material relevant to the learning outcomes?
3. Is the introductory material familiar but new to the examinees?
4. Is the introductory material brief and at the appropriate reading level?
5. Do the test items call forth the performance specified in the learning outcomes?
6. Do the test items call for interpretation (rather than recognition or recall)?
7. Do the test items meet the criteria of effective item writing that apply to the item type used?
8. Is the interpretive exercise free of extraneous clues?

SUMMARY OF POINTS

1. A good practice is to start with multiple-choice items and switch to other selection-type items when more appropriate.
2. The true-false or alternative-response item is appropriate when there are only two possible alternatives.
3. The true-false item is used primarily to measure knowledge of specific facts, although there are some notable exceptions.
4. Each true-false statement should contain only one central idea, be concisely stated, be free of clues and irrelevant sources of difficulty, and have an answer on which experts would agree.
5. Modifications of the true-false item are especially useful for measuring the ability to "distinguish between fact and opinion" and "identify cause-effect relations."
6. Modifications of the true-false item can be used in interpretive exercises to measure various types of complex learning outcomes.
7. The matching item is a variation of the multiple-choice form and is appropriate when it provides a more compact and efficient means of measuring the same achievement.
8. The matching item consists of a list of *premises* and a list of the *responses* to be related to the premises.
9. A good matching item is based on homogeneous material, contains a brief list of premises and an uneven number of responses (more or less) that can be used more than once, and has the brief responses in the right-hand column.
10. The directions for a matching item should indicate the basis for matching and that each response can be used more than once.
11. The interpretive exercise consists of a series of selection-type items based on some type of introductory material (e.g., paragraph, table, chart, graph, map, or picture).
12. The interpretive exercise uses both multiple-choice and alternative-response items to measure a variety of complex learning outcomes.
13. The introductory material used in an interpretive exercise must be relevant to the outcomes to be measured, new to examinees, at the proper reading level, and as brief as possible.
14. The test items used in an interpretive exercise should call for the intended type of interpretation, and the answers to the items should be dependent on the introductory material.
15. The test items used in an interpretive exercise should be in harmony with the rules for constructing that item type.

ADDITIONAL READING

Ebel, R. L., and Frisbie, D. A., *Essentials of Educational Measurement,* 5th ed. (Englewood Cliffs, NJ: Prentice-Hall, 1991). See Chapter 8, "True-False Test Items," for a more favorable treatment of this item type than that found in most educational measurement books.

Educational Testing Service, *Multiple Choice Questions: A Close Look* (Princeton, NJ: Test Development Division, ETS, 1973). Illustrates the use of maps, graphs, diagrams, pictures, and written materials for measuring complex achievement.

Linn, R. L., and Gronlund, N. E., *Measurement and Assessment in Teaching,* 7th ed. (Englewood Cliffs, NJ: Prentice-Hall, 1995). See Chapter 8, "Measuring Complex Achievement: The Interpretive Exercise," for a variety of illustrative exercises for different subject areas, grade levels, and types of introductory material.

Mehrens, W. A., and Lehmann, I. J., *Measurement and Evaluation in Education and Psychology,* 4th ed. (New York: Holt, Rinehart and Winston, 1991). See Chapter 7, "Writing the Objective Test Item: Multiple-Choice and Context-Dependent," for sample interpretive exercises and rules for writing them.

Payne, D. A., *Measuring and Evaluating Educational Outcomes* (New York: Macmillan, 1992). See Chapter 6, for general guidelines for item writing and for rules for writing true-false items.

▶ 6

Writing Supply Items
Short Answer and Essay

Studying this chapter should enable you to

1. Describe the strengths and limitations of short-answer items.
2. Distinguish between well-stated and poorly stated short-answer items.
3. Identify and correct faults in poorly stated short-answer items.
4. Match short-answer items to intended learning outcomes.
5. Construct short-answer items that are well-stated, relevant to important learning outcomes, and free of defects.
6. Describe the strengths and limitations of essay questions.
7. Distinguish between restricted-response and extended-response essay questions.
8. Describe the strengths and limitations of essay questions.
9. Write essay questions that present a clear task, are relevant to important learning outcomes, and provide guidelines for scoring.
10. Score essay answers more effectively.

As noted in the last two chapters, selection-type items can be designed to measure a variety of learning outcomes, ranging from simple to complex. They tend to be favored in achievement tests because they provide (1) greater control of the type of response students can make, (2) broader sampling of achievement, and (3) quicker and more objective scoring. Despite these advantages, supply-type items can also play an important role in measuring achievement.

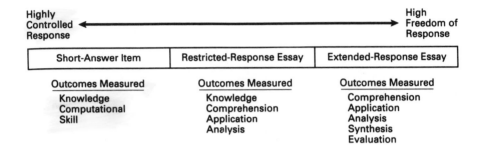

FIGURE 6.1   Supply-Type Items Arranged along a "Control of Response" Continuum and a List of Learning Outcomes Typically Measured by Each Item Type

Supply-type items require students to produce the answer. This may be a single word or a several-page response. Although the length of response ranges along a continuum, supply-type items are typically divided into (1) short-answer items, (2) restricted-response essay, and (3) extended-response essay (see Figure 6.1).

SHORT-ANSWER ITEMS

The short-answer (or completion) item requires the examinee to supply the appropriate words, numbers, or symbols to answer a question or complete a statement.

EXAMPLE

What are the incorrect responses in a multiple-choice item called? *(distracters)*
The incorrect responses in a multiple-choice item are called *(distracters)*

This item type also includes computational problems and any other simple item form that requires supplying the answer rather than selecting it. Except for its use in computational problems, the short-answer item is used primarily to measure simple knowledge outcomes.

The short-answer item appears to be easy to write and use but there are two major problems in constructing short-answer items. First, it is extremely difficult to phrase the question or incomplete statement so that only one answer is correct. In the example we have noted, for instance, a student might respond with any one of a number of answers that could be defended as appropriate. The student might write "incorrect alternatives," "wrong an-

---

Short-Answer Items

Strengths

1. It is easy to write test items.
2. Guessing is less likely than in selection-type items.
3. This item type is well-suited to computational problems and other learning outcomes where supplying the answer is important.
4. A broad range of knowledge outcomes can be measured.

Limitations

1. It is difficult to phrase statements so that only one answer is correct.
2. Scoring is contaminated by spelling ability when responses are verbal.
3. Scoring is tedious and time consuming.
4. This item type is not very adaptable to measuring complex learning outcomes.

---

swers," "inappropriate options," "decoys," "foils," or some other equally descriptive response. Second, there is the problem of spelling. If credit is given only when the answer is spelled correctly, the poor spellers will be prevented from showing their true level of achievement and the test scores will become an uninterpretable mixture of knowledge and spelling skill. On the other hand, if attempts are made to ignore spelling during the scoring process, there is still the problem of deciding whether a badly spelled word represents the intended answer. This, of course, introduces an element of subjectivity that tends to make the scores less dependable as measures of achievement.

Due to these weaknesses, the short-answer item should be reserved for those special situations where supplying the answer is a necessary part of the learning outcome to be measured; for example, where the intent is to have students *recall* the information, where computational problems are used, or where a selection-type item would make the answer obvious. In these situations, the use of the short-answer item can be defended despite its shortcomings.

Rules for Writing Short-Answer Items

1. *State the item so that only a single, brief answer is possible.* This requires great skill in phrasing and the use of precise terms. What appears to be a simple, clear question to the test maker can frequently be answered in many different ways, as we noted with the previous sample item. It helps to review the item with this rule in mind and revise as needed.

2. *Start with a direct question and switch to an incomplete statement only when greater conciseness is possible by doing so.* The use of a direct question increases the likelihood that the problem will be stated clearly and that only one answer will be appropriate. Also, incomplete statements tend to be less ambiguous when they are based on problems that were first stated in question form.

EXAMPLE

What is another name for true-false items? *(alternative-response items)*
True-false items are also called *(alternative-response items)*.

In some cases, it is best to leave it in question form. This may make the item clearer, especially to younger students.

3. *It is best to leave only one blank and it should relate to the main point of the statement.* Leaving several blanks to be filled in is often confusing and the answer to one blank may depend on the answer in another.

EXAMPLE

Poor: In terms of type of response, the (matching) item is most like the *(multiple-choice)* item.

Better: In terms of type of responses, which item is most like the matching item? *(multiple-choice)*.

In the "poor" version, a number of different responses would have to be given credit, such as "short answer" and "essay," and "true-false" and "multiple-choice." Obviously, the item would not function as originally intended.

It is also important to avoid asking students to respond to unimportant or minor aspects of a statement. Focus on the main idea of the item and leave a blank only for the key response.

4. *Place the blanks at the end of the statement.* This permits the student to read the complete problem before coming to the blank to be filled. With this procedure, confusion and rereading of the item is avoided and scoring is simplified. Constructing incomplete statements with blanks at the end is more easily accomplished when the item is first stated as a direct question, as suggested earlier. In some cases, it may be a matter of rewording the item and changing the response to be made.

EXAMPLE

Poor: *(Reliability)* is likely to increase when a test is lengthened.

Better: When a test is lengthened, reliability is likely to *(increase)*.

With this particular item, the "better" version also provides a more clearly focused item. The "poor" version could be answered by "validity," "time for testing," "fatigue," and other unintended but clearly correct responses. This again illustrates the great care needed in phrasing short-answer items.

5. ***Avoid extraneous clues to the answer.*** One of the most common clues in short-answer items is the length of the blank. If a long blank is used for a long word and a short blank for a short word, this is obviously a clue. Thus, all blanks should be uniform in length. Another common clue is the use of the indefinite article "a" or "an" just before the blank. It sometimes gives away the answer, or at least rules out some possible incorrect answers.

EXAMPLE

Poor: The supply-type item used to measure the ability to organize and integrate material is called an *(essay item)*.

Better: Supply-type items used to measure the ability to organize and integrate material are called *(essay items)*.

The "poor" version rules out "short-answer item," the only other supply-type item, because it does not follow the article "an." One solution is to include both articles, using a(an). Another solution is to eliminate the article by switching to plural, as shown in the "better" version.

6. ***For numerical answers, indicate the degree of precision expected and the units in which they are to be expressed.*** Indicating the degree of precision (e.g., to the nearest whole number) will clarify the task for students and pre-

---

Checklist for Evaluating Short-Answer Items

1. Is this type of item appropriate for measuring the intended learning outcome?
2. Does the item task match the learning task to be measured?
3. Does the item call for a single, brief answer?
4. Has the item been written as a direct question or a well-stated incomplete sentence.
5. Does the desired response relate to the main point of the item?
6. Is the blank placed at the end of the statement?
7. Have clues to the answer been avoided (e.g., "a" or "an," length of the blank)?
8. Are the units and degree of precision indicated for numerical answers?

vent them from spending more time on an item than is required. Indicating the units in which to express the answer will aid scoring by providing a more uniform set of responses (e.g., minutes rather than fractions of an hour). When the learning outcome requires knowing the type of unit in common use and the degree of precision expected, this rule must then be disregarded.

ESSAY QUESTIONS

The most notable characteristic of the essay question is the freedom of response it provides. As with the short-answer item, students must produce their own answers. With the essay question, however, they are free to decide how to approach the problem, what factual information to use, how to organize the answer, and what degree of emphasis to give each aspect of the response. Thus, the essay question is especially useful for measuring the ability to organize, integrate, and express ideas. These are the types of performance for which selection-type items and short-answer items are so inadequate.

In deciding when and how to use essay questions, it may be desirable to compare their relative merits with those of selection-type items, as shown in Table 6.1. As can be seen in the table, both item types are efficient for certain purposes and inefficient for others. It is also apparent that the two types tend to complement each other in terms of the types of learning outcomes measured and the effect they are most likely to have on learning. Thus, it is not a matter of using either selection-type items or essay questions, but rather when should each be used. Tests may frequently require both types in order to obtain adequate coverage of the intended learning outcomes.

Types of Essay Questions

The freedom of response permitted by essay questions varies considerably. Students may be required to give a brief and precise response, or they may be given great freedom in determining the form and scope of their answers. Questions of the first type are commonly called *restricted-response questions* and those of the second type are called *extended-response questions*. This is an arbitrary but convenient pair of categories for classifying essay questions.

Restricted-Response Questions.   The restricted-response question places strict limits on the answer to be given. The boundaries of the subject matter to be considered are usually narrowly defined by the problem, and the specific form of the answer is also commonly indicated (by words such as "list," "define," and "give reasons"). In some cases the response is limited further by the use of introductory material or by the use of special directions.

TABLE 6.1 Summary Comparison of Selection-Type Items and Essay

	SELECTION-TYPE ITEMS	ESSAY QUESTIONS
Learning Outcomes Measured	Good for measuring outcomes at the knowledge, comprehension, and application levels of learning; inadequate for organizing and expressing ideas.	Inefficient for measuring knowledge outcomes; best for ability to organize, integrate, and express ideas.
Sampling of Content	The use of a large number of items results in broad coverage, which makes representative sampling of content feasible.	The use of a small number of items limits coverage, which makes representative sampling of content infeasible.
Preparation of Items	Preparation of good items is difficult and time consuming.	Preparation of good items is difficult but easier than selection-type items.
Scoring	Objective, simple, and highly reliable.	Subjective, difficult, and less reliable.
Factors Distorting Scores	Reading ability and guessing.	Writing ability and bluffing.
Probable Effect on Learning	Encourages students to remember, interpret, and use the ideas of others.	Encourages students to organize, integrate, and express their own ideas.

EXAMPLE

Describe the relative merits of selection-type test items and essay questions for measuring learning outcomes at the comprehension level. Confine your answer to one page.

EXAMPLE

Mr. Rogers, a ninth-grade science teacher, wants to measure his students' "ability to interpret scientific data" with a paper-and-pencil test.

1. Describe the steps that Mr. Rogers should follow.
2. Give reasons to justify each step.

Restricting the form and scope of the answers to essay questions has both advantages and disadvantages. Such questions can be prepared more easily, related more directly to specific learning outcomes, and scored more easily.

On the other hand, they provide little opportunity for the students to demonstrate their abilities to organize, to integrate, and to develop essentially new patterns of response. The imposed limitations make restricted-response items especially useful for measuring learning outcomes at the comprehension, application, and analysis levels of learning. They are of relatively little value for measuring outcomes at the synthesis and evaluation levels. At these levels the extended-response question provides the more appropriate measure.

Extended-Response Questions.   The extended-response question gives the student almost unlimited freedom to determine the form and scope of their responses. Although in some instances rather rigid practical limits may be imposed, such as time limits or page limits, restrictions on the material to be included in the answer and on the form of response are held to a minimum. The student must be given sufficient freedom to demonstrate skills of synthesis and evaluation, and just enough control to assure that the intended intellectual skills and abilities will be called forth by the question. Thus, the amount of structure will vary from item to item depending on the learning outcomes being measured, but the stress will always be on providing as much freedom as the situation permits.

EXAMPLE

Synthesis Outcome: For a course that you are teaching or expect to teach, prepare a complete plan for assessing student achievement. Be sure to include the procedures you would follow, the instruments you would use, and the reasons for your choices.

EXAMPLE

Evaluation Outcome: (The student is given a complete achievement test that includes errors or flaws in the directions, in the test items, and in the arrangement of the items.) Write a critical evaluation of this test using as evaluative criteria the rules and standards for test construction described in your textbook. Include a detailed analysis of the test's strengths and weaknesses and an evaluation of its overall quality and probable effectiveness.

The extended-response question provides for the creative integration of ideas, the overall evaluation of materials, and a broad approach to problem solving. These are all important learning outcomes and ones that cannot be measured by other types of test items. The biggest problem, of course, is to evaluate the answers with sufficient reliability to provide a useful measure of learning. This is a difficult and time-consuming task, but the importance of the outcomes would seem to justify the additional care and effort required.

Essay Questions

Strengths

1. The highest level learning outcomes (analysis, synthesis, evaluation) can be measured.
2. Preparation time is less than that for selection-type items.
3. The integration and application of ideas is emphasized.

Limitations

1. There is an inadequate sampling of achievement due to time needed for answering each question.
2. It is difficult to relate to intended learning outcomes because of freedom to select, organize, and express ideas.
3. Scores are raised by writing skill and bluffing and lowered by poor handwriting, misspelling, and grammatical errors.
4. Scoring is time consuming, subjective, and tends to be unreliable.

Rules for Writing Essay Questions

The construction of clear, unambiguous easy questions that call forth the desired responses is a much more difficult task than is commonly presumed. The following rules will not make the task any easier, but their application will result in essay items of higher quality.

1. *Use essay questions to measure complex learning outcomes only.* Most knowledge outcomes profit little from being measured by easy questions. These outcomes can usually be measured more effectively by objective items that lack the sampling and scoring problems that essay questions introduce. There may be a few exceptions, as when supplying the answer is a basic part of the learning outcome, but for most knowledge outcomes essay questions simply provide a less reliable measure with no compensating benefits.

At the comprehension, application, and analysis levels of learning, both objective tests and essay tests are useful. Even here, though, the objective test would seem to have priority, the essay test being reserved for those situations that require the student to *give* reasons, *explain* relationships, *describe* data, *formulate* conclusions, or in some other way produce the appropriate answer. Where supplying the answer is vital, a properly constructed restricted-response question is likely to be most appropriate.

At the synthesis and evaluation levels of learning, both the objective test and the restricted-response test have only limited value. These tests may be used to measure some specific aspects of the total process, but the production of a complete work (such as a plan of operation) or an overall evaluation of a work (for instance, an evaluation of a novel or an experiment) requires the use of extended-response questions. It is at this level that the essay form contributes most uniquely.

2. *Relate the questions as directly as possible to the learning outcomes being measured.* Essay questions will not measure complex learning outcomes unless they are carefully constructed to do so. Each question should be specifically designed to measure one or more well-defined outcomes. Thus, the place to start, as is the case with objective items, is with a precise description of the performance to be measured. This will help determine both the content and form of the item and will aid in the phrasing of it.

The restricted-response item is related quite easily to a specific learning outcome because it is so highly structured. The limited response expected from the student also makes it possible for the test maker to phrase the question so that its intent is communicated clearly to the student. The extended-response item, however, requires greater freedom of response and typically involves a number of learning outcomes. This makes it more difficult to relate the question to the intended outcomes and to indicate the nature of the desired answer through the phrasing of the question. If the task is prescribed too rigidly in the question, the students' freedom to select, organize, and present the answer is apt to be infringed upon. One practical solution is to indicate to the students the criteria to be used in evaluating the answer. For example, a parenthetical statement such as the following might be added: "Your answer will be evaluated in terms of its comprehensiveness, the relevance of its arguments, the appropriateness of its examples, and the skill with which it is organized." This clarifies the task to the students without limiting their freedom, and makes the item easier to relate to clearly defined learning outcomes.

3. *Formulate questions that present a clear task to be performed.* Phrasing an essay question so that the desired response is obtained is no simple matter. Selecting precise terms and carefully phrasing and rephrasing the question with the desired response in mind will help clarify the task to the student. Since essay questions are to be used as a measure of complex learning outcomes, avoid starting such questions with "who," "what," "when," "where," "name," and "list." These terms tend to limit the response to knowledge outcomes. Complex achievement is most apt to be called forth by such words as "why," "describe," "explain," "compare," "relate," "contrast," "interpret," "analyze," "criticize," and "evaluate." The specific terminology to be used will be determined largely by the specific behavior described in the learning outcome to be measured (see Table 6.2).

There is no better way to check on the phrasing of an essay question than to write a model answer, or at least to formulate a mental answer, to the

TABLE 6.2   Types of Complex Outcomes and Related Terms for Writing Essay Questions

OUTCOME	SAMPLE TERMS
Comparing	compare, classify, describe, distinguish between, explain, outline, summarize
Interpreting	convert, draw, estimates, illustrate, interpret, restate, summarize, translate
Inferring	derive, draw, estimate, extend, extrapolate, predict, propose, relate
Applying	arrange, compute, describe, demonstrate, illustrate, rearrange, relate, summarize
Analyzing	break down, describe, diagram, differentiate, divide, list, outline, separate
Creating	compose, design, devise, draw, formulate, make up, present, propose
Synthesizing	arrange, combine, construct, design, rearrange, regroup, relate, write
Generalizing	construct, develop, explain, formulate, generate, make, propose, state
Evaluating	appraise, criticize, defend, describe, evaluate, explain, judge, write

question. This helps the test maker detect any ambiguity in the question, aids in determining the approximate time needed by the student to develop a satisfactory answer, and provides a rough check on the mental processes required. This procedure is most feasible with the restricted-response item, the answer to which is more limited and more closely prescribed. With the extended-response form it may be necessary to ask one or more colleagues to read the question to determine if the form and scope of the desired answer are clear.

4. Do not permit a choice of questions unless the learning outcome requires it. In most tests of achievement, it is best to have all students answer the same questions. If they are permitted to write on only a fraction of the questions, such as three out of five, their answers cannot be evaluated on a comparative basis. Also, since the students will tend to choose those questions they are best prepared to answer, their responses will provide a sample of their achievement that is less representative than that obtained without optional questions. As we noted earlier, one of the major limitations of the essay test is the limited and unrepresentative sampling it provides. Giving students a choice among questions simply complicates the sampling problem further and introduces greater distortion into the test results.

In some situations the use of optional questions might be defensible. For example, if the essay is to be used as a measure of writing *skill* only, some choice of topics on which to write may be desirable. This might also be the case if the essay is used to measure some aspects of creativity, or if the students have pursued individual interests through independent study. Even for these special uses, however, great caution must be exercised in the use of optional questions. The ability to organize, integrate, and express ideas is determined in part by the complexity of the content involved. Thus, an indeterminate amount of contamination can be expected when optional questions are used.

5. *Provide ample time for answering and suggest a time limit on each question.* Since essay questions are designed most frequently to measure intellectual skills and abilities, time must be allowed for thinking as well as for writing. Thus, generous time limits should be provided. For example, rather than expecting students to write on several essay questions during one class period, it might be better to have them focus on one or two. There seems to be a tendency for teachers to include so many questions in a single essay test that a high score is as much a measure of writing speed as of achievement. This is probably an attempt to overcome the problem of limited sampling, but it tends to be an undesirable solution. In measuring complex achievement, it is better to use fewer questions and to improve the sample by more frequent testing.

Informing students of the appropriate amount of time they should spend on each question will help them use their time more efficiently; ideally, it will also provide a more adequate sample of their achievement. If the length of the answer is not clearly defined by the problem, as in some extended-response questions, it might also be desirable to indicate page limits. Anything that will clarify the form and scope of the task without interfering with the measurement of the intended outcomes is likely to contribute to more effective measurement.

Rules for Scoring Essay Answers

As we noted earlier, one of the major limitations of the essay test is the subjectivity of the scoring. That is, the feelings of the scorers are likely to enter into the judgments they make concerning the quality of the answers. This may be a personal bias toward the writer of the essay, toward certain areas of content or styles of writing, or toward shortcomings in such extraneous areas as legibility, spelling, and grammar. These biases, of course, distort the results of a measure of achievement and tend to lower their reliability.

The following rules are desired to minimize the subjectivity of the scoring and to provide as uniform a standard of scoring from one student to another as possible. These rules will be most effective, of course, when the questions have been carefully prepared in accordance with the rules for construction.

1. *Evaluate answers to essay questions in terms of the learning outcomes being measured.* The essay test, like the objective test, is used to obtain evidence concerning the extent to which clearly defined learning outcomes have been achieved. Thus, the desired student performance specified in these outcomes should serve as a guide both for constructing the questions and for evaluating the answers. If a question is designed to measure "the ability to explain cause-effect relations," for example, the answer should be evaluated in terms of how adequately the student *explains the particular cause-effect relations presented in the question.* All other factors, such as interesting but extraneous factual information, style of writing, and errors in spelling and grammar, should be ignored (to the extent possible) during the evaluation. In some cases separate scores may be given for spelling or writing ability, but these should not be allowed to contaminate the scores that represent the degree of achievement of the intended learning outcomes.

2. *Score restricted-response answers by the point method, using a model answer as a guide.* Scoring with the aid of a previously prepared scoring key is possible with the restricted-response item because of the limitations placed on the answer. The procedure involves writing a model answer to each question and determining the number of points to be assigned to it and to the parts within it. The distribution of points within an answer must, of course, take into account all scorable units indicated in the learning outcomes being measured. For example, points may be assigned to the relevance of the examples used and to the organization of the answer, as well as to the content of the answer, if these are legitimate aspects of the learning outcome. As indicate earlier, it is usually desirable to make clear to the student at the time of testing the basis on which each answer will be judged (content, organization, and so on).

3. *Grade extended-response answers by the rating method, using defined criteria as a guide.* Extended-response items allow so much freedom in answering that the preparation of a model answer is frequently impossible. Thus, the test maker usually *grades* each answer by judging its quality in terms of a previously determined set of criteria, rather than *scoring* it point by point with a scoring key. The criteria for judging the quality of an answer are determined by the nature of the question, and thus, by the learning outcomes being measured. If students were asked to "describe a complete plan for preparing an achievement test," for example, the criteria would include such

things as (1) the completeness of the plan (for example, whether it included a statement of objectives, a set of specifications, and the appropriate types of items), (2) the clarity and accuracy with which each step was described, (3) the adequacy of the justification for each step, and (4) the degree to which the various parts of the plan were properly integrated.

Typically, the criteria for evaluating an answer are used to establish about five levels of quality. Then as the answer to a question is read, it is assigned a letter grade or a number from one to five, which designates the reader's rating. One grade may be assigned on the basis of the overall quality of the answer, or a separate judgment may be made on the basis of each criterion. The latter procedure provides the most useful information for diagnosing and improving learning and should be used wherever possible.

More uniform standards of grading can usually be obtained by reading the answers to each question twice. During the first reading the papers should be tentatively sorted into five piles, ranging from high to low in quality. The second reading can then serve the purpose of checking the uniformity of the answers in each pile and making any necessary shifts in rating.

Student Bluffing and Scoring Essays

Students can obtain higher scores on essay questions by clever bluffing. Although this requires skill in writing and some knowledge of the topic, credit should not be given unless the question is specifically answered. Some common types of bluffing are listed below.

1. Student repeats the question in statement form (slightly paraphrased) and tells how important the topic is (e.g., "The role of assessment in teaching is extremely important. It is hard to imagine effective instruction without it, etc.").
2. Student writes on a well-known topic and fits it to the question (e.g., a student who knows testing well but knows little about performance assessment and is asked to compare testing and performance assessment might describe testing in considerable detail and frequently state that performance assessment is much superior for evaluating the type of learning measured by the test).
3. Student liberally sprinkles the answer with basic concepts whether they are understood or not (e.g., asked to write about any assessment technique the importance of "validity" and "reliability" is mentioned frequently).
4. Student includes the teacher's basic beliefs wherever possible (e.g., "The intended learning outcomes must be stated in performance terms before this type of test is constructed or selected").

Bluffing is most effective where plans have not been made for careful scoring of the answers.

4. Evaluate all of the students' answers to one question before proceeding to the next question. Scoring or grading essay tests question by question, rather than student by student, makes it possible to maintain a more uniform standard for judging the answers to each question. This procedure also helps offset the *halo effect* in grading. When all of the answers on one paper are read together, the grader's impression of the paper as a whole is apt to influence the grades assigned to the individual answers. Grading question by question prevents the formation of this overall impression of a student's paper. Each answer is more apt to be judged on its own merits when it is read and compared with other answers to the same question than when it is read and compared with other answers by the same student.

5. Evaluate answers to essay questions without knowing the identity of the writer. This is another attempt to control personal bias during scoring. Answers to essay questions should be evaluated in terms of what is written, not in terms of what is known about the writers from other contacts with them. The best way to prevent prior knowledge from biasing our judgment is to evaluate each answer without knowing the identity of the writer. This can be done by having the students write their names on the back of the paper or by using code numbers in place of names.

6. Whenever possible, have two or more persons grade each answer. The best way to check on the reliability of the scoring of essay answers is to obtain two or more independent judgments. Although this may not be a feasible practice for routine classroom testing, it might be done periodically with a fellow teacher (one who is equally competent in the area). Obtaining two or more independent ratings becomes especially vital where the results are to be used for important and irreversible decisions, such as in the selection of stu-

---

Checklist for Evaluating Essay Questions

1. Is this type of item appropriate for measuring the intended learning outcome?
2. Does the item task match the learning task to be measured?
3. Is the question designed to measure complex learning outcomes?
4. Does the question make clear what is being measured and how the answer will be evaluated?
5. Has terminology been used that clarifies and limits the task (e.g., "describe," not "discuss")?
6. Are all students required to answer the same questions?
7. Has an ample time limit been indicated for each question?
8. Have adequate provisions been made for scoring answers (e.g., model answers or criteria for evaluating)?

dents for further training or for special awards. Here, the pooled ratings of several competent persons may be needed to attain a level of reliability that is commensurate with the significance of the decision being made.

SUMMARY OF POINTS

1. Use supply-type items whenever producing the answer is an essential element in the learning outcome (e.g., *defines* terms, instead of *identifies* meaning of terms).
2. Supply-type items include short-answer items, restricted-response essay, and extended-response essay.
3. The short-answer item can be answered by a word, number, symbol, or brief phrase.
4. The short-answer item is limited primarily to measuring simple knowledge outcomes.
5. Each short-answer item should be so carefully written that there is only one possible answer, the entire item can be read before coming to the answer space, and there are no extraneous clues to the answer.
6. In scoring short-answer items, give credit for all correct answers and score for spelling separately.
7. Essay questions are most useful to measuring the ability to organize, integrate, and express ideas.
8. Essay questions are inefficient for measuring knowledge outcomes because they provide limited sampling, are influenced by extraneous factors (e.g., writing skills, bluffing, grammar, spelling, handwriting), and scoring is subjective and unreliable.
9. Restricted-response essay questions can be more easily written and scored, but due to limitations on the responses they are less useful for measuring the higher-level outcomes (e.g., integration of diverse material).
10. Extended-response essay questions provide the freedom to select, organize, and express ideas in the manner that seems most appropriate; therefore, they are especially useful for measuring such outcomes.
11. Essay questions should be written to measure complex learning outcomes, to present a clear task, and to contain only those restrictions needed to call forth the intended response and provide for adequate scoring.
12. Essay answers should be scored by focusing on the intended response, by using a model answer or set of criteria as a guide, by scoring question by question, and by ignoring the writer's identity. Be wary of student bluffing. If an important decision is to be based on the results, two or more competent scores should be used.

ADDITIONAL READING

Linn, R. L., and Gronlund, N. E., *Measurement and Assessment in Teaching*, 7th ed. (Englewood Cliffs, NJ: Prentice-Hall, 1995). See Chapter 9, "Measuring Complex Achievement: Essay Questions," for a comparison of the essay test to the interpretive exercise and illustrative thought questions for use in essay tests.

Mehrens, W. A., and Lehmann, I. J., *Measurement and Evaluation in Education and Psychology*, 4th ed. (New York: Holt, Rinehart & Winston, 1991). See Chapter 5, "The Essay Test: Preparing the Questions and Grading the Responses," for examples of essay questions and rules for constructing and scoring.

Oosterhof, A. C., *Classroom Applications of Educational Measurement* (Columbus, OH: Merrill Publishing Co., 1990). See Chapter 5, "Constructing and Scoring Essay Items," for guidelines to follow and sample essay items.

Popham, W. J., *Modern Educational Measurement: A Practitioner's Perspective*, 2nd ed. (Englewood Cliffs, NJ: Prentice-Hall, 1990). See Chapter 11, "Constructed-Response Tests," for suggestions for constructing short-answer and essay items and for using a scoring guide.

Stiggins, R. J., *Student Centered Classroom Assessment* (New York: Macmillan, 1994). See Chapter 7, "Essay Assessment: Vast Untaped Potential," for using essay tests to measure complex learning outcomes, and for descriptions of how to prepare exercises and specify scoring criteria.

Assembling, Administering, and Evaluating the Test

Studying this chapter should enable you to

1. Review, edit, and improve test items.
2. Select and arrange items for efficient test taking.
3. Write clear, concise, and complete test directions.
4. Reproduce a well-spaced, error-free test copy.
5. Administer and score a test under controlled conditions.
6. Compute indexes of item difficulty and item discrimination.
7. Interpret item-analysis data.
8. Prepare a test item file.
9. Describe how the computer can contribute to more effective achievement testing.

When constructing items for an achievement test, it is usually desirable to prepare them at least a week or two in advance. A useful practice is to prepare a few items each day while instruction is under way and the material discussed in class is still fresh in mind. In any event, early preparation makes it possible to set the items aside for a time so that they can be reviewed later with a fresh outlook. It is also desirable to prepare more items than the test specifications call for, since defects are likely to become apparent in some items during the later review. The extra items will make it easier for you to maintain the distribution of items reflected in the set of specifications. If you are fortunate enough to end up with more good items than the specifications call for, you can store the extra items in an item file for future use.

Each test item prepared should be written on a separate card (such as a 5 × 8 index card). This simplifies the task of reviewing the items, arranging them in the test, and filing them for future use. The index card is also a convenient place for recording item-analysis data after the effectiveness of each item has been evaluated. If a microcomputer is being used, the items can, of course, be written and stored directly in the computer.

REVIEWING AND EDITING THE ITEMS

The pool of items for a particular test, after being set aside for a time, can be reviewed by the individual who constructed them or by a colleague. In either case it is helpful for the reviewer to read and answer each item as if taking the test. This provides a check on the correct answer and a means of spotting any obvious defects. A more careful evaluation of the items can be made by considering them in light of each of the following questions.

1. *Does each test item measure an important learning outcome included in the test specifications?* Each test item should relate to one of the outcomes in the specifications, since each item is designed to measure one aspect of the subject matter and student performance specified there. If the outcome to which the item refers was noted on the card at the time the item was constructed, the task is simply to read the item and recheck its appropriateness. Essay questions and complex objective items may have to be checked against several outcomes in the specifications. In the final analysis each item should be related directly to the type of performance specified by the learning outcome(s) to be measured.

2. *Is each item type appropriate for the particular learning outcome to be measured?* Some learning outcomes can be measured by any of the common item types. In such cases the multiple-choice item should be favored. However, if the learning outcome calls for supplying the answer, the completion or essay test must be used. If only two alternatives are plausible, the true-false item might be the most useful, and if the outcome calls for relating a series of homogeneous elements, the matching item might be more efficient. Reviewing the items provides for a second check on the appropriateness of each item type for the outcomes to be measured.

3. *Does each item present a clearly formulated task?* The problem presented by a test item, regardless of item type, should be so clear and unambiguous that all students understand the task they are being called on to perform. Those who fail an item should do so only because they lack the knowledge or intellectual skill called for by the item. Although ambiguity is a major problem in test construction, it is fortunately a flaw that becomes more apparent during a follow-up review of the items.

4. *Is the item stated in simple, clear language?* This point is obviously related to the previous one, but here we are concerned more with the appropriateness of the reading level of the item for the age group to be tested. Except for technical terms that are a necessary part of the problem, the vocabulary should be simple. Similarly, short and simple sentences are to be favored over long and complex ones. Meeting these two standards is likely to help remove ambiguity but, equally important, they enable poor readers to demonstrate their levels of achievement more adequately. Reading ability is well worth measuring in its own right, but attempts should be made to keep it from interfering with the measurement of other learning outcomes. Ideally the reading level of the items should be adapted to the least able reader in the group to be tested.

5. *Is the item free from extraneous clues?* Although we do not want students to fail an item if they have achieved the outcome being measured, neither do we want them to answer an item correctly when they have *not* achieved the intended outcome. Thus, the review of items provides another opportunity to ferret out clues that might lead the uninformed to the correct answer. Verbal associations, grammatical inconsistencies, and other clues that are easily overlooked during the construction of the items frequently become obvious during review.

6. *Is the difficulty of the item appropriate?* The difficulty of the items in a criterion-referenced test should match the difficulty of the learning tasks set forth in the specific learning outcomes. No attempt should be made to alter item difficulty simply to obtain a spread of test scores. The important question here becomes: Is the difficulty of the test item the same as that of the specified learning task? We assume, of course, that the appropriateness of the learning task for the age group to be tested was checked at the time the list of learning outcomes was prepared.

In evaluating the difficulty of the items in a norm-referenced test, we shift our focus to the question: How effectively will this item discriminate among students? Recall that the purpose of a norm-referenced test is to obtain a dependable ranking of students, and to do this we need items that discriminate. As we see later in this chapter item analysis can be used to

Reviewing and Improving Test Items

1. Improving the match between item and outcome.

   Intended Outcome: Identifies the meaning of a term.

   Item: Define the term *taxonomy*.

   Improved: The term *taxonomy* means
   *A. classification.
   B. cognitive objectives.
   C. preparation.
   D. specification.

2. Improving the multiple-choice item and the match.

   Intended Outcome: Identifies the use of tests.

   Item: Formative testing is
   A. used for grading students.
   *B. used for monitoring student progress.
   C. given at the beginning of instruction.
   D. more important than summative testing.

   Improved: Formative testing is used primarily for
   A. grading students.
   *B. monitoring student progress.
   C. forming student groups.
   D. selecting students for scholarships.

3. Improving the short-answer item and the match.

   Intended Outcome: Names the parts of test items.

   Item: The wrong answers in a multiple-choice item are
   (*distracters*).

   Improved: The incorrect alternatives in a multiple-choice item
   are called (*distracters*).

4. Improving the true-false item and the match.

   Intended Outcome: Identifies the limitations of test items.

   Item: *T   F   The true-false item has a number of limitations and one of the difficulties is the ambiguity that enters into some of the
   statements.

   Improved: *T   F   It is difficult to write true-false statements
   that are free of ambiguity.

determine the discriminating power of test items. Items that are difficult enough to discriminate between high and low achievers are to be favored.

7. *Is each test item independent, and are the items as a group free from overlapping?* Knowing the answer to one item should not depend on knowing the answer to another item. Thus, each item should be a separate scorable unit. Interlocking items are especially likely to occur when several items are based on common introductory material. A closely related problem occurs when information in one item helps the student determine the answer to another item. This is most common in tests that include both selection and supply items. Frequently the information given in selection items is useful in answering the supply items. These defects can easily be remedied by an overall review of the items during the final selection of the items to be included in the test.

8. *Do the items to be included in the test provide adequate coverage of the test specifications?* The review, elimination, and revision of test items may result in a pool of items that deviates somewhat from the set of specifications. Thus, it may be necessary to further revise some of the items or to construct new ones. In any event the final selection of items for the test must be made in light of the test specifications in order to assure adequate sampling of the intended learning outcomes.

In addition to these general questions that apply to all item types, the rules for constructing each specific type of item provide criteria for item evaluation. In the review of multiple-choice items, for example, the completeness of the problem given in the stem, the inclusion of one clearly best answer, and the plausibility of the distracters all warrant special attention. Just before reviewing a pool of items, you should consult the checklist for evaluating each item type.

ARRANGING THE ITEMS IN THE TEST

After the final selection of the items to be assembled into a test, a decision must be made concerning the best arrangement of the items. This arrangement will vary somewhat with the type of test being prepared. The following are useful guidelines for arranging items.

1. *For instructional purposes it is usually desirable to group together items that measure the same learning outcome.* The instructional uses of test results tend to be enhanced when the items are arranged according to the learning outcomes measured. Typically all items measuring the same outcome are placed together and identified by an appropriate heading. The headings might be simply the major taxonomy categories (knowledge, comprehension, application, and so forth), statements of the general instructional objectives (for example, "Knows terms," "Knows basic principles"), or statements of the specific learning outcomes (for example, "Defines terms," "Writes a sentence using each term"). Whether to group the items by general categories or by specific outcomes depends to a large extent on the type of test being prepared. For norm-referenced tests the general categories are usually sufficient. For criterion-referenced tests, which are used typically to measure mastery and provide feedback concerning specific learning errors, arranging the items under each specific learning outcome is favored. The inclusion of the stated headings in the test helps you to identify the types of learning outcomes causing difficulty and to plan group and individual remedial instruction.

2. *Where possible, the items should be arranged so that all items of the same type are grouped together.* It is desirable to group together all multiple-choice items, all short-answer items, all true-false items, all essay questions, and so on. This arrangement makes it possible to provide only one set of directions for each item type. It also contributes to efficient test taking, since the student can maintain a uniform method of responding throughout each section. Finally, arranging by item type tends to simplify the scoring of the test and the analysis of the results.

If arrangement by item type conflicts with arrangement by learning outcome, grouping items by outcome should probably be favored because of the instructional value of doing so. Both types of arrangement can usually be accommodated, however, because achievement tests are typically limited to just a few item types, and because all items measuring a particular learning outcome tend to be of the same type.

3. *The item should be arranged in order of increasing difficulty.* It is desirable to start with easy items and to establish an order of ascending difficulty throughout the test. Doing so will have a desirable motivational effect on students and will prevent the weaker students from "bogging down" on difficult items early in the test. If the items have been grouped by learning outcome, the outcomes can be arranged in order of increasing difficulty (for example, knowledge, comprehension, and application) and the items within each section can be arranged the same way. This system will closely approximate the desired order of increasing difficulty, while maintaining the basic arrangement by learning outcome.

It is obvious that only a limited number of different methods of arranging items can be applied to the same test. However, since most tests include only a few item types, it is usually possible to honor all three of the suggestions for item arrangement. If this is not feasible, the item arrangement that best fits the nature of the test and its intended use should be preferred. For most instructional purposes this means favoring arrangement by learning outcome.

PREPARING DIRECTIONS

The directions for an achievement test should be simple and concise and yet contain information concerning each of the following: (1) purpose of the test, (2) time allowed to complete the test, (3) how to record the answers, and (4) whether to guess when in doubt about the answer. The following sample directions for a multiple-choice test cover these four points.

EXAMPLE

Directions: This is a test of what you have learned during the first five weeks of the course. The results of this test will be used to clarify any points of difficulty and thus, help you complete the course successfully.

There are 60 multiple-choice items, and you have one hour to complete the test.

For each item, select the answer that *best* completes the statement, or answers the question, and circle the letter of that answer.

Since your score will be the number of items answered correctly, *be sure to answer every item.*

When two or more item types are included in the same test, it is usually desirable to provide general directions for the test as a whole and specific directions for each part. When this is done, the general directions should contain the information about purpose, time allowed, and what to do about guessing, and the specific directions should describe how to record the answers for that particular part. Also, some items, such as keytype exercises, require special directions for each item.

The use of separate answer sheets requires some elaboration of the instructions for recording the answers. If students are not familiar with the use of separate answer sheets, it might also be desirable to present a sample item with the correct answer properly marked. There is a variety of separate answer sheets, and the specific instructions will have to be adapted to the particular type used. Unless machine scoring is to be used, however, a teacher-made answer sheet that simply lists the letters of the alternatives for each item is usually satisfactory:

ITEM	ANSWER
1.	A B C D E
2.	A B C D E
3.	A B C D E
4.	A B C D E

An answer sheet of this type should instruct the students to "put an X through the letter of the correct or best answer." Crossing out the answer is better than circling it, since an X is more visible than a circle through the holes in a scoring stencil. With this type of answer sheet, preparing a scoring key is simply a matter of punching out the letter of the correct answer for each item.

The Problem of Guessing

In our set of sample directions, the students were told, "Since your score will be the number of items answered correctly, be sure to answer every item." This is an attempt to equalize the variation among students in their tendency to guess when in doubt about the answer. Such directions make it unnecessary for the instructor to correct for guessing. When students answer all items in a test, corrected and uncorrected scores rank students in exactly the same order. It is only when some items are omitted in a test that the correction makes a difference in student ranking.

There is considerable controversy concerning the issue of correcting test scores for guessing, but most of it is concerned with standardized testing. Since standardized achievement tests typically contain some material that is inappropriate for the group tested, and since all students may not have an opportunity to complete the test, directions warning them that there will be a penalty for guessing may be defensible. The aim here, of course, is to discourage students from attempting to improve their scores by guessing blindly at some of the answers. These directions do not have a uniform effect on students, however. The bold student is likely to continue to guess wildly, whereas the more hesitant student may even give up guessing on the basis of considerable knowledge.

Generally student scores on informal achievement tests should not be corrected for guessing. The material in the test is closely related to the learning experiences of the students, and the time limits are usually liberal enough to permit the students to carefully consider all items in the test. Under these conditions any guessing that is done is apt to be informed guessing. Although permitting such guessing may be objectionable under some conditions, guessing is quite similar to the behavior called for in making inferences, in identifying the probable causes and effects of an action, and in various decision-making aspects of problem solving. Thus, guessing is not entirely objectionable from an educational standpoint.

There may be some courses or some units within a course in which preciseness receives so much emphasis during instruction that it is desirable to stress it also during testing. In this case, "do-not-guess" instructions would be appropriate. They would also be appropriate in a speed test—that is, a test in which the students have insufficient time to consider all the items. In both instances the students should be told that there will be a correction for guessing, and the following correction-for-guessing formula should be applied during the scoring.

$$\text{Score} = \text{Right} - \frac{\text{Wrong}}{n-1}$$

In this formula, n equals the number of alternatives in each item. Thus, for a multiple-choice test where items contained four alternatives, the formula would be as follows:

$$\text{Score} = \text{Right} - \frac{\text{Wrong}}{3}$$

Applying this correction-for-guessing formula involves simply counting the number of right answers and the number of wrong answers on a student's test paper and inserting these numbers in the formula. The omitted items are not counted. Thus, student who answered 40 items correctly and 6 items incorrectly on a 50-item multiple-choice test using four alternatives would receive a corrected score that is computed as follows:

$$40 - \frac{6}{3} = 40 - 2 = 38$$

The assumption here is that the student guessed on 8 items and had chance success (that is, 2 right, 6 wrong). The formula simply removes those 2 right answers that can be accounted for by chance success in guessing.

REPRODUCING THE TEST

When the test is typed for reproduction, the items should be spaced on the page so that they are easy for students to read and easy for the instructor to score. If multiple-choice items are used, the alternatives should be listed underneath the stem, as in the examples presented in Chapter 3. All of the parts of an item should be on the same page. For interpretive exercises, however,

Checklist for Evaluating the Assembled Test

1. *Balance*   Do the items measure a representative sample of the learning tasks in the achievement domain?

2. *Relevance*   Do the test items present relevant tasks?

3. *Conciseness*   Are the test tasks stated in simple, clear language?

4. *Soundness*   Are the items of proper difficulty, free of defects, and do they have answers that are defensible?

5. *Independence*   Are the items free from overlapping, so that one item does not aid in answering another?

6. *Arrangement*   Are items measuring the same outcome grouped together?

                         Are items of the same type grouped together?

                         Are items in order of increasing difficulty?

7. *Numbering*   Are the items numbered in order throughout the test?

8. *Directions*   Are there directions for the whole test and each part?

                         Are the directions concise and at the proper reading level?

                         Do the directions include time limits and how to record answers?

                         Do the directions tell what to do about guessing?

9. *Spacing*   Does the spacing on the page contribute to ease of reading and responding?

10. *Typing*   Is the final copy free of typographical errors?

it may be necessary to place the introductory material on a facing page or on a separate sheet to be handed out with the test.

If the answers are to be marked on the test itself, provision should be made for recording the answers on the left side of the page. This simplifies the scoring. If separate answer sheets are to be used and the test is to be administered to more than one group of students, it is usually necessary to warn the students not to make any marks on the test booklets. It is also wise to make more copies of the test than are needed because some students will ignore your warning.

Achievement tests for classroom use are commonly reproduced by the mimeograph, ditto, photocopy, or photo-offset processes. Although mimeographing is satisfactory for most purposes, the use of drawings or pictures requires one of the other methods. Regardless of the method of reproduction used, the master copy should be checked carefully for item arrangement, legibility, accuracy of detail in drawings, and freedom from typographical errors.

ADMINISTERING AND SCORING THE TEST

The administration of a carefully prepared informal achievement test is largely a matter of providing proper working conditions, keeping interruptions to a minimum, and arranging enough space between students to prevent cheating. The written directions should be clear enough to make the test self-administering, but in some situations it may be desirable to give the directions orally as well. With young students a blackboard illustration may also be useful. Above all, make certain that all the students know exactly what to do, and then provide them with the most favorable conditions in which to do it.

Scoring is facilitated if all answers are recorded on the left side of each test page, as we suggested earlier. Under this arrangement, scoring is simply a matter of marking the correct answers on a copy of the test and placing it next to the column of answers on each student's paper. If a separate answer sheet is used, it is usually better to punch out the letters of the correct answers on a copy of the answer sheet and use this as a scoring stencil. The stencil is laid over each answer sheet and the correctly marked answers appear through the holes. Where no mark appears, a red line can be drawn across the hole. This indicates to the student the correct answer for each item missed. If machine scoring is to be used, simply scan the students' papers to make certain that only one answer was marked for each item.

Unless corrected for guessing, a student's score on an objective test is typically the number of answers marked correctly. Thus, each test item is counted as one point. Although teachers frequently desire to count some items more heavily than others because of their importance or difficulty, such weighting of scores complicates the scoring task and seldom results in an improved measure of achievement. A better way to increase the relative weight of an area is to construct more items in that area.

ANALYZING THE EFFECTIVENESS OF TEST ITEMS

After a test has been administered, the items should be analyzed for their effectiveness. One method of evaluating the test is to review the test item-by-item when it is handed back to students for a discussion of the results. Significant comments made during the discussion can be recorded on a blank copy of the test. The flexibility of this procedure makes it possible to pursue comments about particular items, to ask students why they selected the response they did (both correct and incorrect selections), and to spend as much time on each item as seems warranted. This procedure may bring forth some unjustified criticisms of the test, but it will also help identify defective items in need of revision. The extra time used in discussing the test results will not be wasted because students will be obtaining a review of the course material covered by the test.

Simple Item Analysis Procedure

The discussion of test results and review of the items can be much more effective if a simple tally of student responses is made on the master copy of the test. By recording the results of the 10 highest scoring students (H) and 10 lowest scoring students (L), like that in Figure 7.1, make the results easily interpretable. The answer is circled and the numbers to the left of each alternative indicate how many students in each group selected that alternative.

The result in Figure 7.1 provide all the information we need to estimate the following types of item analysis information.

1. The difficulty of the item (percentage of students answering the item correctly).
2. The discriminating power of the item (how well the item discriminates between high and low scorers).
3. The effectiveness of each alternative (all should be chosen and each one more frequently by the low scoring group).

By simply looking at the answer sheet in Figure 7.1, we can see that 8 students in the high scoring group and 4 students in the low scoring group selected the correct answer. Also, more students in the low scoring group selected each wrong alternative than in the high scoring group, indicating that the distracters seem to be distracting those students who haven't learned the meaning of the term.

Because we are using 10 students in the high scoring group and 10 students in the low scoring group, we can mentally calculate the usual indexes of difficulty and discriminating power by using the following simple steps.

1. Determine the percentage of high scorers and low scorers passing the item by adding a zero.

   H = 8 out of 10 = 80
   L = 4 out of 10 = 40

2. Obtain *item difficulty* by adding the percentage correct in the high and low groups and dividing by 2. Add a percent sign to the answer.

$$\frac{80 + 40}{2} = 60\%$$

UNIT TEST

Name _____ Date _____

Directions:

This test measures the knowledge, understandings, and applications you have acquired during the first four weeks.

There are 65 objective items, and you will have the full class period to complete the test.

Select the best answer for each item and circle the letter of that answer.

Your score will be the number of items answered correctly, so *be sure to answer every item.*

KNOWLEDGE OF TERMS

H   L

1   3   1. An assessment instrument is properly classified as *objective* when

1   2   A. the instrument uses objective-type questions.

0   1   B. the responses called forth by the instrument are free of opinion.

         C. those preparing the instrument used standard procedures of construction.

8   4   (D.) there is agreement among scorers concerning the correctness of the answers.

FIGURE 7.1   Test Copy with Item Analysis Data to Left of Items (H = 10 Highest Scorers, L = 10 Lowest Scorers)

3. Obtain *discriminating power* by subtracting the percentage correct in the low group from the percentage correct in the high group. Add a decimal point to the answer.

$$80 - 40 = .40$$

The description of the procedure makes it sound more complicated than it is, but making a few mental calculations like this will reveal its simplicity. Item difficulty typically uses the percent sign and, of course, can range from 0% to 100%. Our **difficulty index** is based on the high and low scoring group only but this provides a satisfactory approximation of item difficulty. The **discrimination index** typically uses the decimal point and, thus, ranges from 0 to 1.00.

This simple method of analyzing the test results can be used as an aid in discussing the items when reviewing the test. Items that most students answer correctly can be skipped over or treated lightly, items missed by most

---

Common Reasons for Selecting Multiple-Choice Alternatives

Bases for Correct Choice

1. Possesses required information or skill.
2. Uses partial information that favors answer.
3. Uses clues given in the item.
4. Uses information from other items in the test.
5. Makes a blind, lucky guess.

Bases for Incorrect Choice

1. Lacks the information or skill required by the item.
2. Uses partial information that favors a distracter.
3. Uses misinformation that favors a distracter.
4. Makes a blind, unlucky guess.
5. Marks wrong answer through carelessness.

---

students can be discussed in more detail, and defective items can be pointed out to students rather than defended as fair. Also, the frequency with which each incorrect answer is chosen may reveal common errors and misconceptions that can be corrected on the spot, or serve as a basis for remedial work. In discussing the reasons students have selected the right or wrong answer for an item can sometimes be revealing. We assume that if they selected the correct answer they had learned the material. Not necessarily so, when using selection-type items (see box for common reasons for selecting alternatives). Having students discuss the reasons for their choices provides insights into student thinking that may contribute to both improved teaching and improved test construction skills.

Although the method of **item analysis** presented here is a crude one, it is probably satisfactory for most classroom tests. We are using it primarily as a basis for reviewing the items with students and for any insights the results might give us for improving test items in the future. A more detailed description of norm-referenced item analysis and cautions in interpreting item-analysis data can be found in Linn and Gronlund (1995).

Because of the small number of students involved in classroom testing, item-analysis information must be interpreted with great caution. If a test item is reused with a new group, the results may be quite different, due to changes in the instruction, the study habits of students, or some other factor. The tentative nature of the item-analysis data is not of great concern, however, when used to review tests with students for the purpose of improving learning.

ITEM ANALYSIS OF CRITERION-REFERENCED TESTS

Since criterion-referenced tests are designed to describe which learning tasks a student can and cannot perform rather than to discriminate among students, the traditional indexes of item difficulty and item discriminating power are of little value. A set of items in a criterion-referenced mastery test, for example, might be answered correctly by all students (zero discriminating power) and still be effective items. If the items closely match an important learning outcome, the results simply tell us that here is an outcome that all students have mastered. This is valuable information for describing the types of tasks students can perform, and to eliminate such items from the test would distort our description of student learning.

The difficulty of an item in a criterion-referenced test is determined by the learning task it is designed to measure. If the task is easy, the item should be easy. If the task is difficult, the item should be difficult. No attempt should be made to eliminate easy items or to alter item difficulty simply to obtain a spread of test scores. Although an index of item difficulty can be computed for items in a criterion-referenced test, there is seldom a need to do so. If mastery is being measured and the instruction has been effective, criterion-referenced test items are typically answered correctly by a large percentage of the students.

Item-Analysis Procedure for Criterion-Referenced Tests

A basic concern in evaluating the items in a criterion-referenced mastery test is the extent to which each item is measuring the *effects of instruction*. If an item can be answered correctly by all students both *before* and *after* instruction, the item obviously is not measuring instructional effects. Similarly, if an item is answered incorrectly by all students both before and after instruction, the item is not serving its intended function. These are extreme examples, of course, but they highlight the importance of obtaining a measure of instructional effects as one basis for determining item quality.

To obtain a measure of item effectiveness based on instructional effects, the teacher must give the same test before instruction and after instruction. Effective items will be answered correctly by a larger number of students after instruction than before instruction. An index of *sensitivity to instructional effect(s)*[1] can be computed by using the following formula:

$$S = \frac{R_A - R_B}{T}$$

[1]W. J. Kryspin and J. T. Feldhusen, *Developing Classroom Tests* (Minneapolis: Burgess Publishing Co., 1974) p. 166.

where R_A the number of students answering the item correctly *after* instruction, R_B = the number answering correctly *before* instruction, and T = the total number answering the item both times. Applying this formula to an item that was answered incorrectly by all students before instruction and correctly by all students after instruction (N = 32), our result would be as follows:

$$S = \frac{32 - 0}{32} = 1.00$$

Thus, maximum sensitivity to instructional effects is indicated by an index of 1.00. The index for effective items will fall between .00 and 1.00, with larger positive values indicating items with greater sensitivity to the effects of instruction.

There are several limitations in the use of the sensitivity index: (1) the test must be given twice to compute the index, (2) a low index may be due to either an ineffective item or ineffective instruction, and (3) the item responses after instruction may be influenced to some extent by having taken the same test earlier. The last limitation is likely to be more serious where the instruction time is short. Despite these limitations, the sensitivity index provides a useful means of evaluating the effectiveness of items in a criterion-referenced mastery test. Items are of little value for measuring the intended outcomes of instruction unless they are sensitive to instructional effects.

USING A TEST-ITEM FILE

After test items have been used and evaluated, it is desirable to make any corrections needed (e.g., change wording, replace poor distracters) and then to place the items in a test file. If each item has been placed on a 5 × 8 index card, as suggested earlier, item-analysis data can be placed on the back of the card and the cards can be filed by content area and objective measured. The sample card in Figure 7.2, for example, would be filed under the first subcategory of the general content heading "Test Planning," as follows:

Test Planning

Knowledge

Understanding

Application

If a more detailed filing system is desired, Test Planning can be subdivided into such categories as Instructional Objectives, Test Specifications, and the like. Similarly, the general categories for objectives can also be further

---

Course *Test Construction*   Unit *Test Planning*
Objective *Identifies the meaning of terms (Knowledge)*

ITEM

The term *taxonomy* means
 *A. classification
  B. identification
  C. interpretation
  D. specification

(Front of item card)

ITEM DATA

Date	Students	A	B	C	D	Total	Diff.	Disc.
		ALTERNATIVES					INDEXES	
1/5/96	Upper	10	0	0	0	10	80%	.40
	Lower	6	1	1	2	10		
4/25/96	Upper	9	0	0	1	10	65%	.50
	Lower	4	3	0	3	10		
	Upper							
	Lower							
	Upper							
	Lower							

(Back of item card)

FIGURE 7.2   Test Item Card with Item-Analysis Data Recorded on Back

subdivided (e.g., Knowledge of Terms, Knowledge of Facts, Knowledge of Principles). The amount of detail in the filing system depends on how extensive the file is to become and how the items are to be used. A test file for a mastery learning program, for example, will need to be very detailed so that test items for brief learning units can be easily selected.

The test-item file is valuable in its own right and is assuming increasing importance as computers become more widely used in school testing. Item files maintained by teachers provide good beginning pools of items for starting computer item banks needed in computer-assisted test construction.

COMPUTER USE IN TESTING

As computers have become more widely used in schools, teachers have been able to turn over many of the procedures of test development and use to the computer. A complete system can provide for item banking, item analysis, test printing, test scoring, statistical analysis, and the maintenance of student records. Some test publishers provide complete instructional measurement systems that use microcomputer software for banking items and preparing locally developed tests. Computerized "adaptive" or "tailored" testing is also being developed and in the future may make paper-and-pencil testing obsolete.

Item Banking

Computers are especially useful for maintaining files of items (called *item banks* or *item pools*) that can be retrieved later for the preparation of tests. Typically the items are coded by subject area, instructional level, instructional objective measured, and various pertinent item characteristics (e.g., item difficulty and discriminating power). The coded information for each item makes it possible to retrieve items with known characteristics and thus build tests that match given test specifications. Item bank software can be used that permit the addition and deletion of items and the modification of items in the bank. The flexibility and efficiency of the computer should contribute to the more effective uses of item banks and relieve the test user of many of the routine tasks involved in maintaining an item file.

Test Printing

Custom-designed tests, based on the items selected from the computer item bank, can also be printed by the computer. The coded information recorded for each item makes it possible to arrange the test in the form desired. For example, the computer might be directed to arrange the items by instructional objective with the set of items under each objective in order of increasing difficulty.

Test Scoring and Statistical Analysis

After the test is administered, the computer can be used to score the test, analyze and arrange the scores in various ways, compute item-analysis data for each item, and provide reliability information. The specific nature of the data provided depends on the computer program that is used. The role of the computer in scoring and statistical analysis is especially helpful in relieving test users of tasks that can be very time consuming. Thus, it is likely to encourage test users to analyze and use the test results in ways that otherwise tend to be neglected.

Maintenance of Student Records

Records of student performance can be maintained in the computer in various forms so that learning progress can be readily determined. In a mastery learning program, for example, a student's record might indicate what objectives have been mastered, what areas show lack of mastery, and what types of learning errors are occurring in the nonmastered areas. The detailed information that can be stored in the computer, and easily retrieved when needed, should contribute to greater instructional use of achievement tests.

Computerized Adaptive Testing

In addition to the various ways that the computer can assist in paper-and-pencil testing, it can also be used directly in "adaptive" or "tailored" testing. This involves the computer administration of a set of test items that is most appropriate for each individual's achievement or ability level. The examinee is presented with test items on the computer screen; the answer to each item (or to all previous items) determines which item will be administered next by the computer. Thus, each person is tested with an individually tailored test drawn from the same pool of items. Adapting the test to each examinee's performance level eliminates those items that are too easy and too difficult for the individual. This makes it possible to obtain a more effective measure of achievement with fewer test items than is possible with the typical paper-and-pencil test.

In addition to the psychometric efficiency of computer **adaptive testing,** it provides for more controlled conditions of test administration and for the immediate availability of results. All examinees are tested under the same standard conditions, and the computer can score and report the results without the usual delays involved in the scoring and reporting of test data. This immediate availability of results saves time, avoids errors, and should contribute to the greater instructional use of test scores.

As computers become more widely used in the classroom, we can expect computer-assisted testing and computer adaptive testing to play an increasingly important role. This will relieve teachers of many of the time-consuming, routine tasks presently connected with testing and, hopefully, will bring about a better integration of testing and teaching.

SUMMARY OF POINTS

1. Test items should be written and set aside for a time before reviewing them.

2. A review of each test item should focus on its importance, relevance, clarity, difficulty, independence, and freedom from extraneous clues.

3. Where needed, items should be edited to remove nonfunctioning material, barriers that might prevent a knowledgeable person from responding (e.g., ambiguity), and clues that might lead the uninformed to the correct answer (e.g., verbal associations).

4. The items selected for the final copy of the test should be guided by the test specifications to assure balanced coverage of the outcomes to be measured.

5. Item arrangement within the test will vary with the type of test used. Where possible, however, items should be grouped by the major outcome measured (e.g., knowledge, comprehension, application), similar item types should be grouped together, and the items should be arranged in order of increasing difficulty within sections.

6. Test directions should be written at the proper reading level and indicate the purpose of the test, the time allowed, how to record the answers, and whether to guess when in doubt.

7. On most classroom tests, students should be told to answer every question. The correction for guessing should be limited to speed tests and to those few areas where guessing is contrary to the learning outcomes being measured.

8. Before the test copy is reproduced it should be checked for proper item arrangement, spacing, legibility, accuracy of detail in drawings, and freedom from typographical errors.

9. Test administration should provide conditions that permit all students to demonstrate their best performance (e.g., good work space, no interruptions) without the aid of others (e.g., sufficient space between seats).

10. Scoring is typically based on one point for each objective test item. Greater weight to an area can be obtained by adding more items.

11. Item analysis of classroom tests provides an index of item difficulty and item discriminating power, and provides for an evaluation of the effectiveness of each distracter. It aids in reviewing tests with students.

12. One item-analysis procedure used with criterion-referenced tests provides an index of sensitivity to instructional effects. This index is based on a comparison of test responses before and after instruction.

13. Item analysis of classroom tests must be interpreted with caution because of the small number of students that is typically used.

14. A test-item file is useful for building up a pool of items for future use. The item file can be kept on index cards or stored directly in a computer.

15. Computers can be used for item banking, item analysis, test printing, test scoring, statistical analysis, maintenance of student records, and the direct administration of tests "adapted" or "tailored" to each individual's ability or achievement level.
16. The use of computers should contribute to the more effective use of tests in the instructional program.

ADDITIONAL READING

Baker, F. B., "Computer Technology in Test Construction and Processing." Chapter 10 in Linn, R. L., Ed., *Educational Measurement*, 3rd ed. (New York: Macmillan Publishing Co., 1989). Describes use of microcomputers in item writing, item banking, test construction, test printing, test scanning and scoring, and reporting of results. Several computer systems are reviewed.

Geisert, P. G., and Futrell, M. K., *Teachers, Computers, and Curriculum*, 2nd ed. (Boston: Allyn & Bacon, 1995). This book emphasizes practical applications of computers in teaching. See Chapter 7, "Using Microcomputers to Measure and Manage."

Linn, R. L., and Gronlund, N. E., *Measurement and Assessment in Teaching*, 7th ed. (Englewood Cliffs, NJ: Prentice-Hall, 1995). See Chapter 12, "Assembling, Administering, and Appraising Classroom Tests and Assessments," for a more comprehensive treatment of material covered in this chapter.

Popham, W. J., *Classroom Assessment* (Boston: Allyn & Bacon, 1995). See Chapter 11, "Improving Teacher Developed Assessments," for a discussion of judgmental and empirical methods for evaluating and improving tests.

▶ 8

Making Performance Assessments

Studying this chapter should enable you to

1. Describe how performance assessments differ from traditional paper-and-pencil testing.
2. Identify the strengths and limitations of performance assessments.
3. Distinguish between restricted and extended performance assessment.
4. Describe the general procedure for making a performance assessment.
5. Write intended learning outcomes for a restricted performance assessment.
6. Prepare a plan for arranging, observing, recording, and evaluating a restricted performance task.
7. Describe the steps in an extended research project.
8. Construct a checklist that is well-stated, relevant, and easy to use.
9. Construct a rating scale that is well-stated, relevant, and easy to use.
10. Construct a scoring rubric for a performance assessment.
11. Describe how to use a portfolio in collecting, exhibiting, and evaluating student work.
12. List ways to improve performance assessments.

As noted in Chapter 2, performance assessment can be distinguished from the traditional paper-and-pencil test by a number of characteristics. Performance assessment is characterized by:

1. greater realism of tasks (i.e., more like those in the real world).
2. greater complexity of tasks (i.e., less structured problems that encourage originality and thinking skills, and may have multiple solutions).
3. greater time needed for assessment (due to the difficulty of designing the tasks, the comprehensive nature of the tasks, and the increased time needed to evaluate the results).
4. greater use of judgment in scoring (due to the complexity of tasks, originality of the responses, and in some cases the variety of possible solutions).

Performance tasks appear in many different forms but the majority of them fall into one of the following categories.

1. Solving realistic problems (e.g., how to reduce drug use in the United States).
2. Oral or psychomotor skills without a product (e.g., giving a speech, speaking a foreign language, using a microscope, repairing an engine).
3. Writing or psychomotor skills with a product (e.g., writing a theme, writing a lab report, typing a letter, building a book case).

These various types of performance may be very restricted to fit a specific instructional objective or they may be so extended and comprehensive that numerous instructional objectives are involved. For example, we may judge how well students can select and use laboratory equipment, or we may have them conduct an experiment that involves planning the experiment and writing a report of the findings. We might also have them present their findings to the class and defend their procedures and conclusions. Because performance tasks can vary so widely in comprehensiveness, it is helpful to use the designations *restricted performance* tasks and *extended performance* tasks.

Restricted performance tasks tend to be highly structured and limited in scope, as illustrated in the following examples.

Write a one-page report describing a science field trip.

Give a one minute speech on a given topic.

Read aloud a selection of poetry.

Construct a graph from a given set of data.

Demonstrate how to set up laboratory equipment.

By limiting the scope of the task, it is easier to relate it to a particular objective, to administer it, and to judge the response. However, the limited nature of the task prevents students from demonstrating their ability to deal with comprehensive, poorly structured problems that are more like those in the "real world."

With the use of extended performance tasks, we are better able to obtain information about the students' ability to identify the crux of a problem, to gather and integrate information for solving it, and to provide original, well supported conclusions. Extended performance in the skill area enable us to determine how well students can integrate a series of specific skills into a complex pattern of movements or in the production of as superior product. Some extended performance projects combine all three types of performance tasks: problem solving, communication skills, and psychomotor skills that result in a product.

Extended performance tasks tend to be less structured and broad in scope, as illustrated by the following examples.

Design and conduct an experiment on a selected topic and present and defend the findings.

Write a short story, followed by a criticism of it, and then rewrite a second draft.

Read a novel and write a critical review of it.

Assume you are investing $40,000 in the stock market for your college education. Select the stocks, make a record of their value for 30 days, then write a report describing your success and indicating what changes you would make in your portfolio of stocks.

Design and build a bookcase and write an evaluation of how well it meets a given set of criteria.

Performance Assessments

Strengths

1. Can evaluate complex learning outcomes and skills that cannot be evaluated with traditional paper-and-pencil tests.
2. Provides a more natural, direct, and complete evaluation of some types of reasoning, oral, and physical skills.
3. Provides greater motivation for students by clarifying goals and making learning more meaningful.
4. Encourages the application of learning to "real life" situations.

Limitations

1. Requires considerable time and effort to use.
2. Judgment and scoring performance is subjective, burdensome, and typically has low reliability.
3. Evaluation must frequently be done individually, rather than in groups.

Extended performance assessment projects typically give students greater freedom in selecting projects, in carrying them out, in self assessment, and in defense of their quality. Discussions of the results with the teacher focus on both the quality of the project and the students' self-assessment skills.

NEED FOR PERFORMANCE ASSESSMENT

Performance assessments provide a systematic way of evaluating those reasoning and skill outcomes that cannot be adequately measured by the typical objective or essay test. These outcomes are important in many different types of courses. For example, science courses are typically concerned with solving problems and with laboratory skills, mathematics courses are concerned with various types of practical problem-solving skills, English and foreign-language courses are concerned with communication skills, and social studies courses are concerned with such skills as map and graph construction and operating effectively in a group. In addition, skill outcomes are emphasized heavily in art and music courses, industrial education, business education, agricultural education, home economics courses, and physical education. Thus, in most instructional areas performance assessment provides a useful adjunct to the traditional paper-and-pencil tests. Although tests can tell us whether students know what to do in a particular situation, performance assessments are needed to evaluate their actual performance skills.

In addition to the traditional needs for performance assessment in the various areas of instruction, two educational trends have provided renewed emphasis on performance assessment. First, the shift from norm-referenced measurement (ranking students in order of achievement) to criterion-referenced measurement (describing what students can do) in classroom assessment has created a need for more direct measures of how well students can perform. Thus, if you want to describe a student's "proficiency in performing an activity or skill," a performance assessment is required. A test of "knowledge about" the performance will not substitute for the actual performance, no matter how highly the two may be related. Second, modern learning theory emphasizes the need for focusing on the more complex learning outcomes (e.g., reasoning and thinking skills), on using more comprehensive student projects based on "real world" problems, and on engaging students in the activities and in the construction of meaning from them. In short, modern learning theory calls for the use of extended performance assessment as a basic means of improving learning.

It is our view that performance assessment is a useful adjunct to traditional testing and not a replacement for it. How large a role performance assessment plays in a classroom assessment program depends on the area of instruction and the particular instructional objectives being stressed. Most learning programs can benefit from the use of both tests and performance assessments.

Effective performance assessments are most likely to result when a systematic approach is used. The following procedural steps outline the main factors to consider when making performance assessments.

1. Specifying the performance outcomes.
2. Selecting the focus of the assessment (procedure, product, or both).
3. Selecting an appropriate degree of realism.
4. Selecting the performance situation.
5. Selecting the method of observing, recording, and scoring.

Each of these steps will be described in turn.

SPECIFYING THE PERFORMANCE OUTCOMES

If the intended learning outcomes have been prespecified for the instruction, it is simply a matter of selecting those that require the use of performance assessment. If performance outcomes are not available, they should be identified and defined for the areas of performance to be assessed. Restricted performance outcomes, commonly use verbs such as *identity, construct,* and *demonstrate* (and their synonyms). A brief description of these verbs and some illustrative objectives for restricted performance outcomes are shown in Table 8.1.

The specification of performance outcomes typically include a job or task analysis to identify the specific factors that are most critical in the performance. Because it is frequently impossible to focus on all of the specific procedures involved in a particular performance, it is necessary to obtain a representative sample of the most crucial ones. Keeping the list to a reasonable length increases the possibility of more accurate observations and judgments. The following examples illustrate realistic sets of performance tasks for restricted performance assessments.

Demonstrates Skill in Oral Reporting

1. Stands in a natural manner.
2. Maintains good eye contact.
3. Uses appropriate facial expressions.
4. Uses gestures effectively.
5. Speaks clearly and with good volume.
6. Speaks at an appropriate rate.
7. Presents ideas in an organized manner.
8. Uses appropriate language.
9. Maintains interest of the group.

TABLE 8.1 Typical Action Verbs and Illustrative Instructional Objectives for Restricted Performance Outcomes

ACTION VERBS	ILLUSTRATIVE INSTRUCTIONAL OBJECTIVES
IDENTIFY: selects the correct objects, part of the object, procedure, or property (*typical verbs:* identify, locate, select, touch, pick up, mark, describe)	Select the proper tool. Identify the parts of a typewriter. Choose correct laboratory equipment. Select the most relevant statistical procedure. Locate an automobile malfunction. Identify a musical selection. Identify the experimental equipment needed. Identify a specimen under the microscope.
CONSTRUCT: make a product to fit a given set of specifications (*typical verbs:* construct, assemble, build, design, draw, make, prepare)	Draw a diagram for an electrical circuit. Design a pattern for making a dress. Assemble equipment for an experimental study. Prepare a circle graph. Construct a weather map. Prepare an experimental design.
DEMONSTRATE: performs a set of operations or procedures (*typical verbs:* demonstrate, drive, measure, operate, perform, repair, set up)	Drive an automobile. Measure the volume of a liquid. Operate a filmstrip projector. Perform a modern dance step. Repair a malfunctioning TV set. Set up laboratory equipment. Demonstrate taking a patient's temperature. Demonstrate the procedure for tuning an automobile.

Repairs a Malfunctioning Motor
1. Identifies the nature of the malfunction.
2. Identifies the system causing the malfunction.
3. Selects the tests to be made.
4. Conducts the tests in proper sequence.
5. Locates the malfunctioning component.
6. Replaces or repairs the component.
7. Removes and replaces parts in proper sequence.
8. Uses proper tools in a correct manner.
9. Follows safety precautions throughout procedure.

In some cases, the order in which the performance tasks are listed is unimportant, as illustrated by the first example. In other performance assessments, the sequence of steps provides a systematic approach to be followed. In these cases, as illustrated by the second example, placing the tasks in proper sequence will make it easier to observe and record the performance and to note errors in procedure.

Extended performance projects typically involve multiple instructional objectives and it is important to consider all of them when designing a project. A research project, for example, might include intended learning outcomes as follows:

Selects an appropriate research task.

Uses the library effectively.

Locates, analyzes, and integrates relevant information.

Designs and conducts an experiment.

Writes an accurate account of the study.

States valid conclusions.

Writes a critique of the procedure and findings.

Presents and defends the study in class.

These outcomes would need to be defined in more specific terms, like the two described earlier, but stating the general objectives first and then specifying them in more detail provides a useful procedure. In defining each major outcome, it may be desirable to divide some in two (e.g., Designs an experiment, Conducts an experiment). In other cases some may be combined. For example "states valid conclusions" may be included as part of "Writes an accurate account of the study." In any event, the final list should provide a major list of the intended learning outcomes, each clearly specified by descriptions of what students can do to demonstrate achievement of the outcomes. More detailed descriptions of how to state intended learning outcomes and define them in performance terms can be found in Gronlund (1995).

SELECTING THE FOCUS OF THE ASSESSMENT

Performance assessment can focus on the procedure, the product, or some combination of the two. The nature of the performance frequently dictates where the emphasis should be placed, but in some cases there are other considerations also.

Assessing the Procedure

Those types of performance that don't result in a product (e.g., speaking, reading aloud, physical skills, musical performance) require that the performance be evaluated in progress.

In many cases, both procedure and product are important aspects of a performance. For example, skill in locating and correcting a malfunction in a television set involves following a systematic procedure (rather than using trial and error) in addition to producing a properly repaired set. Frequently, procedure is emphasized during the early stages of learning and products later, after the procedural steps have been mastered. In assessing typing skill, for example, proper use of the "touch system" would be evaluated at the beginning of instruction, but later evaluation would focus on the neatness and accuracy of the typed material and the speed with which it was produced. Similarly, in such areas as cooking, woodworking, and painting, correct procedure is likely to be stressed during the early stages of instruction and the quality of the product later. Procedure evaluation may also be used during later stages of instruction, of course, in order to detect errors in procedure that might account for an inferior product.

In general, focus the performance assessment on the procedure when:

1. There is no product, or product evaluation is infeasible (e.g., unavailable or too costly).
2. The procedure is orderly and directly observable.
3. Correct procedure is crucial to later success.
4. Analysis of procedural steps can aid in improving a product.

Assessing the Product

In some areas of performance, the product is the focus of attention and the procedure (or process) is of little or no significance. In evaluating a student's theme, drawing, or insect display, for example, the teacher is not likely to assess the procedures used by the student. This might be because various procedures could lead to an equally good product, or because the product was the result of a take-home project and the process was therefore not observable by the teacher. Also, some in-class activities are nonobservable because they involve primarily mental processes (such as mathematical reasoning). Some elements of the process can be obtained by having students "think aloud" and by using oral questioning, but the main focus is on the product. The quality of the product is typically guided by specific criteria that have been prepared especially for that purpose.

Where both the procedure and product are observable, the emphasis given to each will depend on the skill being assessed and the stage of skill development. However, when the procedure has been sufficiently mastered, product evaluation is favored because it typically provides a more objective basis for judgment, it can be done at a convenient time, and judgments can be rechecked if necessary.

Performance assessment should be focused on the product when:

1. Different procedures can result in an equally good product (e.g., writing a theme).
2. The procedure is not available for observation (e.g., take-home work).
3. The procedural steps have been mastered.
4. The product has qualities that can be clearly identified and judged.

SELECTING AN APPROPRIATE DEGREE OF REALISM

Performance assessment in instructional settings typically falls somewhere between the usual paper-and-pencil test and performance in "real-life situations." Although we can't expect to duplicate the natural situation in which the learning will later be used, we can strive for performance assessments that approximate "real world" conditions. This, then, is another dimension to consider in preparing performance assessments. How much "realism" can we incorporate into our assessment? The more the better, of course, but authenticity is a matter of degree.

The presence of varying degrees of realism in a performance assessment can be illustrated by the simple example of applying arithmetic skills to the practical problem of determining correct change while shopping in a store (adapted from Fitzpatrick and Morrison, 1971). A simulation of this situation might range from the use of a story problem (low realism) to an actual purchase in a storelike situation (high realism). The various problem situations that might be contrived for this performance measure are shown in Figure 8.1. It should be noted that even though solving a story problem is relatively low in realism, it simulates the criterion situation to a greater degree than simply asking students to subtract 69 from 100. Thus, even with paper-and-pencil testing it is frequently possible to increase the degree of realism to a point where the results are useful in assessing performance outcomes.

The degree of realism selected for a particular situation depends on a number of factors. First, the nature of the instructional objectives must be considered. Acceptable performance in paper-and-pencil applications of skill, or in other measures with a low degree of realism, might be all that the instruction is intended to achieve. This is frequently the case with introductory courses that are to be followed by more advanced courses emphasizing applied performance. Second, the sequence of instruction within a particular

Low realism — Have students solve this story problem: "If you bought a toy for 69¢ and you gave the clerk $1.00, how much change would you get?"

Demonstrate the problem situation with actual money and ask each student to judge whether the change is correct.

Pair off the students, give them actual money, and have them role-play the problem situation.

High realism — Set up a mock toy store, and have each student demonstrate the "purchase" of a toy with actual money.

FIGURE 8.1   Illustration of Various Degrees of Realism in Measuring the Ability to Determine Correct Change while Making a Purchase in a Store

course may indicate that it would be desirable to measure paper-and-pencil applications before "hands-on" performance is attempted. Locating the source of a malfunction on a diagram, for example, might precede working with actual equipment. Third, numerous practical constraints, such as time, cost, availability of equipment, and difficulties in administering and scoring, may limit the degree of realism that can be obtained. Fourth, the task itself may restrict the degree of realism in a test situation. In testing first aid skills, for example, it would be infeasible (and undesirable) to use actual patients with wounds, broken bones, and other physical conditions needed for realistic assessment. Thus, although we should strive for as high a degree of realism as the performance outcomes dictate, it is frequently necessary to make compromises in preparing performance assessments.

SELECTING THE PERFORMANCE SITUATION

Performance assessments can be classified by the type of situation or setting used. The following classification system closely approximates the degree of realism present in the situation and includes the following types: (1) paper-

and-pencil performance, (2) identification test, (3) structured performance test, (4) simulated performance, (5) work sample, and (6) extended research project. Although these categories overlap to some degree, they are useful for describing and illustrating the various approaches used in performance assessment.

Paper-and-Pencil Performance

Paper-and-pencil performance differs from the more traditional paper-and-pencil test by placing greater emphasis on the application of knowledge and skill in a simulated setting. These paper-and-pencil applications might result in desired terminal learning outcomes, or they might serve as an intermediate step to performance that involves a higher degree of realism (for example, the actual use of equipment).

In a number of instances, paper-and-pencil performance can provide a product of educational significance. A course in test construction, for example, might require students to perform activities such as the following:

Construct a set of test specifications for a unit of instruction.

Construct test items that fit a given set of specifications.

Construct a checklist for evaluating an achievement test.

The action verb "construct" is frequently used in paper-and-pencil performance testing. For instance, students might be asked to construct a weather map, bar graph, diagram of an electrical circuit, floor plan, design for an article of clothing, poem, short story, or plan for an experiment. In such cases, the paper-and-pencil product is a result of both knowledge and skill, and it provides a performance measure that is valued in its own right.

In other cases, paper-and-pencil performance might simply provide a first step toward hands-on performance. For example, before using a particular measuring instrument, such as a micrometer, it might be desirable to have students read various settings from pictures of the scale. Although the ability to read the scale is not a sufficient condition for accurate measurement, it is necessary one. In this instance, paper-and-pencil performance would be favored because it is a more convenient method of testing a group of students. Using paper-and-pencil performance as a precursor to hands-on performance might be favored for other reasons. For example, if the performance is complicated and the equipment is expensive, demonstrating competence on paper-and-pencil situations could avoid subsequent accidents or damage to equipment. Similarly, in the health sciences, skill in diagnosing and prescribing for hypothetical patients could avoid later harm to real patients.

Identification Test

The identification test includes a wide variety of situations representing various degrees of realism. In some cases, a student may be asked simply to identify a tool or piece of equipment and to indicate its function. A more complex situation might present the student with a particular performance task (e.g., locating a short in an electrical circuit) and ask him or her to identify the tools, equipment, and procedures needed in performing the task. An even more complex type of identification test might involve listening to the operation of a malfunctioning machine (such as an automobile motor, a drill, or a lathe) and, from the sound, identifying the most probable cause of the malfunction.

Although identification tests are widely used in industrial education, they are by no means limited to that area. The biology teacher might have students identify specimens that are placed at various stations around the room, or identifying the equipment and procedures needed to conduct a particular experiment. Similarly, chemistry students might be asked to identify "unknown" substances, foreign-language students to identify correct pronunciation, mathematics students to identify correct problem-solving procedures, English students to identify the "best expression" to be used in writing, and social studies students to identify various leadership roles as they are acted out in a group. Identifying correct procedures is also important, of course, in art, music, physical education, and such vocational areas as agriculture, business education, and home economics.

The identification test is sometimes used as an *indirect* measure of performance skill. The experienced plumber, for example, is expected to have a broader knowledge of the tools and equipment used in plumbing than the inexperienced plumber. Thus, a tool identification test might be used to eliminate the least skilled in a group of applicants for a position as plumber. More commonly, the identification test is used as an instructional device to prepare students for actual performance in real or simulated situations.

Structured Performance Test

A structured performance test provides for an assessment under standard, controlled conditions. It might involve such things as making prescribed measurements, adjusting a microscope, following safety procedures in starting a machine, or locating a malfunction in electronic equipment. The performance situation is structured and presented in a manner that requires all individuals to respond to the same set of tasks.

The construction of a structured performance test follows somewhat the same pattern used in constructing other types of achievement tests but there are some added complexities. The test situation can seldom be fully controlled and standardized, they typically take more time to prepare and administer, and they are frequently more difficult to score. To increase the likelihood that the test situation will be standard for all individuals, instructions should be used that describe the test situation, the required performance, and the conditions under which the performance is to be demonstrated. Instructions for locating a malfunction in electronic equipment, for example, would typically include the following:

1. Nature and purpose of the test
2. Equipment and tools provided
3. Testing procedure:
    a. Type and condition of equipment
    b. Description of required performance
    c. Time limits and other conditions
4. Method of judging performance

When using performance tests, it may be desirable to set performance standards that indicate the minimum level of acceptable performance. These might be concerned with accuracy (e.g., measure temperature *to the nearest two tenths of a degree*), the proper sequencing of steps (e.g., adjust a microscope *following the proper sequence of steps*), total compliance with rules (e.g., check *all safety guards* before starting a machine), or speed of performance (e.g., locate a malfunction in electronic equipment *in three minutes*). Some common **standards** for judging performance are shown in the accompanying box.

Performance standards are, of course, frequently used in combination. A particular performance may require correct form, accuracy, and speed. How much weight to give to each depends on the stage of instruction as well as the nature of the performance. In assessing laboratory measurement skills, for example, correct procedure and accuracy might be stressed early in the instruction, and concern about speed of performance delayed until the later stages of instruction. The particular situation might also influence the importance of the dimension. In evaluating typing skill, for example, speed might be stressed in typing routine business letters, whereas accuracy would be emphasized in typing statistical tables for economic reports.

Simulated Performance

Simulated performance is an attempt to match the performance in a real situation—either in whole or in part. In physical education, for example, swinging a bat at an imaginary ball, shadow boxing, and demonstrating various swimming or tennis strokes are simulated performances. In science, vocational, and business courses, skill activities are frequently designed to simulate portions of actual job performance. In mathematics, the use of calculators in solving lifelike problems represents simulated performance. Sim-

---

Some Common Standards for Judging Performance

Type	Examples
Rate	Solve ten addition problems in two minutes. Type 40 words per minute.
Error	No more than two errors per typed page. Count to 20 in Spanish without error.
Time	Set up laboratory equipment in five minutes. Locate an equipment malfunction in three minutes.
Precision	Measure a line within one eighth of an inch. Read a thermometer within two tenths of a degree.
Quantity	Complete 20 laboratory experiments. Locate 15 relevant references.
Quality (rating)	Write a neat, well-spaced business letter. Demonstrate correct form in diving.
Percentage Correct	Solve 85 percent of the math problems. Spell correctly 90 percent of the words in the word list.
Steps Required	Diagnose a motor malfunction in five steps. Locate a computer error using proper sequence of steps.
Use of Material	Build a bookcase with less than 10 percent waste. Cut out a dress pattern with less than 10 percent waste.
Safety	Check all safety guards before operating machine. Drive automobile without breaking any safety rules.

---

ilarly, in social studies, student roleplaying of a jury trial, a city council meeting, or a job interview provides the instructor with opportunities to evaluate the simulated performance of an assigned task. In some cases, specially designed equipment is used for instructional and assessment purposes. In both driver training and flight training, for example, students are frequently trained and tested on simulators. Such simulators may prevent personal injury or damage to expensive equipment during the early stages of skill development. Simulators are also used in various types of vocational training programs.

In some situations, simulated performance testing might be used as the final assessment of a performance skill. This would be the case in assessing students' laboratory performance in chemistry, for example. In many situations, however, skill in a simulated setting simply indicates readiness to attempt actual performance. The student in driver training who has demonstrated driving skill in the simulator, for example, is now ready to apply his or her skill in the actual operation of an automobile.

Work Sample

The work sample requires the student to perform actual tasks that are representative of the total performance to be measured. The sample tasks typically include the most crucial elements of the total performance, and are performed under controlled conditions. In being tested for automobile driving skill, for example, the student is required to drive over a standard course that includes the most common problem situations likely to be encountered in normal driving. The performance on the standard course is then used as evidence of the ability to drive an automobile under typical operating conditions.

Performance assessments in business education and industrial education are frequently of the work-sample type. When students are required to take and transcribe shorthand notes from dictation, type a business letter, or operate a computer in analyzing business data, a work-sample assessment is being employed. Similarly, in industrial education, a work-sample approach is being used when students are required to complete a metal-working or woodworking project that includes all of the steps likely to be encountered in an actual job situation (steps such as designing, ordering materials, and constructing). Still other examples are the operation of machinery, the repair of equipment, and the performance of job-oriented laboratory tasks. The work-sample approach to assessing performance is widely used in occupations involving performance skills, and many of these situations can be duplicated in the school setting.

Extended Research Project

One of the most comprehensive types of performance assessments involves the extended research project. This approach involves a combination of academic, communication, and thinking skills in the solving of unstructured "real world" problems, the construction of a unique product, or both. It typically involves multiple outcomes and criteria for each; student participation in developing criteria, selecting the problem to investigate, in designing and carrying out the study, and in evaluating the results; and written reports and an oral presentation and defense of the findings. Throughout, the focus is on higher-level learning outcomes used in problem solving (e.g., analysis, synthesis, evaluation), the effective use of communication skills, the development of self-assessment skills, and independent learning.

A common outline for an extended project includes the following items.

1. Establishing criteria and standards.
2. Selection of the problem.
3. Doing the research.
4. Writing the report.
5. Designing and constructing a product.
6. Orally presenting and defending the project.

Each of these steps is guided by the teacher and involves considerable student-teacher interaction.

Establishing Criteria and Standards.   Because of the multiple outcomes expected from a project, criteria must be established in many areas. For example, criteria for each of the major areas (i.e., problem selection, research skills, report writing, product design and construction, and oral presentation). Throughout these areas, or as a separate category, criteria must also be established for level of thinking shown and general problem-solving skills. These criteria may be developed by the teacher or they may be cooperatively prepared with the students. The latter procedure tends to provide greater understanding of the criteria by students and tends to be more motivating.

Standards that describe levels of success on each criterion should be set at the same time as the criteria are prepared, and may be stated separately as scoring rubrics (i.e., scoring guides) or may be included as part of a rating scale to be used in evaluating the project.

Selection of the Problem.   Students should be free to select a problem that interests them but the selection requires considerable help from the teacher. In a traditional classroom, many students are in the "tell me what to do" mode and one or two conferences may be needed to help them think about possible problems to study. The listing of criteria for selecting a problem is helpful (e.g., Is in harmony with present knowledge and skill, provides opportunity for new learning, fits present vocational interests, etc.). Describing to the student the range of problems the past students have studied and what their projects were like is also helpful.

Doing the Research.   After stating the problem clearly, the student is expected to go to reference books and other sources to gather information. Other sources might include interviews with knowledgeable people in the community (e.g., banker, accountant, doctor, scientist) observation of a process (e.g., council meeting, trial, bakery operation) or writing a letter to a congressman requesting information. The point is, students are expected to

obtain information from any source that can provide help with the problem—as we do in "real life."

Writing the Report.   The report should be written in accordance with the set
of criteria that were established for judging the report (e.g., clearly stated
problem, procedure described in detail, good organization, analysis and synthesis of the findings, validity of the conclusions). To assess higher-order
thinking skills, the criteria should also include those concerned with reasoning (e.g., quality of questions raised and suggestions proposed, relevance of
arguments, the adequacy of supporting data). In some cases there may be
separate criteria on the mechanics of writing (e.g., tone, style, grammar,
spelling). In any event, the student should be aware of the criteria before
writing the report, use them to evaluate the report and to then revise the report as needed. It is helpful for the teacher to evaluate the report and compare
the ratings with those of the student in a conference, before the student re-
vises the report.

Designing and Constructing a Product.   In some cases the product may be
the report itself but in others the research report may serve as a basis for a
product. This might be a poster, chart, graph, model, or some other type of
exhibit illustrating the findings. Or it might be a wood or metal product as in
the vocational area. In this case, the focus of the project may be on designing
and constructing the product but the research phase is still important. For a
woodworking project, for example, the research may involve a study of different types of wood, various construction procedures, or a history of the
product (e.g., in making a replica of an antique chair). The research phase provides for the combining of academic and vocational skills in carrying out the
project, and increases the opportunities for including higher-level thinking
skills in the project.

Orally Presenting and Defending the Project.   Upon completion of the extended project, each student is expected to give an oral description of the procedures and findings, and to display the product (if there is one). This
presentation may be made to the class, a panel of teachers, or to both plus
members of the community. The nature of the group depends on the purpose
of the assessment, the type of project, and how the school is organized.

The final presentation gives the student practice in public speaking and in
defending his work. This, of course, also provides another opportunity to evaluate higher-order thinking skills through use of questions concerning the research findings, the procedures used, and the resulting product. As with other
phases of the project, evaluation of the presentation is guided by the criteria
developed at the beginning of the project and fully shared with the students.

The extended research project described here includes multiple outcomes, such as research skills, writing skills, speaking skills, thinking skills, self-assessment skills, and in some cases vocational skills. The specific nature of such a project will, of course, vary with the area of instruction and the purpose of the project. It is helpful to review descriptions of how this and other types of performance assessments are functioning in the schools. The list of references at the end of this chapter provide numerous descriptions and examples of performance assessment in action.

SELECTING THE METHOD OF OBSERVING, RECORDING, AND SCORING

Whether judging procedures, products, or some combination of the two, some type of guided observation and method of recording and scoring the results is needed. Commonly used procedures include (1) systematic observation and anecdotal records, (2) checklists, and (3) rating scales.

Systematic Observation and Anecdotal Records

Observing students in natural settings is one of the most common methods of assessing performance outcomes. Unfortunately, the observations are typically unsystematic and frequently no record is made of the observation. For minor performance tasks that are easily corrected, like how to hold a paint brush or how to label a graph, informal observation may be all that is needed. For more comprehensive performance situations, however, the observations should be systematic and typically some record of the observation should be made. This will enhance their objectivity, meaningfulness, and usefulness at a later date.

Observations are frequently guided by checklists or rating scales but there is some advantage in making and recording less structured observations. For example, noting how students approach a task, how persistent they are in completing it, and how carefully they work has significance for evaluating their success in performing the task. Similarly, one student may need assistance on every step of the performance, while another student completes the task early and turns to help others. These important aspects of performance are apt to be overlooked by more structured observational devices but can be described in anecdotal records.

An **anecdotal record** is a brief description of some significant event. It typically includes the observed behavior, the setting in which it occurred, and a separate interpretation of the event. Although keeping anecdotal records can be time consuming, the task can be kept manageable by limiting the records to certain types of behavior (e.g., safety) and to those individuals needing the most help (e.g., slow, careless). The records are likely to be most useful when (1) they focus on meaningful incidents, (2) they are recorded soon after the incident, (3) they contain enough information to be understandable later, and (4) the observed incident and its interpretation are kept separate. What is desired is a brief, objective, self-sufficient description of a meaningful incident, and a separate interpretation (if needed) of what the incident means. As these records of events accumulate for a particular individual, a typical pattern of behavior is obtained.

Checklists

The **checklist** is basically a list of measurable dimensions of a performance or product, with a place to record a simple "yes" or "no" judgment. If a checklist were used to evaluate a set of procedures, for example, the steps to be followed might be placed in sequential order on the form; the observer would then simply check whether each action was taken or not taken. Such a checklist for evaluating the proper use of an oral thermometer is shown in Figure 8.2. A checklist for evaluating a product typically contains a list of the dimensions that characterize a good product (size, color, shape, and so on), and a place to check whether each desired characteristic is present or absent. Thus, the checklist simply directs attention to the elements to be observed and provides a convenient means of recording judgments.

Construction of a checklist for performance assessment involves the following steps.

Directions: Place a check in front of each step as it is performed

———— 1. Removes thermometer from container by grasping nonbulb end.
———— 2. Wipes thermometer downward from nonbulb end with fresh wiper.
———— 3. Shakes thermometer down to less than 96° while holding nonbulb end.
———— 4. Places bulb end of thermometer under patient's tongue.
———— 5. Tells patient to close lips but to avoid biting on thermometer.
———— 6. Leaves thermometer in patient's mouth for three minutes.
———— 7. Removes thermometer from patient's mouth by grasping nonbulb end.
———— 8. Reads temperature to the nearest *two tenths* of a degree.
———— 9. Records temperature reading on patient's chart.
———— 10. Cleans thermometer and replaces in container.

FIGURE 8.2 Checklist for Evaluating the Proper Use of an Oral Thermometer

1. List the procedural or product characteristics to be evaluated.
2. Add common errors to the list, if such is useful in diagnosing poor performance.
3. Arrange the list in some logical order (e.g., sequence of steps).
4. Provide instructions and a place for checking each item.
5. Add a place for comments at the bottom of the form, if needed.

Rating Scales

The **rating scale** is similar to the checklist and serves somewhat the same purpose in judging procedures and products. The main difference is that the rating scale provides an opportunity to mark the degree to which an element is present instead of using the simple "present-absent" judgment. The scale for rating is typically based on the frequency with which an action is performed (e.g., always, sometimes, never), the general quality of a performance (e.g., outstanding, above average, average, below average), or a set of descriptive phrases that indicates degrees of acceptable performance (e.g., completes task quickly, slow in completing task, cannot complete task without help). Like the checklist, the rating scale directs attention to the dimensions to be observed and provides a convenient form on which to record the judgments.

A sample rating scale for evaluating both procedures and product is shown in Figure 8.3. Although this numerical rating scale uses fixed alternatives, the same scale items could be described by descriptive phrases that vary from item to item.

In this case, each rated item would be arranged as follows:

(a) Plan for the project

1	2	3	4	5
Plan is too general and vague.		Plan is in proper form but needs more detail		Plan is detailed and complete.

A space for comments might also be added under each item, or at the bottom of each set of items, to provide a place for clarifying the ratings or describing how to improve performance.

The construction of a rating scale for performance assessment typically includes the following steps.

1. List the procedural or product characteristics to be evaluated.
2. Select the number of points to use on the scale and define them by descriptive terms or phrases.
3. Arrange the items on the rating scale so that they are easy to use.

Directions: Rate each of the following items by circling the appropriate number. The numbers represent the following values: 5—outstanding; 4—above average; 3—average; 2—below average; 1—unsatisfactory.

PROCEDURE RATING SCALE

How effective was the student's performance in each of the following areas?

5 4 3 2 1 (a) Preparing a detailed plan for the project.
5 4 3 2 1 (b) Determining the amount of material needed.
5 4 3 2 1 (c) Selecting the proper tools.
5 4 3 2 1 (d) Following the correct procedures for each operation.
5 4 3 2 1 (e) Using tools properly and skillfully.
5 4 3 2 1 (f) Using materials without unnecessary spoilage.
5 4 3 2 1 (g) Completing the work within a reasonable amount of time.

PRODUCT RATING SCALE

To what extent does the product meet the following criteria?

5 4 3 2 1 (a) The product appears neat and well constructed.
5 4 3 2 1 (b) The dimensions match the original plan.
5 4 3 2 1 (c) The finish meets specifications.
5 4 3 2 1 (d) The joints and parts fit properly.
5 4 3 2 1 (e) The materials were used effectively.

FIGURE 8.3   Rating Scale for a Woodworking Project

4. Provide clear, brief instructions that tell the rater how to mark items on the scale.
5. Provide a place for comments, if needed for diagnostic or instructional purposes.

Analytic Versus Holistic Scoring

Rating scales are especially useful for **analytic** scoring. That is, when we want a judgment on each criterion by which the performance or product is to be judged. In evaluating writing skill, for example, such things as organization, vocabulary, style, ideas, and mechanics might be judged separately. The rating scale then becomes an instrument for directing observation to these criteria and provides a convenient means of recording and scoring our judgments.

Holistic scoring is based on an overall impression of the performance or product rather than a consideration of the individual elements. The global judgment is made by assigning a numerical score to each performance or product. Typically, between 4 and 8 points are used, and an even number of points is favored to avoid a "middle dumping ground." Evaluation consists of quickly examining the performance or product and assigning the number that matches the general impression of the performance or product. In the case of writing assessment, for example, the reader will read each writing sample quickly for overall impression and place it in one of the piles ranging from 4 to 1. It is assumed that good writing is more than a sum of the individual elements that go into writing and that holistic scoring will capture this total impression of the work.

Holistic scoring can be guided by scoring rubrics that clarify what each level of quality is like. A **scoring rubric** (i.e., scoring guide) for writing and a psychomotor skill are shown in the accompanying boxes. These descriptions of each level do not provide for analysis of the product or the performance but simply list the criteria to keep in mind when making the overall judgment. Another way to clarify the meaning of each score level for a product is to use a *product scale*. This consists of a series of sample products that represent various degrees of quality. In writing assessment, for example, a writing sample representing each level of quality from 4 to 1 are reviewed and each writing product is compared to the sample models and assigned the number of the sample it matches most closely. Product scales are especially useful where the quality of the product is difficult to define (e.g., art, creative writing).

For most instructional purposes, both holistic and analytic scoring are useful. One gives the global judgment of the performance or product and the

---

Sample Scoring Rubric for Writing

4—Interesting throughout
    Flows smoothly, good transitions
    Well-organized for topic
    Good use of mechanics and sentence structure
3—Interesting most of the time
    Flows smoothly but some poor transitions
    Organized but some weaknesses
    Minor mechanical errors
2—Interest lowered by lapses in focus
    Flow is interrupted by many poor transitions
    Organization weak, strays from topic
    Some serious mechanical errors
1—No clear focus
    Jerky and rambling
    Poorly organized
    Many mechanical errors and weak sentence structure

General Scoring Rubric for a Psychomotor Skill

EXCELLENT   Uses procedure rapidly and skillfully

                                 Explains function of each step in procedure

                                 Modifies procedure to fit changing conditions

GOOD   Uses procedure correctly but with some hesitation

                                 Gives general explanation of steps in procedure

                                 Modifies procedure but needs some instructor guidance

ACCEPTABLE   Uses procedure correctly but is slow and clumsy

                                 Explanation of procedure is limited

                                 Modifies procedures but only after demonstration by instructor

INADEQUATE   Fails to use procedure correctly

                                 Explanation of procedure shows lack of understanding

                                 Uses trial and error in adjusting procedure

---

other provides diagnostic information useful for improving performance. Where both are used, the global judgment should be made first so some specific element does not distort the general impression of the product.

PORTFOLIOS

Portfolios have been used for many years by artists, photographers, writers, and others to collect and display the best samples of their work. This approach has been adopted by some educators as a basic, or sole, method of performance assessment. The term **portfolio assessment** is used to identify this comprehensive use of portfolios in the school. These portfolios include many of the different types of performance assessments we talked about throughout this chapter plus evaluations of them, observations, notes on teacher-student conferences, and other information relevant to students' learning progress. This broad approach to performance assessment has been used as one method for bringing about school reform. It has been stated that this comprehensive use of portfolio assessment "requires a total rethinking of how we organize curriculum, instruction, scheduling, and a host of other institutional issues" (Johnson, 1996).

    The use of portfolios in the traditional classroom has more modest goals. It is not considered a unique type of performance assessment but a useful method of collecting, organizing, and evaluating samples of students' work. The work samples in the portfolio provide a basis for judging learning progress and for communicating it to students, parents, and other interested parties.

Advantages of Using Classroom Portfolios

Portfolios have a number of advantages that make their use worthwhile in the classroom.

1. Learning progress over time can be clearly shown (e.g., changes in writing skills).
2. Focus on students' best work provides a positive influence on learning (e.g., best writing samples).
3. Comparing work to past work provides greater motivation than comparison to the work of others (e.g., growth in writing skills).
4. Self-assessment skills are increased due to the student selection of best samples of work and justifying choice (e.g., focus is on criteria of good writing).
5. Provides for adjustment to individual differences (e.g., students write at their own level but work toward common goals).
6. Provides for clear communication of learning progress to students, parents, and others (e.g., writing samples obtained at different times can be shown and compared).

Despite the numerous advantages of using portfolios, they are time consuming to maintain and use. The selection of students' work samples and a periodic review of the portfolio to evaluate learning progress requires considerable student-teacher conference time. Simply collecting samples of student work and putting it in a file does not provide for effective use of the portfolio.

Deciding What to Include

The collection of student work samples is guided by the purpose of the portfolio, as reflected in the intended learning outcomes and the use to be made of the results. In some cases, the portfolio might be limited to a specific area. For example, a collection of students' writing samples may be obtained to measure progress in writing skill. The writing samples may be confined to a particular type of writing or may be concerned with different types of writing (letter, essay, poetry) depending on the goals of the instruction. A more comprehensive portfolio may include work samples of various types depending on the area of instruction. In math, for example, work samples might include examples such as problem solving, written explanation of how to solve a problem, math theories and print-outs of computer use in solving problems. What to include will, of course, vary with the subject and with the purpose for using the portfolio. Typically, the focus is on the best samples of student performance and the student participates in selecting the samples.

Deciding on Criteria and Standards

The procedures for developing criteria and standards for evaluating the work samples are the same here as for any performance assessment, like those discussed earlier in this chapter. The criteria should define the type of performance we are willing to accept as evidence that the intended learning outcomes are being achieved, and the standard should identify the levels of acceptable performance. These are then used in preparing rating scales or scoring rubrics to be used in evaluating the work samples, as described earlier.

Students should be made aware of the criteria and standards by which performance will be judged, at the beginning of instruction. It is desirable to have students participate in defining the criteria and in preparing the rating scales or other evaluation forms, whenever possible.

Collecting the Work Samples

Typically, file folders are used for the portfolio and these are stored in a file cabinet. The work samples included in the portfolio should represent a student's best work. This means that the student must be able to judge which samples are best. The samples are dated when entered and may be accompanied by a student evaluation of the sample. Student participation in selecting the samples, thus, enhances students' self-assessment skills. As noted earlier, performance assessment focuses on the improvement of both performance skills and self-assessment skills and the portfolio should be designed and used with these goals in mind.

Maintaining and Using the Portfolio

Students should actively participate in the maintenance of the portfolio. It is a collection of their work, so they should aid in setting the guidelines for what goes into the portfolio, in selecting the work samples, and in evaluating the progress reflected in the samples of work. Unless students are active participants, they are less likely to feel that it is their portfolio.

The portfolio is reviewed periodically during a student-teacher conference. Here, they can view the content together, compare student and teacher evaluations, and discuss strengths in learning progress and areas where improvement is needed. The portfolio is also used in parent-teacher conferences to demonstrate and discuss student learning progress. There is no better way to make clear to parents what a student is learning than by the use of actual samples of student work.

Getting Started

If portfolios have not been used in the school before, one might start on a small scale. A safe approach is to start with one specific area such as writing, drawing, problem solving, laboratory work, or some other specific type of relevant work sample, and then expanding it to other areas as experience is obtained and time constraints are worked out.

The purpose, content, and use of portfolios varies so widely from one area of instruction to another and from one level of instruction to another that it is wise to consult some of the numerous references on portfolio design and use before getting started. The references at the end of this chapter describe

---

Improving Performance Assessments

1. Specify the intended performance outcomes in observable terms and describe the use to be made of the results.
2. Limit the observable dimensions of the performance to a reasonable number.
3. Provide clear, definite criteria for judging the procedure or product.
4. Select the performance setting that provides the most relevant and realistic situation.
5. If a structured performance situation is used, provide clear and complete instructions.
6. Be as objective as possible in observing, judging, and recording the performance.
7. Observe the performance under various conditions and use multiple observations whenever possible.
8. Make a record as soon as possible after an observation.
9. Use evaluation forms that are clear, relevant, and easy to use.
10. Use a scoring procedure that is appropriate for the use to be made of the results (e.g., holistic for global evaluation, analytic for diagnostic purposes).
11. Inform students of the method and criteria to be used in evaluating the performance.
12. Supplement and verify performance assessments with other evidence of achievement.
13. Use a portfolio for collecting and exhibiting samples of student work.
14. Have students participate in all phases of the performance assessment.

and illustrate a variety of types of portfolios and the varied uses of them. Especially useful, are the examples of forms and criteria used in different subjects and in different schools.

IMPROVING PERFORMANCE ASSESSMENTS

Performance assessments can provide useful information concerning student achievement but they are subject to all of the errors of observation and judgment, such as personal bias, generosity error (tendency to overrate), and halo effect (judging individual characteristics in terms of a general impression). Thus, if performance assessments are to provide valid information, special care must be taken to improve the objectivity, reliability, and meaningfulness of the results. A set of guidelines in the accompanying box list ways to improve the usefulness of performance assessments.

SUMMARY OF POINTS

1. Performance assessments provide greater realism of tasks and greater complexity of tasks than traditional paper-and-pencil testing, but they are time consuming to use and require greater use of judgment in scoring.
2. Restricted performance tasks are highly structured and limited in scope (e.g., construct a graph). Extended performance tasks are typically poorly structured and broad in scope (e.g., solve a "real world" problem).
3. The need for performance assessment arises out of the nature of the course (e.g., communication, laboratory, and problem-solving skills), the shift from norm-referenced measurement to criterion-referenced measurement (e.g., describing achievement rather than ranking scores), and modern learning theory that emphasizes complex learning outcomes and active student participation in the construction of meaning.
4. The first step in performance assessment is to specify the intended performance outcomes.
5. Performance assessment may focus on a procedure (e.g., giving a speech), a product (e.g., a theme), or both (e.g., uses tools properly in building a bookcase).
6. In some cases, it may be desirable to emphasize procedure evaluation during the early stages of instruction (e.g., touch system in typing) and product evaluation later (typed letter).
7. There are varying degrees of realism in performance assessment, and the aim is to obtain as high a degree of realism as possible within the various constraints operating (e.g., time, cost, availability of equipment).

8. Paper-and-pencil performance assessment is useful as a terminal measure in many areas (e.g., writing, drawing, problems solving) and can serve as a first step toward "hands-on" performance in others (e.g., procedure for repairing an automobile engine).

9. The identification test is typically concerned with identifying the tools, equipment, and procedures needed for a performance task and serves as an *indirect* measure of performance, or as an instructional device to prepare students for actual performance.

10. A structured performance test provides for an assessment under standard, controlled conditions (e.g., locating a malfunction in electronic equipment). The tools, equipment, conditions, and standards of performance are all carefully prescribed.

11. Performance assessment based on simulated performance (e.g., driver's training simulator) and the work sample (e.g., analyze business data on a computer) has a high degree of realism. Many performance skills in laboratory courses, business education, and industrial education can be evaluated at this level.

12. The extended research project provides for assessment of multiple outcomes (e.g., research, writing, speaking, thinking, and self-assessment skills) and can be adapted to various areas of instruction.

13. Observing students in natural settings and keeping anecdotal records can aid in evaluating aspects of performance that are likely to be overlooked by more structured methods (e.g., work habits).

14. Rating scales provide for analytic scoring, direct attention to the performance dimensions to be observed, and provide a convenient form on which to record the judgments.

15. Scoring rubrics (i.e., scoring guides) and product scales are especially useful where holistic judgments are being made (e.g., creative writing, works of art).

16. A portfolio is a collection of student work (e.g., writing or drawing samples) that can be used for evaluating learning progress and communicating it to students and parents. A portfolio provides for adjustment to individual differences, emphasis on learning strengths, development of self-assessment skills, and the active participation of students in the learning process—but they are time consuming to maintain and use.

17. Improving performance assessments involves making clear what is to be observed, how it is to be observed, how the observations are to be recorded, and how the results are to be scored and used. In addition, any procedure that contributes to more objective observations and records will aid in increasing the reliability and meaningfulness of the results. Also, the use of portfolios and student participation can contribute to the improvement of performance assessments.

ADDITIONAL READING

Darling-Hamond, L., Ancess, J., and Falk, B., *Authentic Assessment in Action* (New York: Teachers College Press, Columbia University, 1995). Descriptions of how two elementary schools and three secondary schools developed and used performance-based assessments in the creation of learner-centered educational programs. The use of projects, portfolios, and performance tasks are described and illustrated.

Fitzpatrick, R., and Morrison, E. J., "Performance and Product Evaluation." Chapter 9 in R. L. Thorndike, Ed., *Educational Measurement*, 2nd ed. (Washington, DC: American Council on Education, 1971). An older but worthwhile discussion of the principles and procedures of performance assessment.

Gronlund, N. E., *How to Write and Use Instructional Objectives*, 5th ed. (Englewood Cliffs, NJ: Prentice-Hall, 1995). See Chapter 9, "Writing Performance Objectives," for descriptions and examples.

Herman, J., Aschbacher, P., and Winters, L., *A Practical Guide to Performance Assessment* (Alexandria, VA: ASCD, 1992). Describes and illustrates performance assessment procedures and scoring rubrics.

Johnson, B., *Performance Assessment Handbook: Volume 1, Portfolios and Socratic Seminars* (Princeton, NJ: Eye on Education, 1996). A practical guide for understanding performance assessment programs and how they are changing secondary schools. Numerous illustrations of forms, criteria, and scoring rubrics used in the programs.

Johnson, B., *Performance Assessment Handbook: Volume 2, Performances and Exhibitions* (Princeton, NJ: Eye on Education, 1996). A practical guide, like Volume 1, that describes and illustrates various assessment programs in schools.

Kulm, G., *Mathematics Assessment: What Works in the Classroom* (San Francisco, CA: Jossey-Bass, 1994). Describes how to develop and use performance assessments with numerous examples from the elementary and secondary levels. Although focusing on mathematics, much of the material would be useful to all teachers.

Linn, R. L., and Gronlund N. E., *Measurement and Assessment in Teaching*, 7th ed. (Englewood Cliffs, NJ: Prentice-Hall, 1995). See Chapter 10, "Measuring Complex Achievement: Performance-Based Assessment," for descriptions of performance assessments and procedures for preparing and using checklists and rating scales.

McMillan, J. H., *Classroom Assessment* (Boston: Allyn & Bacon, 1997). See Chapter 9, "Using Portfolios to Assess Reasoning, Skills, and Products," for a practical and comprehensive treatment of how to use portfolios in student assessment.

▶ 9

Assigning Grades

Studying this chapter should enable you to

1. Distinguish between absolute grading and relative grading.
2. Describe how to select a proper frame of reference, or standard, for assigning grades.
3. Explain why learning ability, improvement, and effort provide a poor basis for grading.
4. Describe and defend the grading system you would use in your area of instruction.
5. Demonstrate how to properly weight components to be included in a grade.
6. Describe a rationale for making the pass-fail decision.
7. Write a statement, to be given to students, that describes your grading procedures.

Grades assigned to student work should represent the extent to which the instructional objectives (i.e., the intended learning outcomes) have been achieved, and should be in harmony with the grading policies of the school. Some schools have both clearly defined objectives and grading policies; many schools have neither. With or without the guidance of clear-cut policies and procedures, the assigning of grades is a difficult and frustrating task. It is somewhat easier if valid evidence of achievement has been gathered throughout the course.

Assessment of learning during instruction might include the use of objective and essay tests, ratings, papers, and various types of performance assessment. The problem of grading is that of summarizing this diverse collection of information into a single letter grade or brief report. Because the single letter grade (e.g., A, B, C, D, F) is the most widely used grading system, we shall focus on how best to assign such grades. This involves several important considerations: (1) What frame of reference, or standard, should be used to report level of performance? (2) How should the performance data be combined for grading? (3) What guidelines should be followed to provide the most effective and fair grading system? Each of these will be discussed in turn.

SELECTING THE BASIS FOR GRADING

Letter grades are typically assigned by comparing a student's performance to a prespecified standard of performance (absolute grading) or to the performance of the members of a group (relative grading). In some cases, grades are based on or modified by the learning ability of the student, the amount of improvement shown over a given instructional period, or student effort. As we shall see later, these factors provide an inadequate basis for assigning grades.

Absolute Grading

A common type of absolute grading is the use of letter grades defined by a 100-point system. Whether assigning grades to an individual set of test scores, or as a basis for the final grades in a course, the set of grades might be expressed as one of the following:

	Points	*Points*	*Points*
A =	90–100	95–100	91–100
B =	80–89	85–94	86–90
C =	70–79	75–84	81–85
D =	60–69	65–74	75–80
F =	below 60	below 65	below 75

In the case of an individual test, this 100-point system might represent the percentage of items correct or the total number of points earned on the test. When used as a final grade, it typically represents a combining of scores from various tests and other assessment results. In any event, it provides an absolute basis for assigning letter grades.

Which set of points provides the best basis for assigning grades? There is no way of knowing. The distribution of points is arbitrary. Whatever distribution is used, however, should be based on the teacher's experience with this and past groups of students, knowledge concerning the difficulty of the intended learning outcomes, the difficulty of the tests and other assessments used, the conditions of learning, and the like. These are all subjective judgments, however, and shifts in the proportion of students getting the letter grade of A or F are difficult to evaluate. Do a larger number of grades of A represent improved instruction and better study habits by students, or easier tests and less rigid grading of papers and projects? Do more failures indicate poor teaching, inadequate study, or assessments that have inadvertently increased in difficulty?

Despite the problem of setting meaningful standards for an absolute grading system, this method is widely used in schools. It is most appropriate in programs where the set of learning tasks has been clearly specified, the standards have been defined in terms of the learning tasks, and the tests and other assessment techniques have been designed for criterion-referenced interpretation. All too frequently, however, absolute grading is based on some hodgepodge of ill-defined achievement results. When the distribution of points does not fit the grading scale, the points are adjusted upward or downward by some obscure formula to get a closer fit. Needless to say, such grades do not provide a meaningful report of the extent to which the intended learning outcomes have been achieved.

Relative Grading

When assigning grades on a relative basis, the students are typically ranked in order of performance (based on a set of test scores or combined assessment results) and the students ranking highest receive a letter grade of A, the next highest receive a B, and so on. What proportion of students should receive each grade is predetermined and might appear as one of the following:

	Percent of Students	Percent of Students
A	15	10–20
B	25	20–30
C	45	40–50
D	10	10–20
F	5	0–10

The percent of students to be assigned each grade is just as arbitrary as the selection of points for each grade in the absolute grading system. The use of a range of percents (e.g., A = 10–20 percent) should probably be favored because it makes some allowance for differences in the ability level of the class. It does not make sense to assign 15 percent As to both a regular class and a gifted class. Likewise, in an advanced course a larger proportion of As and Bs should be assigned and fewer (if any) Fs because the low-achieving students have been "weeded out" in earlier courses. When these percentages have been set by the school system, one has little choice but to follow the school practice—at least until efforts to change it are successful.

Older measurement books recommended using the normal curve to assign grades. This resulted in the same percent of As and Fs (e.g., 7 percent) and Bs and Ds (e.g., 38 percent). Although some teachers may still use such a system, its use should be discouraged. Measures of achievement in classroom groups seldom yield normally distributed scores. Also, to maintain the same proportion of grades, especially failures, at different grade levels does not take into account that the student population is becoming increasingly select as the failing students are held back or drop out of school.

The relative grading system requires a reliable ranking of students; thus, it is most meaningful when the achievement measures provide a wide range

---

Absolute Grading and Relative Grading

ABSOLUTE GRADING

Strengths

1. Grades can be described directly in terms of student performance, without reference to the performance of others.
2. All students can obtain high grades if mastery outcomes are stressed and instruction is effective.

Limitations

1. Performance standards are set in an arbitrary manner and are difficult to specify and justify.
2. Performance standards tend to vary unintentionally due to variations in test difficulty, assignments, student ability, and instructional effectiveness.
3. Grades can be assigned without clear reference to what has been achieved (but, of course, they should not be).

RELATIVE GRADING

Strengths

1. Grades can be easily described and interpreted in terms of rank in a group.
2. Grades distinguish among levels of student performance that are useful in making prediction and selection decisions.

Limitations

1. The percent of students receiving each grade is arbitrarily set.
2. The meaning of a grade varies with the ability of the student group.
3. Grades can be assigned without clear reference to what has been achieved (but, of course, they should not be).

of scores. This makes it possible to draw the lines between grades with greater assurance that misclassifications will be kept to a minimum. Ideally, of course, the spread of scores should be based on the difficulty and complexity of the material learned. For example, an A should not simply represent more knowledge of factual material, but a higher level of understanding, application, and thinking skills. Thus, although norm-referenced interpretation is being utilized, the real meaning of the grades comes from referring back to the nature of the achievement that each grade represents.

Learning Ability, Improvement, and Effort

In some cases, attempts are made to base grades on achievement in relation to learning ability, the amount of improvement in achievement, or the amount of effort a student puts forth. All of these procedures have problems that distort the meaning of grades.

Grading on the basis of *learning ability* has sometimes been used at the elementary level to motivate students with less ability. At first glance, it seems sensible to give a grade of A to students who are achieving all that they are capable of achieving. There are two major problems with this procedure, however. First, it is difficult, if not impossible, to get a dependable measure of learning ability apart from achievement. Both bests have similar type items and measure similar concepts. Second, the meaning of the grades become distorted. A low-ability student with average performance might receive an A, whereas a high-ability student with average performance receives a grade of C. Obviously the grades are no longer very meaningful as indicators of achievement.

Using the amount of *improvement* as a basis for grading also has its problems. For one, the difference scores between measures of achievement over short spans of time are very unreliable. For another, students who score high on the entry test cannot possibly get a high grade because little improvement can be shown. Students who know about this grading procedure ahead of time can, of course, do poorly on the first test and be assured of a fairly good grade. This is not an uncommon practice where grades are based on improvement. Finally, the grades lack meaning as indicators of achievement when increase in achievement becomes more important than level of achievement. For example, a low-achieving student with considerable improvement might receive an A, while a high-achieving student with little improvement receives a B or C.

Grading on the basis of *effort*, or adjusting grades for effort, also distorts the meaning of the results. Low-achieving students who put forth great effort receive higher grades than their achievement warrants and high-achieving students who put forth little effort are likely to receive lower grades than deserved. Although such grading seems to serve a motivational function for low-achieving students, the grades become meaningless as measures of the extent to which students are achieving the intended learning outcomes.

In summary, assigning grades that take into account learning ability, amount of improvement, or effort simply contaminates the grades and distorts their meaning as indicators of student achievement. A letter grade is most useful when it represents achievement and only achievement. Other factors may be rated separately on a report card, but they should not be allowed to distort the meaning of the letter grade.

A Combination of Absolute and Relative Grading

Grades should represent the degree of which instructional objectives (i.e., intended learning outcomes) are achieved by students. Some of the objectives of instruction are concerned with minimum essentials that must be mastered if a student is to proceed to the next level of instruction. Other objectives are concerned with learning outcomes that are never fully achieved but toward which students can show varying degrees of progress. The first are called *minimal objective* and the second *developmental objectives.*

Minimal objectives are concerned with the knowledge, skill, and other lower-level learning outcomes that represent the minimum essentials of the course. In order to receive a passing grade, a student must demonstrate that this basic knowledge and skill, which are prerequisite to further learning in the area, have been learned to a satisfactory degree. *Developmental objectives* are concerned with higher-level learning outcomes such as understanding, application, and thinking skills. Although we can identify degrees of progress toward these objectives, we cannot expect to ever fully achieve them. In science, for example, we might expect all students to master basic terms, concepts, and skills, but encourage each student to proceed as far as he can in understanding and applying the scientific process, and in developing the intellectual skills used by scientists. Similarly, all students in math might be expected to master the fundamental operations, but show wide diversity in problem-solving ability and mathematical reasoning. In all instructional areas there are lower-level objectives that should be mastered by all students and higher-level objectives that provide goals that never can be fully achieved. Thus, with minimal objectives we attempt to obtain a uniformly high level of performance for all students, and with developmental objectives we encourage each student to strive for maximum development.

As indicated earlier, the pass-fail decision should be based on whether or not the minimal objectives have been mastered. Students demonstrating that they have achieved the minimal objectives, and thus have the necessary prerequisites for success at the next level of instruction, should be passed. Those who do not should fail. This requires an *absolute* judgment, not a relative one. Students should not be failed simply because their achievement places them near the bottom of some group. It is the nature of the achievement that is significant.

Above the pass-fail cutoff point, grades should be assigned on a relative basis. This is because students' scores will tend to be spread out in terms of their degree of development beyond the minimal level. Students cannot be expected to master the more complex learning outcomes described by developmental objectives, but they can show varying degrees of progress toward their attainment. Although it would be ideal to have a scale of achievement ranging from simple to complex so that absolute grading could be used, this is not possible at this time. The best we can do is obtain a spread of student achievement scores in terms of the complexity of the learning outcomes attained and use relative grading. If properly done, a grade of A would represent greater achievement of the higher-level learning outcomes and not simply a high relative position in the group. This would assume, of course, that tests and other assessment techniques would measure a range of achievement from simple to complex, and not just knowledge of factual information and simple skills, as is commonly done now (see Terwilliger, 1989).

In many cases the school will dictate the grading policy, including the basis on which the grades are to be assigned. Regardless of the system used, it is important to relate the grades back to student achievement so that different grades represent different levels of performance. Letter grades without an achievement referent tend to have little meaning.

COMBINING DATA FOR GRADING

Assigning grades typically involves combining results from various types of assessment, including such things as tests, projects, papers, and laboratory work. If each element is to be included in the grade in terms of its relative importance, the data must be combined in a way that proper weights are used. For example, if we want test scores to count 50 percent, papers 25 percent, and laboratory work 25 percent of the grade, we need a method that will result in grades that reflect this emphasis. The process is simplified if all assessment results are converted to numerical scores first. It is then simply a matter of following a systematic procedure of combining scores.

The method of combining scores so that proper weights are obtained for each element is not as simple as it seems. A common procedure is simply to add scores together if they are to have equal weight and to multiply by 2 if an element is to count twice as much as the other. This typically will not result in each element receiving its proper weight, even if the highest possible scores is the same for all sets of scores. How much influence each element has in a composite score is determined by the spread, or variability, of scores and not the number of total points.

The problem of weighting scores when combining them can be best illustrated with a simple example. Let's assume we only have two measures of achievement and we want to give them equal weight in a grade. Our two sets of achievement scores have score ranges as follows:

Test scores	20 to 100
Laboratory work	30 to 50

If we simply added together a student's test score and score on laboratory work, the grade the student received would be determined largely by the test score because of its wide spread of scores. This can be shown by comparing a student who had the highest test score and lowest laboratory score (Student 1) with a student who had the lowest test score and highest laboratory score (Student 2).

	Student 1	*Student 2*
Test score	100	20
Laboratory score	30	50
Composite score	130	70

It is quite obvious that the composite score does not represent equal weighting.

With sets of scores like those for our test and laboratory work, it is not uncommon for teachers to attempt to give them equal weight by making the top possible score equal. This can be done, of course, by multiplying the score on laboratory work by 2, making the highest possible score 100 for both measures. Here is how the two composite scores for our hypothetical students would compare under this system:

	Student 1	*Student 2*
Test score	100	20
Laboratory score ($\times 2$)	60	100
Composite score	160	120

Our composite scores make clear that equalizing the maximum possible score does not provide equal weights either. As noted earlier, the influence a measure has on the composite score depends on the spread, or variability, of scores. Thus, the greater the spread of scores, the larger the contribution to the composite score.

We can give equal weight to our two sets of scores by using the **range** of scores in each set. Because our test scores have a range of 80 (100–20) and our laboratory scores have a range of 20 (50–30), we must multiply each laboratory score by 4 to equalize the spread of scores and, thus, given them equal weight in the composite score. Here are the composite scores for our two hypothetical students:

	Student 1	*Student 2*
Test score	100	20
Laboratory score (× 4)	120	200
Composite score	220	220

At last we have a system that gives the two measures equal weight in the composite score. Note that if we wanted to count our test score *twice* as much

---

Computing Composite Scores for Grading

1. Select assessments to be included in the composite score and assign percentages.
2. Record desired weight for each assessment.
3. Equate range of scores by using multiplier.
4. Determine weight to apply to each score by multiplying "desired weight" by "multiplier to equate ranges."

Components		Desired Weight	Range of Scores	Multiplier to Equate Ranges	Weight to Apply to Each Score
1. Test scores	50%	2	20 to 100	1	$2 \times 1 = 2$
2. Laboratory work	25%	1	30 to 50	4	$1 \times 4 = 4$
3. Homework	25%	1	0 to 10	8	$1 \times 8 = 8$

COMPUTING THE COMPOSITE SCORES

Students	Raw Scores			Weighted Scores			Composite
	1.	2.	3.	1.(×2)	2.(×4)	3.(×8)	1.(w)+2.(w)+3.(w)
Dave	93	42	8	186	168	64	418
Derek	84	45	10	168	180	80	428
Maria	85	47	7	170	188	56	414
Tricia	95	35	10	190	140	80	410

Note that Derek had the highest composite score but would have had the lowest if the raw scores were simply added together, or even if the test score was multiplied by 2 (the desired weight). That is because the measure with the biggest range of scores has the greatest influence on the combined scores unless adjustments are made to equate the spread of scores. Compare Tricia's raw scores and composite scores to Derek's.

as the laboratory score, we would multiply it by 2 and the laboratory score by 4. However, if we wanted to have our laboratory score count twice as much as the test score, we would have to multiply each laboratory score by 8. Thus, when we originally multiplied our laboratory scores by 4, we simply adjusted the spread of those scores to match the spread of the test scores. When the two sets of scores have the same range of scores, we can then assign additional weights in terms of their relative importance.

The range of scores provides only a rough approximation of score variability but it is satisfactory for most classroom grading purposes. A more dependable basis for weighting grade components can be obtained with the standard deviation (see Ebel and Frisbie, 1991).

Some teachers obtain a composite grade by converting all test scores and other assessments to letter grades, converting the letter grades to numbers (e.g., A = 4, B = 3, C = 2, D = 1, F = 0) and then averaging them for a final grade. When this procedure is followed, information is lost because the data are reduced to only five categories. For example, a student with a high A and high B would receive the same average grade as a student with a low A and a low B. To overcome this problem, pluses and minuses are sometimes added (e.g., A+ = 12, A = 11, A– = 10, B+ = 9, B = 8, B– = 7, etc.). This provides more categories but some information is still lost. A better solution is to use numerical scores on all assessments and then combine these numerical scores into a composite score before assigning grades.

GUIDELINES FOR EFFECTIVE AND FAIR GRADING

Assigning grades that provide a valid measure of student achievement, that have a meaning beyond the classroom in which they are given, and that are considered to be fair by students is a difficult but important part of teaching. The following guidelines provide a framework that should help clarify and standardize the task.

1. *Inform students at the beginning of instruction what grading procedures will be used.* This should include what will be included in the final grade (e.g., tests, projects, laboratory work) and how much weight will be given to each element. It should also include a description, in achievement terms, of what each letter grade represents. A descriptive handout may be helpful.

2. *Base grades on student achievement, and achievement only.* Grades should represent the extent to which the intended learning outcomes were achieved by students. They should *not* be contaminated by student effort, tardiness, misbehavior, or other extraneous factors. These can be reported on separately, but they should not influence the achievement grade. If they are permitted to become a part of the grade, the meaning of the grade as an indicator of achievement is lost.

3. Base grades on a wide variety of valid assessment data. All too frequently, grades are based primarily, if not entirely, on test scores. If grades are to be sound indicators of achievement, all important learning outcomes must be assessed and the results included in the final grade. Evaluations of papers, projects, and laboratory work are not as reliable as objective test scores but to eliminate them lowers the validity of the grades.

4. When combining scores for grading, use a proper weighting technique. As noted earlier, the influence of a component on the overall grade is determined by the spread, or variability, of the scores. Thus, in combining scores to obtain a composite for assigning grades, be sure the spread of scores is equalized before weighting and combining them.

5. Select an appropriate frame of reference for grading. If the entire instruction is based on mastery learning, it is necessary to use an *absolute* standard for grading and to define the grades in mastery terms. For conventional classroom instruction, the pass-fail distinction should be described in absolute terms and the grades above that determined by relative position in the group. However, these relative letter grades should have achievement referents representing learning outcomes ranging from simple to complex.

6. Review borderline cases by reexamining all achievement evidence. When setting cutoff points for each grade, there is typically a student or two just below the cutoff line. Measurement errors alone might be responsible for a student being just below (or above) the line. Also, the composite score may contain a clerical error, or one low test score contributing to the composite score may be due to illness or some other extraneous factor. In any event, it is wise to review the data for borderline cases and make any needed adjustments. When in doubt, fair grading would favor giving the student the higher grade.

Although in this chapter we focused on assigning grades, it does not imply that all student assignments and activities should be graded. Using brief tests, written assignments, and projects as learning tools is frequently more effective if the focus is on detecting and overcoming learning errors rather than on assigning grades. Formative assessment emphasizes this function of assessment results. Whether graded or not, however, all assessments of student achievement should include plans for the effective feedback of results along with suggestions for improving learning. As noted in Chapter 8, the portfolio is useful for this purpose, as well as for reporting learning progress to parents. Grading is an important and necessary task in teaching but it is secondary to our main purpose—improving student learning.

SUMMARY OF POINTS

1. Grades should represent achievement of the intended learning outcomes and be uncontaminated by other factors.
2. Grades should be assigned in accordance with the grading policies and procedures of the school.
3. Absolute grading requires predetermined standards based on clearly specified learning tasks and measures designed for criterion-referenced interpretation.
4. If instruction is based on a mastery learning program, absolute grading should be used with defined cutoff points and a stated rationale for the selection of the cutoff points.
5. Relative grading is based on the ranking of individuals in a group but relative grades also should have content meaning. Higher grades should represent higher levels of understanding, application, thinking skills, and performance skills.
6. Where relative grading is used, the pass-fail decision still should be determined on an absolute basis. The important question is: Does this student have the minimum knowledge and skill needed to succeed at the next level of instruction?
7. A grading system based on minimal objectives (to determine the pass-fail decision) and developmental objectives that spread students out in terms of the difficulty and complexity of the material learned, provides a good compromise between absolute and relative grading for use in conventional classroom instruction.
8. Basing grades on achievement in relation to learning ability, amount of improvement, or effort will only distort the meaning of grades as measures of achievement.
9. Grades should be based on valid measures of achievement. Validity is built in during the construction of tests and other assessment procedures by designing instruments that measure the intended outcomes of instruction.
10. Grades should be based on a variety of achievement assessments. Test scores should be supplemented by various types of performance assessment that measure the intended outcomes of instruction more directly (e.g., writing samples, laboratory work).
11. Components entering into an overall grade should be adjusted for the spread of scores before weighting them in terms of their importance.
12. Borderline cases should be given the benefit of the doubt and assigned the higher grade, unless a review of the achievement data indicates otherwise.

13. Attitude, effort, tardiness, misbehavior, and other nonachievement factors might be rated separately on a report card but should not be allowed to influence the achievement grade.
14. Some tests and assessment techniques can be used for learning purposes only and need not be assigned a grade (e.g., formative use of learning assessments).
15. Plans should be made for the effective feedback of all assessment results with suggestions for improving student learning. Portfolios are useful for this.
16. Whatever grading system is used, the grading procedures should be described for students at the beginning of instruction. A descriptive handout may be useful for this.

ADDITIONAL READING

Airasian, P. W., *Classroom Assessment*, 3rd ed. (New York: McGraw-Hill, 1997). See the chapter on grading for a comprehensive discussion of grading with illustrative report cards.

Ebel, R. L., and Frisbie, D. A., *Essentials for Educational Measurement*, 5th ed. (Englewood Cliffs, NJ: Prentice-Hall, 1991). See Chapter 15, "Grading and Reporting Achievements," for methods of assigning grades, including problems, procedures, combining grade components, and how to locate grading software for a microcomputer.

Linn, R. L., and Gronlund, N. E., *Measurement and Assessment in Teaching*, 7th ed. (Englewood Cliffs, NJ: Prentice-Hall, 1995). See Chapter 13, "Marking and Reporting," for various types of marking and reporting systems and their use in the schools.

Macmillan, J. H., *Classroom Assessment* (Boston: Allyn & Bacon, 1997). See Chapter 11, "Using Assessment for Grading and Reporting," for descriptions of the functions and types of grades, how to combine different types of scores in grading, and how to report to parents. Appendix B contains a list of computer software packages for grading and item banking.

Terwilliger, J. S., "Classroom Standard Setting and Grading Practices," *Educational Measurement: Issues and Practice*, 1989, 8(2), 15–19. Describes the use of minimal and developmental objectives in assigning grades.

▶ 10

Interpreting Standardized Achievement Test Scores

Studying this chapter should enable you to

1. Distinguish between norm-referenced and criterion-referenced interpretation of standardized test results.
2. Describe the basic features of a standardized achievement test.
3. Explain the meaning of each of the scores used in norm-referenced interpretation and list the cautions when interpreting each one.
4. Describe how standard scores are derived from the mean and standard deviation.
5. Convert standard scores to each other and to percentile ranks, using the normal curve.
6. Explain the stanine system and describe the advantages of using stanine scores.
7. Describe the procedures for making criterion-referenced interpretations with standardized tests.
8. List the cautions to observe when making criterion-referenced interpretations with standardized tests.

Standardized achievement tests have been widely used in the schools as a means of determining how well schools are doing. These tests have been primarily norm-referenced tests that compared local student performance to the performance of a representative sample of students in a norm group (e.g., a group of students at the national, regional, or state level). In the past, the test items were selection-type items, primarily multiple choice. In recent years, the tests have been modified to provide for criterion-referenced interpretations as well (e.g., by including more items per task, using open-ended tasks, and providing for interpretation by clusters of tasks). Both types of interpretation will be discussed in turn.

Being able to interpret the various types of norm-referenced test scores and to understand how criterion-referenced interpretations are used in standardized tests is important, if the tests are to play a role in the instructional program. It is also important, of course, to understand them well enough to be able to explain them to students and parents. To start with, it is important to keep in mind that norm-referenced interpretation indicates a student's relative level of performance in comparison to others and criterion-referenced interpretation describes the tasks a student can perform.

FEATURES OF STANDARDIZED ACHIEVEMENT TESTS

Standardized achievement tests are designed to determine how well students are achieving a common set of broadly based goals. Well-constructed standardized achievement tests typically have the following features.

1. The content of the test is based on widely used textbooks and curriculum guides.
2. The test items are written by test experts in consultation with subject-matter experts, and are based on a clear set of specifications.
3. The test items are tried out, reviewed, analyzed for difficulty and discriminating power, and either revised or eliminated.
4. The final set of items is selected on the basis of the test specifications.
5. Directions for administering and scoring the test are rigidly prescribed.
6. The test is administered to select groups of students to establish national, regional, or state-wide norms for interpretation of the test scores.
7. The final version of the test is published along with a test manual that describes the test's technical qualities, and the procedures for administering, scoring, interpreting, and using the results.

Thus, a standardized test measures a standard set of broadly based educational outcomes, uses standard directions and standard scoring procedures, and provides for a comparison of a student's score to that of similar students who have taken the same test under the same conditions. If a **battery of tests** is used, and all tests have been standardized on the same norm group, a student's performance on the different tests can also be compared. On a basic skill battery, for example, we can determine a student's relative level of performance in reading, language, and mathematics. With comparable forms of the test, we can also examine learning progress over a series of grade levels. All of these norm-referenced interpretations and comparisons of standardized test scores requires an understanding of the various types of test scores that are used in describing students' test performance.

INTERPRETING NORM-REFERENCED SCORES

The score a student receives when a test has been scored according to the directions is called the **raw score.** On a classroom test, this is typically the number of items a student answers correctly. Although raw scores are used in classroom testing, the interpretations and comparisons made with standardized tests require that the raw scores be converted to some type of **derived score.** Comparison of performance on two different tests (e.g., reading and math), for example, require that both tests be on the same scale. Raw scores won't work because the two tests may differ in the number of items in the test and the difficulty of the items. By converting both sets of raw scores to the same derived score scale, we provide a common basis for comparing relative performance. Although there are many different types of derived scores, the most common types used in school achievement testing are:

1. Percentile ranks
2. Grade equivalent scores
3. Standard scores

The raw scores on a standardized test are converted to derived scores during the norming of the test. Attempts are made to obtain norm groups that contain a sample of students like those for whom the test is intended. National **norms,** for example, typically include students from the various geographic regions of the United States, urban and rural schools, and schools of different size. A balance of boys and girls, socioeconomic levels and ethnic groups is also sought. Thus, national norms should approximate as closely as possible the student population throughout the United States. The same care is typically also followed in obtaining regional, state, and special group norms (e.g., private schools). Despite the care in obtaining norm groups, however, the obtained sample of students only approximates the ideal sample, due to such constraints as the needed cooperation of selected schools to administer the tests and the time limits for obtaining the norm sample.

After the norm groups have been selected and the tests administered and scored, the raw scores are converted to derived scores and presented in the test manual in tables of norms. These tables present the raw scores and derived scores in columns so that a raw score can be converted into a derived score by going across the parallel columns from the raw score to the derived score. Of course, the printout from machine scoring will give both the raw score and the derived score.

Before using the derived scores from a standardized test, it is wise to consider the nature of the norm group. Does the norm group provide a relevant basis for interpreting student performance? How was the norm group obtained? When were the norms obtained? We can obtain the most meaningful norm-referenced interpretation of test scores when the norms are relevant, representative, and up to date.

A final caution. The scores in the norm group should not be viewed as goals or standards. They are simply the scores that a representative group of students have earned on the test. They aid in interpreting and comparing test performance but they do not represent levels of performance to strive for. They are average or typical scores obtained in average or typical schools.

PERCENTILE RANKS

The percentile rank is one of the easiest scores to understand and to interpret to parents. A percentile rank indicates a student's relative position in a group in terms of the percentage of group members scoring at or below the student's raw score. For example, if a raw score of 33 equals a percentile rank of 80, it means 80 percent of the group members had raw scores equal to or lower than 33. By converting raw scores to percentile ranks, the raw scores are put on a scale that has the same meaning with different size groups and for different length tests.

To further clarify the meaning of percentile ranks, Table 10.1 illustrates how raw scores are converted to percentile ranks. The following steps illustrate the procedure.

1. The raw scores are ranked from high to low (column 1).
2. The number of students obtaining each score is listed in the frequency column (column 2).
3. The score frequencies are added from the bottom up (i.e., adding each score frequency to the total frequency of all lower scores) to obtain the cumulative frequency (column 3).

4. Applying the following formula at each score level to get the percentile rank for that raw score (column 4).

$$PR = \frac{CF\ below\ score + 1/2\ of\ frequency\ at\ score}{number\ in\ group\ (N)} \times 100$$

where   PR = percentile rank
         CF = cumulative frequency

To illustrate the computation, let's compute the percentile ranks for two scores.

Score 33 $PR = \dfrac{23 + 1}{30} \times 100 = 80$

Score 30 $PR = \dfrac{17 + .5}{30} \times 100 = 58.3$

TABLE 10.1   Frequency Distribution and Percentile Ranks for an Objective Test of 40 Items

1 TEST SCORE	2 FREQUENCY	3 CUMULATIVE FREQUENCY	4 PERCENTILE RANK*
38	1	30	98
37	1	29	95
36	0	28	93
35	2	28	90
34	1	26	85
33	2	25	80
32	3	23	72
31	2	20	63
30	1	18	58
29	4	17	50
28	2	13	40
27	2	11	33
26	2	9	27
25	3	7	18
24	1	4	12
23	0	3	10
22	1	3	8
21	1	2	5
20	0	1	3
19	1	1	2
	N = 30		

*Rounded to nearest whole number.

Percentile ranks are rounded to the nearest whole number, so the percentile rank for the raw score of 30 is listed in Table 10.1 as 58. To be sure you understand this procedure, you can compute the percentile ranks of other raw scores in the table and check your answers.

When interpreting percentile ranks there are a number of cautions to be kept in mind. (1) Percentile ranks describe test performance in terms of the *percentage of persons* earning a lower score and *not* the percentage of items answered correctly. The **percentage correct score** is a criterion-referenced interpretation; **percentile rank** indicates relative standing and, therefore, is a norm-referenced score. (2) Percentile ranks are always specific to a particular group. For example, a percentile rank of 90 in a gifted group represents higher test performance than a percentile rank of 90 in an average group. Thus, whenever we are describing a student's relative performance, knowing the nature of the group is just as important as knowing the student's relative standing. (3) Percentile ranks are not equally spaced on the scale. A difference of 5 percentile ranks near the middle of the distribution of scores represents a smaller difference in test performance than a 5 percentile rank difference at the ends of the distribution. This is because percentile ranks are based on the percentage of persons being surpassed and there is a larger percentage of persons in the middle of a score distribution to surpass than at the ends of the distribution. For example, at the high end of the distribution, a raw score difference of several points will make little difference in percentile rank because there are so few high scores. Although this limits some uses of percentile ranks (e.g., they can't be directly averaged), they remain one of the most useful and easiest to interpret types of derived scores.

Percentile Bands

Some test manuals use **percentile bands** in presenting test norms. Instead of a specific percentile rank for each raw score, a range of percentile ranks is presented. For example, a table of norms may show that a raw score of 52 has a percentile band of 60–64. This allows for the possible error in the test score. The band tells us that we can be fairly certain that a student who earns a raw score of 52 on the test has a relative standing that falls somewhere between the 60th and 64th percentile rank. We cannot be more precise than this because our estimates of test performance (i.e., raw scores) always contain some error, due to such factors as fluctuations in attention, memory, effort, and luck in guessing during testing.

The width of the percentile band is determined by the reliability of the test. With a highly reliable test the band is narrow. With a test of low reliability the band is wide. The width of the band is computed by using the **standard error of measurement.** This is a statistic computed from the reliability coefficient and used to estimate the amount of error in an individual test score (see Chapter 11). These *error* bands can, of course, be computed for raw scores or for any type of derived score. They are sometimes called *confidence* bands because they indicate how much confidence we can have in the score representing a person's test performance. With a narrow band, we are more confident that the score represents the person's "true" or "real" level of achievement.

In addition to using percentile bands to interpret an individual's test performance, they can also be used to interpret differences in test performance on a battery of tests. In comparing percentile bands for the different tests, we can conclude that where the bands do *not* overlap there is probably a "real" difference in test performance and where they do overlap, the differences are likely to be due to error. For example, the following percentile bands from a test battery for Maria indicate that there is no "real" difference in her performance in reading and language, but she is lower in math.

	Reading	*Language*	*Math*
Maria's percentile bands	70–75	74–79	63–68

The use of percentile bands prevents us from over interpreting small differences in test scores. Test publishers that use percentile bands typically plot them as bars on students' test profiles, making it easy to determine when the ends of the bands overlap and when they don't.

GRADE EQUIVALENT SCORES

Grade equivalent scores provide another widely used method of describing test performance. They are used primarily at the elementary school level. With these scores, a student's raw score on the test is converted to the grade level at which the score matches the average raw score of students in the norm group. As with other derived scores, tables in the test manual present parallel columns of raw scores and grade equivalents. Thus, all we need to do is consult the table and obtain the grade equivalent for any given raw score. Although it is easy to obtain and is apparently easy to interpret, it is probably one of the most misinterpreted types of score. Let's take a look at what the grade equivalent score means and what it doesn't mean.

To clarify the meaning of grade equivalents, let's assume that we obtained the following grade equivalent scores from a test battery for Dave, who is in the middle of the fourth grade.

Reading   4.5
Language   6.5
Math   7.8

First note that the grade equivalent score is expressed in terms of the grade level and the month in that school year. Thus, Dave's score in reading is equal to the average score earned by students (in the norm group) in the middle of the fourth grade. Because Dave is in the middle of the fourth grade, we interpret his performance in reading as average. In language, Dave is two years advanced, and in math, he is more than three years advanced. Does that mean that Dave can do the work at these levels? No, it most likely means that he does fourth-grade work in these areas faster and more efficiently than other fourth-graders. The tests probably did not include sixth- and seventh-grade material. The same misinterpretations can occur with low grade equivalents. If Dave had a math score of 2.0, for example, it wouldn't mean he could only do second-grade math problems. It would more likely mean that he did fourth-grade problems slower and with more errors than other fourth-graders. High and low grade equivalent scores are typically obtained by extrapolation and do not represent average scores earned by those groups. This is often necessary because students at lower grade levels may not have the knowledge and skill needed to take the test and students at higher grade levels may have moved beyond the types of skills measured by the test.

Grade equivalent scores provide a simple method of interpreting test performance, but when using them and interpreting them to parents, the following common misinterpretations should be avoided.

1. They are *not* standards to be achieved but simply the average scores of students in the norm group.
2. They do *not* indicate the grade level at which a student can do the work.
3. Extremely high and low grade equivalent scores are *not* as dependable indicators of test performance as those near the student's grade level.

In addition to these cautions to be observed when interpreting an individual's grade equivalent scores, a comparison of scores on tests in a test battery requires an additional caution. Growth in basic skills, for example, is uneven. In reading, growth is more rapid than in math, which depends more directly on the skills taught in school. Thus, a difference of a year in grade equivalent scores represents a larger difference in achievement on a reading test than on a math test. In addition, growth in achievement tends to slow down at different times for different skills, and when growth slows down, the differences in achievement between grade equivalent scores become smaller. Both the variations in growth of skills from one area to another and the variations in patterns of growth over time contribute to the unevenness of the units on our grade equivalent score scale. In comparing a student's grade equivalent scores on different tests from a test battery, it may be wise to look at the norm table to see how the raw scores spread out on each test. A high or low grade equivalent score might be discounted if the difference from other grade equivalent scores is based on relatively few raw score points.

STANDARD SCORES

A **standard score** describes test performance in terms of how far a raw score is above or below average. It is expressed in units that are computed from the mean and the standard deviation of a set of scores. We are all familiar with the use of the **mean** as an average. It is obtained by summing the test scores and dividing by the number of scores. The standard deviation indicates the

---

Computation of the Standard Deviation Using a Hand Calculator

Steps to Follow

1. Square each score in the set.
2. Add these squared values to obtain a total.
3. Divide the total by the number of scores in the set.
4. Square the mean of the set of scores.
5. Subtract the squared mean in step 4 from the result obtained in step 3.
6. Take the square root of the difference obtained in step 5. This is the standard deviation (*SD* or *s*).

Formula for the Computational Steps

$$SD = \sqrt{\frac{\Sigma X^2}{N} - M^2}$$

where
Σ = "sum of"
X = a test score
N = number of scores
M = mean
$\sqrt{}$ = "square root of"

---

spread of scores in a set. The computation for obtaining the standard deviation is shown in the box but that does not help us understand its meaning or its use in interpreting standard scores. This can best be done by describing its properties and showing how it is used as the basic unit for the various types of standard scores.

The standard deviation (SD or S) is an important and widely applicable statistic in testing. In addition to its use as a basic unit in standard scores, it also serves as a basis for computing reliability coefficients and the standard error of measurement, as we shall see in the next chapter.

The Mean, Standard Deviation, and Normal Curve

The mean and the standard deviation can probably be best understood in terms of the **normal curve,** although a normal distribution is not required for computing them. The normal curve is a symmetrical bell-shaped curve based on a precise mathematical equation. Scores distributed according to the normal curve are concentrated near the mean and decrease in frequency the further one departs from the mean. A sample normal curve is presented in Figure 10.1.

It will be noted in Figure 10.1 that the mean falls at the exact center of a normal distribution. Note also that when the normal curve is divided into standard deviation (SD) units, which are equal distances along the baseline of the curve, each portion under the curve contains a fixed percentage of cases. Thus, 34 percent of the cases fall between the mean and +1 SD, 14 percent between +1 SD and +2 SD, and 2 percent between +2 SD and +3 SD. Since the curve is symmetrical, the same percentages, of course, apply to the intervals below the mean. These percentages have been rounded to the nearest whole number, but only a small fraction of a percent (0.13 percent) of the

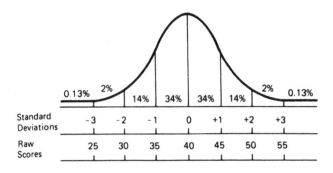

FIGURE 10.1   Normal Curve with the Approximate Percentage of Cases Within Each Interval (percentages have been rounded)

cases fall above and below three standard deviations from the mean. Thus, from a practical standpoint, a normal distribution of scores falls between –3 and +3 standard deviations from the mean.

To aid in understanding the meaning of standard deviation, a set of raw scores with a mean of 40 and a standard deviation of 5 has been placed below the baseline of the curve in Figure 10.1. Note that the mean raw score of 40 has been placed at the zero point and that the distance of one standard deviation is 5 raw score points everywhere along the baseline of the curve. Thus, the point one standard deviation above the mean equals 45 (40 + 5) and the point one standard deviation below the mean equals 35 (40 – 5). In this particular set of scores, then, approximately 68 percent of the scores (about two thirds) fall between 35 and 45, approximately 96 percent fall between 30 and 50, and approximately 99.7 percent fall between 25 and 55 (the figure shows 100 percent because numbers are rounded).

When the standard deviation is being computed for a set of normally distributed scores, we are essentially determining how far we need to go above (or below) the mean in raw score points to include 34 percent of the cases. The scores obtained with standardized tests typically approximate a normal distribution or are normalized by statistical means and thus permit the types of interpretations we are making here.

z-Scores

A number of standard scores are based on the standard deviation unit. The simplest of these and the one that is basic to the others is the z-score. This score simply indicates, in standard deviation units, how far a given raw score is above or below the mean. The raw score of 45 in Figure 10.1, for example, would be assigned a z-score of 1.0 because it is one standard deviation above the mean. The raw score of 30 in Figure 10.1 would be given a z-score of –2.0 because it is two standard deviations below the mean. The formula for z-scores is:

$$z\text{-score} = \frac{\text{Raw score} - \text{Mean}}{\text{Standard deviation}}$$

For example, z-scores for raw scores of 47 and 36 in Figure 10.1 would be computed as follows:

$$z\text{-score} = \frac{47 - 40}{5} = 1.4 \qquad z\text{-score} = \frac{36 - 40}{5} = -.8$$

Thus, a raw score of 47 is 1.4 standard deviations above the mean and a raw score of 36 is .8 of a standard deviation below the mean.

While used in research, z-scores are seldom used directly in test interpretation because of the use of decimal points and minus signs. Instead, z-scores are converted to other types of standard scores that use only whole numbers and positive values. Such scores are more convenient to use and avoid the possibility of misinterpretation due to a forgotten minus sign.

There are a number of different types of standard scores used in test interpretation. All one needs to do is select an arbitrary mean and standard deviation and convert the z-scores into the standard score units. To illustrate, we will describe the procedure for some common standard scores.

T-Scores

T-scores have a mean of 50 and a standard deviation of 10. They are obtained from z-scores by multiplying the z-score by 10 and adding the result to 50, as shown in the following formula.

T-score $= 50 + 10$ (z-score)

Applying the formula to the various z-scores discussed earlier (1.0, –2.0, 1.4, –.8) we would obtain T-scores as follows:

$T = 50 + 10 \ (1.0) = 60$ $T = 50 + 10 \ (-2.0) = 30$
$T = 50 + 10 \ (1.4) = 64$ $T = 50 + 10 \ (-.8) \ = 42$

T-scores can be easily interpreted because they always have the same mean and standard deviation. A T-score of 60 always means one standard deviation above the mean and a T-score of 30 always means two standard deviations below the mean. Thus, with the use of T-scores, an individual's performance on different tests can be directly compared, and the scores can be combined or averaged without the distortion of different size standard deviations, which occur with the raw scores.

Where a normal distribution can be assumed, T-scores can also be interpreted in terms of percentile ranks because, in this case, there is a direct relationship between the two as shown in Figure 10.2. Note that a T-score of 30 is equivalent to a percentile rank of 2, a T-score of 40 is equivalent to a percentile rank of 16, and so on. This relationship makes it possible to use standard scores for those purposes where equal units are needed, and to use percentile ranks when interpreting test performance to students and parents.

Because T-scores and percentile ranks both have a mean of 50 and use similar two-digit numbers, the two types of scores are often confused by those inexperienced in test interpretation. Thus, it is important to keep in mind that percentile rank indicates the percentage of individuals who fall at

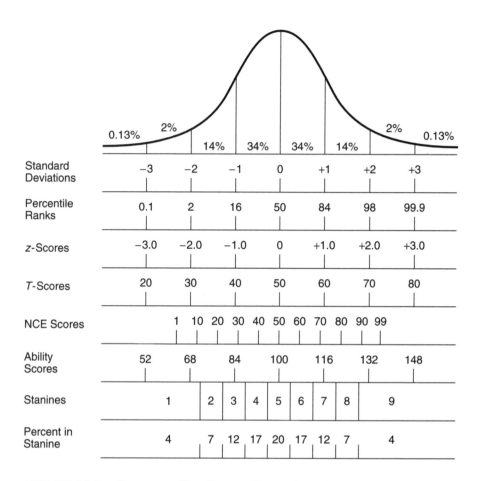

FIGURE 10.2 **Corresponding Percentile Ranks, z-Scores, T-scores, NCE Scores, Ability Scores, and Stanines in a Normal Distribution**

or below a given score, while a *T*-score indicates how many standard deviation units a given score falls above or below the mean. Note in Figure 10.2 that although percentile ranks and *T*-scores have the same mean value of 50, below the mean percentile ranks are smaller than *T*-scores and above the mean they are larger than *T*-scores. This is accounted for, of course, by the fact that percentile ranks are crowded together in the center of the distribution and spread out at the ends, while *T*-scores provide equal units throughout the distribution of scores.

Normal-Curve Equivalent Scores (NCE)

Another standard score that might be confused with both *T*-scores and percentile ranks is the **normal-curve equivalent score** (NCE). This set of scores also has a mean of 50, but a standard deviation of 21.06. This provides a set of scores with equal units, like the *T*-score, but the scores range from 1 to 99. Percentile ranks also range from 1 to 99, but they do not provide equal units. As can be seen in Figure 10.2, percentile ranks are smaller at the middle of the distribution (e.g., one *SD* = 34%) than at the ends (e.g., one *SD* = 2%). Thus, when interpreting NCE scores, don't confuse them with *T*-scores, which have a more restricted range of scores (typically 20 to 80), or with percentile ranks that have the same range of scores (1 to 99) but are based on unequal units.

Ability Scores

Publishers of achievement test batteries typically administer a test of learning ability (also called cognitive ability, school ability, or intelligence) to the same norm groups as the achievement battery, to make comparisons of learning ability and achievement possible. The scores on these tests are now reported as standard scores with a mean of 100 and standard deviation of 16 (15 on some tests). These scores are to be interpreted like any other standard score (see Figure 10.2). A score of 116 means one standard deviation above the mean (percentile rank = 84). These scores were originally called deviation IQs, because they replaced the old ratio IQ (i.e., $\frac{MA}{CA} \times 100$). More recently, however, to avoid the confusion surrounding IQ scores, they have been given more appropriate names, such as school ability scores and standard age scores.

Stanine Scores

Test scores can also be expressed by single-digit standard scores called stanines (pronounced *stay-nines*). The stanine scale divides the distribution of raw scores into nine parts (the term **stanine** was derived from *standard nines*). The highest stanine score is 9, the lowest is 1, and stanine 5 is located in the center of the distribution. Each stanine, except 9 and 1, includes a band of raw scores *one half of a standard deviation wide*. Thus, stanines are standard scores with a mean of 5 and a standard deviation of 2. The distribution of stanines and the percentage of cases in each stanine are shown in Figure 10.2.

The nine point scale is simple to interpret to students and parents because of the single digit score. It is easy to visualize where a person falls on a nine point scale, where 5 is average. Because each stanine includes a band of raw scores, there is also less chance that test performance will be over interpreted.

Interpreting Standardized Test Results to Students and Parents

1. Describe in general terms what the test measures and how it relates to the local curriculum (e.g., The test measures computational skills only. It does not include measures of math reasoning, which is the main focus of our curriculum.).

2. When interpreting percentile ranks, keep the description simple (e.g., The percentile rank of 87 means 87 percent of students in the norm group had lower scores. It is not a percentage-correct score.).

3. When interpreting grade equivalents, make statements that are unlikely to be misinterpreted (e.g., The grade equivalent of 6.5 for a fifth-grader means he can do fifth-grade work as rapidly and efficiently as students in the middle of the sixth grade.).

4. When interpreting stanines, use brief, simple statements (e.g., The stanine of 6 on the reading test is one stanine above average on a scale from 1 to 9, and the stanine of 4 on the math test is one stanine below average.).

5. When interpreting differences between test scores use percentile bands or other ways to take error into account (e.g., The percentile bands for reading and math do not overlap, so there is probably a "real" difference in performance. Or, the stanines indicate a "real" difference because they differ by two stanines.).

When comparing scores on two different tests in a test battery, a difference of two stanines is typically significant. Thus, in interpreting the following scores for a student, we would conclude that the student is higher in math but there is no difference between reading and language.

Reading stanine = 5
Language stanine = 4
Math stanine   = 7

In addition to the ease of interpretation, stanines provide a simple method for combining and averaging test scores. The conversion of raw scores to stanines puts the scores from different tests on the same standard score scale, with equal units. Thus, they have uniform meaning from one part of the scale to another and from one test to another. A difference between stanine 5 and stanine 7 is the same as a difference between a stanine of 4 and a stanine of 6. A difference of two stanines is also the same, if we are referring to a reading test, a language test, a math test, or any other test. Like other standard scores, they provide equal units that can be readily combined. Unlike other standard scores, they are easy to interpret and to explain to others.

CRITERION-REFERENCED INTERPRETATION

To make standardized achievement test batteries more useful for instructional purposes, some test publishers have modified the multiple-choice items to include more "real-life" situations, have added open-ended performance tasks, and have made provisions for criterion-referenced interpretation of test performance.

One of the best known methods of reporting criterion-referenced test results is the *percentage-correct score*. This simply reports the percentage of test items in a test, or subtest, answered correctly. The report can be for individual students, the class, the school, or the entire school district. Percentage-correct scores for the various school groups are compared to the percentage-correct scores in the national norm sample as one basis for evaluating the schools.

Scores for individuals can also be presented by clusters of items representing a content area, skill, or objective, with an indication of the level of performance (e.g., above average, average, below average). Care must be taken in interpreting these results where a small number of items is included in the item clusters.

Some test batteries provide reports that include standards of performance. The standards are typically set by panels of educators and the report indicates a student level of performance by categories ranging from lack of mastery to superior performance.

When making criterion-referenced interpretations of test performance there are a number of questions to keep in mind.

1. Do the objectives the tests were designed to measure match the school's objectives for these subjects (e.g., routine skills versus reasoning)?
2. Are the skills and content measured by the tests appropriate for the grade levels tested?
3. Did elimination of the easy items from the test, to obtain greater discrimination among students for norm-referenced interpretation, result in inadequate description of what low achieving students can do?
4. Was there a sufficient number of test items in each item cluster to permit criterion-referenced interpretation?
5. Was the procedure in setting performance standards adequate for this type of interpretation?

Criterion-referenced interpretation of standardized tests can be useful in classroom instruction but they must be cautiously made.

SUMMARY OF POINTS

1. Standardized achievement tests have been widely used in the schools to determine how student performance compared to that of a sample of students (i.e., a norm group) at the national, regional, or state level.

2. Standardized tests were carefully constructed to fit a set of test specifications, tried out and improved, and administered to a norm group for norm-referenced test interpretation.

3. The most common types of norm-referenced scores used with standardized tests are percentile ranks, grade equivalent scores, and various types of standard scores.

4. A percentile rank indicates relative position in a group in terms of the percentage of group members scoring at or below a given score. It should not be confused with the percentage of items answered correctly (a criterion-referenced interpretation).

5. Percentile bands are used in reporting test performance to allow for possible error in test scores. The width of the band indicates the amount of error to allow for during interpretation, and it prevents the over interpretation of small differences in test scores.

6. A grade equivalent score indicates relative test performance in terms of the grade level at which the student's raw score matches the average score earned by the norm group. Thus, a grade equivalent score of 4.5 indicates performance equal to the average student in the middle of the fourth grade. Grade equivalent scores are easy to interpret but they are subject to numerous misinterpretations.

7. Standard scores are based on the mean (M) and standard deviation (SD) of a set of scores. To fully understand them it is necessary to understand the meaning of these statistics.

8. Standard scores indicate the number of standard deviations a raw score falls above and below the mean. They are more difficult to understand and interpret to others but they have the advantage of providing equal units.

9. The standard scores discussed in this chapter have the following means (M) and standard deviations (SD). The third column shows the score for one standard above the mean.

	M	SD	$+1SD$
z-scores	0	1	1
T-scores	50	10	60
NCE scores	50	21.06	71
Ability scores	100	16	116
Stanines	5	2	7

10. In a normal distribution, any standard score can be converted to percentile rank for easy interpretation. For example, one standard deviation above the mean (see column 3) has a percentile rank of 84, no matter what type of standard score is used to express test performance.

11. Because *T*-scores, NCE scores, and percentile ranks all have a mean of 50 and use similar two-digit numbers, care must be taken not to confuse them when interpreting test performance.

12. Stanines are single-digit standard scores that range from 1 to 9. They are easily explained to students and parents and a difference of two stanines typically indicates a significant (i.e., "real") difference in test performance.

13. Stanines and percentile ranks using percentile bands are the two types of scores that are favored when interpreting test results to others and judging differences between test scores.

14. Criterion-referenced interpretations of test performance have been added to many standardized tests. These include percentage correct scores, the use of performance standards and interpretation by item clusters representing a content area, skill, or objective.

15. Criterion-referenced interpretations of standardized tests require a check on how well the objectives, content, and skills of the test match the local instructional program; whether the construction of the test favors criterion-referenced interpretation; whether there is a sufficient number of test items for each type of interpretation; and how the performance standards are determined.

ADDITIONAL READING

Carey, L. M., *Measuring and Evaluating School Learning*, 2nd ed. (Boston: Allyn & Bacon, 1994). See Chapter 15, "Interpreting Standardized Test Results for a description and illustration of the various norm-referenced test scores used in standardized testing.

Linn, R. L., and Gronlund, N. E., *Measurement and Assessment in Teaching*, 7th ed. (Englewood Cliffs, NJ: Prentice-Hall, 1995). See Chapter 17, "Interpreting Test Scores and Norms," for descriptions, interpretations, and comparisons of test scores. See Appendix A, "Elementary Statistics," for simplified methods of computing statistics used with test scores.

Lyman, H. B., *Test Scores and What They Mean*, 5th ed. (Englewood Cliffs, NJ: Prentice-Hall, 1991). Clear descriptions and comparisons of the many types of scores used in testing. Emphasizes norm-referenced interpretations.

Oosterhoff, A., *Classroom Applications of Educational Measurement*, 2nd ed. (Columbus, OH: Merrill Publishing Co., 1994). See the several chapters on interpreting test scores for a comprehensive treatment of the topic.

Payne, D. A., *Measuring and Evaluating Educational Outcomes.* (New York: Macmillan, 1992). See Chapter 15, "Interpreting the Meaning of Norm-Referenced Test Scores," for a description of the methods of expressing test scores and a list of test-wise principles that influence test scores.

▶ 11

Validity and Reliability

Studying this chapter should enable you to

1. Distinguish between validity and reliability.
2. Describe the essential features of the concept of validity.
3. Describe how content-related evidence of validity is obtained.
4. List factors that can lower the validity of achievement assessments.
5. Describe procedures for obtaining criterion-related evidence of validity.
6. Describe procedures for obtaining construct-related evidence of validity.
7. Describe the role of consequences of using an assessment procedure on its validity.
8. Describe the methods for estimating test reliability and the type of information provided by each.
9. Describe how the standard error of measurement is computed and interpreted.
10. Explain how to determine the reliability of a performance-based assessment.

The two most important questions to ask about a test or other assessment procedure are: (1) to what extent will the interpretation of the results be appropriate, meaningful, and useful?, and (2) to what extent will the results be free from errors? The first question is concerned with *validity*, the second with *reliability*. An understanding of both concepts is essential to the effective construction, selection, interpretation, and use of tests and other assessment instruments. Validity is the most important quality to consider in the preparation and use of assessment procedures. First and foremost we want the results to provide a representative and relevant measure of the achievement domain under consideration. Our second consideration is reliability, which refers to the consistency of our assessment results. For example, if we tested individuals at a different time, or with a different sample of equivalent items, we would like to obtain approximately the same results. This consistency of results is important for two reasons. (1) Unless the results are fairly stable we cannot expect them to be valid. For example, if an individual scored high on a test one time and low another time, it would be impossible to validly describe the achievement. (2) Consistency of results indicates smaller errors of measurement and, thereby, more dependable results. Thus, reliability provides the consistency needed to obtain validity and enables us to interpret assessment results with greater confidence.

Although it is frequently unnecessary to make elaborate validation and reliability studies of informal assessment procedures, an understanding of these concepts provides a conceptual framework that can serve as a guide for more effective construction of assessment instruments, more effective selection of standardized tests, and more appropriate interpretation and use of assessment results.

VALIDITY

Validity is concerned with the interpretation and use of assessment results. For example, if we infer from an assessment that students have achieved the intended learning outcomes, we would like some assurance that our tasks provided a relevant and representative measure of the outcomes. If we infer that the assessment is useful for predicting or estimating some other performance, we would like some credible evidence to support that interpretation. If we infer that our assessment indicates that students have good "reasoning ability," we would like some evidence to support the fact that the results actually reflect that construct. If we infer that our use of an assessment had positive effects (e.g., increased motivation) and no adverse effects (e.g., poor study habits) on students, we would like some evidence concerning the consequences of its use. These are the kinds of considerations we are concerned with when considering the validity of assessment results (see the summary in Figure 11.1).

The meaning of *validity* in interpreting and using assessment results can be grasped most easily by reviewing the following characteristics.

1. Validity is *inferred* from available evidence (not measured).
2. Validity depends on *many different types* of evidence.

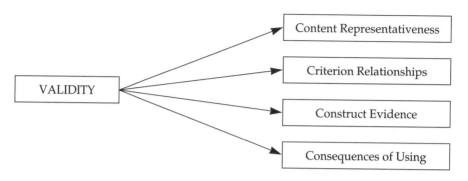

FIGURE 11.1   Types of Considerations in Determining the Validity of Assessment Results

3. Validity is expressed by *degree* (high, moderate, low).
4. Validity is specific to a particular *use.*
5. Validity refers to the *inferences drawn,* not the instrument.
6. Validity is a *unitary concept.*
7. Validity is concerned with the *consequences of using the assessments.*

Describing validity as a unitary concept is a basic change in how validity is viewed. The traditional view that there were several different "types of validity" has been replaced by the view that validity is a single, unitary concept that is based on various forms of evidence. The former "types of validity" (content, criterion-related, and construct) are now simply considered to be convenient categories for accumulating evidence to support the validity of an interpretation. Thus, we no longer speak of "content validity," but of "content-related evidence" of validity. Similarly, we speak of "criterion-related evidence" and "construct-related evidence."

For some interpretations of assessment results only one or two types of evidence may be critical, but an *ideal* validation would include evidence from all four categories. We are most likely to draw valid inferences from assessment results when we have a full understanding of: (1) the nature of the assessment procedure and the specifications that were used in developing it, (2) the relation of the assessment results to significant criterion measures, (3) the nature of the psychological characteristic(s) or construct(s) being assessed, and (4) the consequences of using the assessment. Although in many practical situations the evidence falls short of this ideal, we should gather as much relevant evidence as is feasible within the constraints of the situation. We should also look for the various types of evidence when evaluating standardized tests (see Table 11.1).

TABLE 11.1   Basic Approaches to Validation

TYPE OF EVIDENCE	QUESTION TO BE ANSWERED
Content-Related	How adequately does the sample of assessment tasks represent the domain of tasks to be measured?
Criterion-Related	How accurately does performance on the assessment (e.g., test) predict future performance (predictive study) or estimate present performance (concurrent study) on some other valued measure called a *criterion?*
Construct-Related	How well can performance on the assessment be explained in terms of psychological characteristics?
Consequences	How well did use of the assessment serve the intended purpose (e.g., improve performance) and avoid adverse effects (e.g., poor study habits)?

Content-Related Evidence

Content-related evidence of validity is critical when we want to use performance on a set of tasks as evidence of performance on a larger domain of tasks. Let's assume, for example, that we have a list of 500 words that we expect our students to be able to spell correctly at the end of the school year. To test their spelling ability, we might give them a 50-word spelling test. Their performance on these words is important only insofar as it provides evidence of their ability to spell the 500 words. Thus, our spelling test would provide a valid measure to the degree to which it provided an adequate sample of the 500 words it represented. If we selected only easy words, only difficult words, or only words that represented certain types of common spelling errors, our test would tend to be unrepresentative and thus the scores would have low validity. If we selected a balanced sample of words that took these and similar factors into account, our test scores would provide a representative measure of the 500 spelling words and thereby provide for high validity.

It should be clear from this discussion that the key element in content-related evidence of validity is the adequacy of the *sampling*. An assessment is always a sample of the many tasks that could be included. Content validation is a matter of determining whether the sample of tasks is representative of the larger domain of tasks it is supposed to represent.

Content-related evidence of validity is especially important in achievement assessment. Here we are interested in how well the assessment measures the intended learning outcomes of the instruction. We can provide greater assurance that an assessment provides valid results by (1) identifying the learning outcomes to be assessed, (2) preparing a plan that specifies the sample of tasks to be used, and (3) preparing an assessment procedure that

---

Factors that Lower the Validity of Assessment Results

1. Tasks that provide an inadequate sample of the achievement to be assessed.
2. Tasks that do not function as intended, due to use of improper types of tasks, lack of relevance, ambiguity, clues, bias, inappropriate difficulty, or similar factors.
3. Improper arrangement of tasks and unclear directions.
4. Too few tasks for the types of interpretation to be made (e.g., interpretation by objective based on a few test items).
5. Improper administration—such as inadequate time allowed and poorly controlled conditions.
6. Judgmental scoring that uses inadequate scoring guides, or objective scoring that contains computational errors.

---

closely fits the set of specifications. These are the best procedures we have for ensuring the assessment of a representative sample of the domain of tasks encompassed by the intended learning outcomes.

Although the focus of content-related evidence of validity is on the adequacy of the sampling, a valid interpretation of the assessment results assumes that the assessment was properly prepared, administered, and scored. Validity can be lowered by inadequate procedures in any of these areas (see box). Thus, validity is "built in" during the planning and preparation stages, and maintained by proper administration and scoring. Throughout this book we have described how to prepare assessments that provide valid results, even though we have not used the word validity as each procedure was discussed.

The makers of standardized test follow these same systematic procedures in building achievement tests, but the content and learning outcomes included in the test specifications are more broadly based than those used in classroom assessment. Typically, they are based on the leading textbooks and the recommendations of various experts in the area being covered by the test. Therefore, a standardized achievement test may be representative of a broad range of content but be unrepresentative of the domain of content taught in a particular school situation. To determine relevance to the local situation, it is necessary to evaluate the sample of test items in light of the content and skills emphasized in the instruction.

In summary, content-related evidence of validity is of major concern in achievement assessment, whether you are developing or selecting the assessment procedure. When constructing a test, for example, content relevance and representativeness are built in by following a systematic procedure for specifying and selecting the sample of test items, constructing high quality items, and arranging the test for efficient administration and scoring. In test selection, it is a matter of comparing the test sample to the domain of tasks to be measured and determining the degree of correspondence between them. Similar care is needed when preparing and using performance assessments. Thus, content-related evidence of validity is obtained primarily by careful, logical analysis.

Criterion-Related Evidence

There are two types of studies used in obtaining criterion-related evidence of validity. These can be explained most clearly using test scores, although they could be used with any type of assessment result. The first type of study is concerned with the use of test performance to predict future performance on some other valued measure called a *criterion*. For example, we might use scholastic aptitude test scores to predict course grades (the criterion). For obvious reasons, this is called a *predictive* study. The second type of study is concerned with the use of test performance to estimate current performance on some criterion. For instance, we might want to use a test of study skills to estimate what the outcome would be of a careful observation of students in an actual study situation (the criterion). Since with this procedure both measures (test and criterion) are obtained at approximately the same time, this type of study is called a *concurrent* study.

Although the value of using a predictive study is rather obvious, a question might be raised concerning the purpose of a concurrent study. Why would anyone want to use test scores to estimate performance on some other measure that is to be obtained at the same time? There are at least three good reasons for doing this. First, we may want to check the results of a newly constructed test against some existing test that has a considerable amount of validity evidence supporting it. Second, we may want to substitute a brief, simple testing procedure for a more complex and time-consuming measure. For example, our test of study skills might be substituted for an elaborate rating system if it provided a satisfactory estimate of study performance. Third, we may want to determine whether a testing procedure has *potential* as a predictive instrument. If a test provides an unsatisfactory estimate of current performance, it certainly cannot be expected to predict future performance on the same measure. On the other hand, a satisfactory estimate of present performance would indicate that the test may be useful in predicting future performance as well. This would inform us that a predictive study would be worth doing.

The key element in both types of criterion-related study is the *degree of relationship* between the two sets of measures: (1) the test scores and (2) the criterion to be predicted or estimated. This relationship is typically expressed by means of a correlation coefficient or an expectancy table.

Correlation Coefficients. Although the computation of correlation coefficients is beyond the scope of this book, the concept of correlation can easily be grasped. A **correlation coefficient** (*r*) simply indicates the degree of relationship between two sets of measures. A *positive* relationship is indicated when high scores on one measure are accompanied by high scores on the other; low scores on the two measures are similarly associated. A *negative* relationship is indicated when high scores on one measure are accompanied by low scores on the other. The extreme degrees of relationship it is possible to obtain between two sets of scores are indicated by the following values:

1.00 = perfect positive relationship

.00 = no relationship

−1.00 = perfect negative relationship

When a correlation coefficient is used to express the degree of relationship between a set of test scores and some criterion measure, it is called a *validity coefficient*. For example, a validity coefficient of 1.00 applied to the relationship between a set of aptitude test scores (the predictor) and a set of achievement test scores (the criterion) would indicate that each individual in the group had exactly the same relative standing on both measures, and would thereby provide a perfect prediction from the aptitude scores to the achievement scores. Most validity coefficients are smaller than this, but the extreme positive relationship provides a useful bench mark for evaluating validity coefficients. The closer the validity coefficient approaches 1.00, the higher the degree of relationship and, thus, the more accurate our predictions of each individual's success on the criterion will be.

A more realistic procedure for evaluating a validity coefficient is to compare it to the validity coefficients that are *typically* obtained when the two measures are correlated. For example, a validity coefficient of .40 between a set of aptitude test scores and achievement test scores would be considered small because we typically obtain coefficients in the .50 to .70 range for these two measures. Therefore, validity coefficients must be judged on a relative basis, the larger coefficients being favored. To use validity coefficients effectively, one must become familiar with the size of the validity coefficients that are typically obtained between various pairs of measures under different conditions (e.g., the longer the time span between measures, the smaller the validity coefficient).

Expectancy Table. The expectancy table is a simple and practical means of expressing criterion-related evidence of validity and is especially useful for making predictions from test scores. The **expectancy table** is simply a twofold chart with the test scores (the predictor) arranged in categories down the left side of the table and the measure to be predicted (the criterion) arranged in categories across the top of the table. For each category of scores on the *predictor*, the table indicates the percentage of individuals who fall within each category of the *criterion*. An example of an expectancy table is presented in Table 11.2.

Note in Table 11.2 that of those students who were in the above-average group (stanines 7, 8, and 9) on the test scores, 43 percent received a grade of A, 43 percent a B, and 14 percent a C. Although these percentages are based on this particular group, it is possible to use them to predict the future performance of other students in this science course. Hence, if a student falls in the above-average group on this scholastic aptitude test, we might predict that he or she has 43 chances out of 100 of earning an A, 43 chances out of 100 of earning a B, and 14 chances out of a 100 of earning a C in this particular science course. Such predictions are highly tentative, of course, due to the small number of students on which this expectancy table was built. Teachers can construct more dependable tables by accumulating data from several classes over a period of time.

Expectancy tables can be used to show the relationship between any two measures. Constructing the table is simply a matter of (1) grouping the scores on each measure into a series of categories (any number of them), (2) placing the two sets of categories on a twofold chart, (3) tabulating the number of students who fall into each position in the table (based on the student's standing on both measures), and (4) converting these numbers to percentages (of the total number in that row). Thus, the expectancy table is a clear way of showing the relationship between sets of scores. Although the expectancy table is more cumbersome to deal with than a correlation coefficient, it has special ad-

TABLE 11.2   Expectancy Table Showing the Relation Between Scholastic Aptitude Scores and Course Grades for 30 Students in a Science Course

GROUPED SCHOLASTIC APTITUDE SCORES (STANINES)	PERCENTAGE IN EACH SCORE CATEGORY RECEIVING EACH GRADE				
	E	D	C	B	A
Above Average (7, 8, 9)			14	43	43
Average (4, 5, 6)		19	37	25	19
Below Average (1, 2, 3)	57	29	14		

vantage of being easily understood by persons without knowledge of statistics. Thus, it can be used in practical situations to clarify the predictive efficiency of a test.

Construct-Related Evidence

The construct-related category of evidence focuses on assessment results as a basis for inferring the possession of certain psychological characteristics. For example, we might want to describe a person's reading comprehension, reasoning ability, or mechanical aptitude. These are all hypothetical qualities, or *constructs*, that we assume exist in order to explain behavior. Such theoretical constructs are useful in describing individuals and in predicting how they will act in many different specific situations. To describe a person as being highly intelligent, for example, is useful because that term carries with it a series of associated meanings that indicate what the individual's behavior is likely to be under various conditions. Before we can interpret assessment results in terms of these broad behavior descriptions, however, we must first establish that the constructs that are presumed to be reflected in the scores actually do account for differences in performance.

Construct-related evidence of validity for a test includes (1) a description of the theoretical framework that specifies the nature of the construct to be measured, (2) a description of the development of the test and any aspects of measurement that may affect the meaning of the test scores (e.g., test format), (3) the pattern of relationship between the test scores and other significant variables (e.g., high correlations with similar tests and low correlations with tests measuring different constructs), and (4) any other type of evidence that contributes to the meaning of the test scores (e.g., analyzing the mental process used in responding, determining the predictive effectiveness of the test). The specific types of evidence that are most critical for a particular test depend on the nature of the construct, the clarity of the theoretical framework, and the uses to be made of the test scores. Although the gathering of construct-related evidence of validity can be endless, in practical situations it is typically necessary to limit the evidence to that which is most relevant to the interpretations to be made.

The construct-related category of evidence is the broadest of the three categories. Evidence obtained in both the content-related category (e.g., representativeness of the sample of tasks) and the criterion-related category (e.g., how well the scores predict performance on specific criteria) are also relevant to the construct-related category because they help to clarify the meaning of the assessment results. Thus, the construct-related category encompasses a variety of types of evidence, including that from content-related and criterion-related validation studies. (See Figure 11.2.)

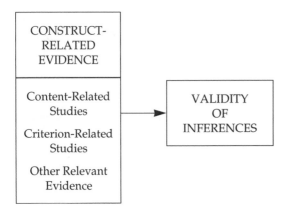

FIGURE 11.2   Construct Validation Includes All Categories of Evidence

The broad array of evidence that might be considered can be illustrated by a test designed to measure mathematical reasoning ability. Some of the evidence we might consider is as follows:

1. Compare the sample of test tasks to the domain of tasks specified by the conceptual framework of the construct. Is the sample relevant and representative (content-related evidence)?
2. Examine the test features and their possible influence on the meaning of the scores (e.g., test format, directions, scoring, reading level of items). Is it possible that some features might distort the scores?
3. Analyze the mental process used in answering the questions by having students "think aloud" as they respond to each item. Do the items require the intended reasoning process?
4. Determine the internal consistency of the test by intercorrelating the test items. Do the items seem to be measuring a single characteristic (in this case mathematical reasoning)?
5. Correlate the test scores with the scores of other mathematical reasoning tests. Do they show a high degree of relationship?
6. Compare the scores of known groups (e.g., mathematical majors and nonmajors). Do the scores differentiate between the groups as predicted?
7. Compare the scores of students before and after specific training in mathematical reasoning. Do the scores change as predicted from the theory underlying the construct?
8. Correlate the scores with grades in mathematics. Do they correlate to a satisfactory degree (criterion-related evidence)?

Other types of evidence could be added to this list but it is sufficiently comprehensive to make clear that no single type of evidence is adequate. Interpreting test scores as a measure of a particular construct involves a comprehensive study of the development of the test, how it functions in a variety of situations, and how the scores relate to other significant measures.

Assessment results are, of course, influenced by many factors other than the construct they are designed to measure. Thus, construct validation is an attempt to account for all possible influences on the scores. We might, for example, ask to what extent the scores on our mathematical reasoning test are influenced by reading comprehension, computation skill, and speed. Each of these factors would require further study. Were attempts made to eliminate such factors during test development by using simple vocabulary, simple computations, and liberal time limits? To what extent do the test scores correlate with measures of reading comprehension and computational skill? How do students' scores differ under different time limits? Answers to these and similar questions will help us to determine how well the test scores reflect the construct we are attempting to measure and the extent to which other factors might be influencing the scores.

Construct validation, then, is an attempt to clarify and verify the inferences to be made from assessment results. This involves a wide variety of procedures and many different types of evidence (including both content-related and criterion-related). As evidence accumulates from many different sources, our interpretations of the results are enriched and we are able to make them with great confidence.

Consequence of Using Assessment Results

Validity focuses on the inferences drawn from assessment results with regard to specific uses. Therefore, it is legitimate to ask, What are the consequences of using the assessment? Did the assessment improve learning, as intended, or did it contribute to adverse effects (e.g., lack of motivation, memorization, poor study habits)? For example, assessment procedures that focus on simple learning outcomes only (e.g., knowledge of facts) cannot provide valid evidence of reasoning and application skills, are likely to narrow the focus of student learning, and tend to reinforce poor learning strategies (e.g., rote learning). Thus, in evaluating the validity of the assessment used, one needs to look at what types of influence the assessments have on students. The following questions provide a general framework for considering some of the possible consequences of assessments on students.

1. Did use of the assessment improve motivation?
2. Did use of the assessment improve performance?
3. Did the use of the assessment improve self-assessment skills?

4. Did the use of the assessment contribute to transfer of learning to related areas?
5. Did the use of the assessment encourage independent learning?
6. Did the use of the assessment encourage good study habits?
7. Did the use of the assessment contribute to a positive attitude toward school work?
8. Did use of the assessment have an adverse effect in any of the above areas?

Judging the consequences of using the various assessment procedures is an important role of the teacher, if the results are to serve their intended purpose of improving learning. Both testing and performance assessments are most likely to have positive consequences when they are designed to assess a broad range of learning outcomes, they give special emphasis to complex learning outcomes, they are administered and scored (or judged) properly, they are used to identify students' strengths and weaknesses in learning, and the students view the assessments as fair, relevant, and useful for improving learning.

RELIABILITY

Reliability refers to the consistency of assessment results. Would we obtain about the same results if we used a different sample of the same type task? Would we obtain about the same results if we used the assessment at a different time? If a performance assessment is being rated, would different raters rate the performance the same way? These are the kinds of questions we are concerned about when we are considering the reliability of assessment results. Unless the results are generalizable over similar samples of tasks, time periods, and raters, we are not likely to have great confidence in them.

Because the methods for estimating reliability differ for tests and performance assessments these will be treated separately.

ESTIMATING THE RELIABILITY OF TEST SCORES

The score an individual receives on a test is called the *obtained score, raw score,* or *observed score.* This score typically contains a certain amount of error. Some of this error may be *systematic error,* in that it consistently inflates or lowers the obtained score. For example, readily apparent clues in several test items might cause all students' scores to be higher than their achievement would warrant, or short time limits during testing might cause all students' scores to be lower than their "real achievement." The factors causing systematic errors are mainly due to inadequate testing practices. Thus, most of these errors can be eliminated by using care in constructing and administering tests. Removing systematic errors from test scores is especially important because they have a direct effect on the validity of the inferences made from the scores.

Some of the error in obtained scores is *random error,* in that it raises and lowers scores in an unpredictable manner. Random errors are caused by such things as temporary fluctuations in memory, variations in motivation and concentration from time to time, carelessness in marking answers, and luck in guessing. Such factors cause test scores to be inconsistent from one measurement to another. Sometimes an individual's obtained score will be higher than it should be and sometimes it will be lower. Although these errors are difficult to control and cannot be predicted with accuracy, an estimate of their influence can be obtained by various statistical procedures. Thus, when we talk about estimating the *reliability* of test scores or the amount of *measurement error* in test scores, we are referring to the influence of random errors.

Reliability refers to the *consistency* of test scores from one measurement to another. Because of the ever present measurement error, we can expect a certain amount of variation in test performance from one time to another, from one sample of items to another, and from one part of the test to another. Reliability measures provide an estimate of how much variation we might expect under different conditions. The reliability of test scores is typically reported by means of a *reliability coefficient* or the **standard error of measurement** that is derived from it. Since both methods of estimating reliability require score variability, the procedures to be discussed are useful primarily with tests designed for norm-referenced interpretation.

As we noted earlier, a correlation coefficient expressing the relationship between a set of test scores and a criterion measure is called a *validity coefficient.* A *reliability coefficient* is also a correlation coefficient, but it indicates the correlation between two sets of measurements taken from the same procedure. We may, for example, administer the same test twice to a group, with a time interval in between (*test-retest* method); administer two equivalent forms of the test in close succession (*equivalent-forms* method); administer two equivalent forms of the test with a time interval in between (*test-retest with equivalent forms* method); or administer the test once and compute the consistency of the response within the test (*internal-consistency* method). Each of these methods of obtaining reliability provides a different type of information. Thus, reliability coefficients obtained with the different procedures are not interchangeable. Before deciding on the procedure to be used, we must determine what type of reliability evidence we are seeking. The four basic methods of estimating reliability and the type of information each provides are shown in Table 11.3.

TABLE 11.3   Methods of Estimating Reliability of Test Scores

METHOD	TYPE OF INFORMATION PROVIDED
Test-retest method	The stability of test scores over a given period of time.
Equivalent-forms method	The consistency of the test scores over different forms of the test (that is, different samples of items).
Test-retest with equivalent forms	The consistency of test scores over *both* a time interval and different forms of the test.
Internal-consistency methods	The consistency of test scores over different parts of the test.

Note: Scorer reliability should also be considered when evaluating the responses to *supply-type* items (for example, essay tests). This is typically done by having the test papers scored independently by two scorers and then correlating the two sets of scores. Agreement among scorers, however, is not a substitute for the methods of estimating reliability shown in the table.

Test-Retest Method

The test-retest method requires administering the same form of the test to the same group after some time interval. The time between the two administrations may be just a few days or several years. The length of the time interval should fit the type of interpretation to be made from the results. Thus, if we are interested in using test scores only to group students for more effective learning, short-term stability may be sufficient. On the other hand, if we are attempting to predict vocational success or make some other long-range predictions, we would desire evidence of stability over a period of years.

Test-retest reliability coefficients are influenced both by errors within the measurement procedure and by the day-to-day stability of the students' responses. Thus, longer time periods between testing will result in lower reliability coefficients, due to the greater changes in the students. In reporting test-retest reliability coefficients, then, it is important to include the time interval. For example, a report might state: "The stability of test scores obtained on the same form over a three-month period was .90." This makes it possible to determine the extent to which the reliability data are significant for a particular interpretation.

Equivalent-Forms Method

With this method, two equivalent forms of a test (also called **alternate forms** or **parallel forms**) are administered to the same group during the same testing session. The test forms are equivalent in the sense that they are built to measure the same abilities (that is, they are built to the same set of specifications), but for determining reliability it is also important that they be constructed independently. When this is the case, the reliability coefficient indicates the adequacy of the test sample. That is, a high reliability coefficient would indicate that the two independent samples are apparently measuring the same thing. A low reliability coefficient, of course, would indicate that the two forms are measuring different behavior and that therefore both samples of items are questionable.

Reliability coefficients determined by this method take into account errors within the measurement procedures and consistency over different samples of items, but they do not include the day-to-day stability of the students' responses.

Test-Retest Method with Equivalent Forms

This is a combination of both methods. Here, two different forms of the same test are administered with time intervening. This is the most demanding estimate of reliability, since it takes into account all possible sources of variation. The reliability coefficient reflects errors within the testing procedure, consistency over different samples of items, and the day-to-day stability of the students' responses. For most purposes, this is probably the most useful type of reliability, since it enables us to estimate how generalizable the test results are over the various conditions. A high reliability coefficient obtained by this method would indicate that a test score represents not only present test performance but also what test performance is likely to be at another time or on a different sample of equivalent items.

Internal-Consistency Methods

These methods require only a single administration of a test. One procedure, the *split-half* method, involves scoring the odd items and the even items separately and correlating the two sets of scores. This correlation coefficient indicates the degree to which the two arbitrarily selected halves of the test provide the same results. Thus, it reports on the internal consistency of the test. Like the equivalent-forms method, this procedure takes into account errors within the testing procedure and consistency over different samples of items, but it omits the day-to-day stability of the students' responses.

Since the correlation coefficient based on the odd and even items indicates the relationship between two halves of the test, the reliability coefficient for the total test is determined by applying the Spearman-Brown prophecy formula. A simplified version of this formula is as follows:

$$\text{Reliability of total test} = \frac{2 \times \text{reliability for } \frac{1}{2} \text{test}}{1 + \text{reliability for } \frac{1}{2} \text{test}}$$

Thus, if we obtained a correlation coefficient of .60 for two halves of a test, the reliability for the total test would be computed as follows:

$$\text{Reliability of total test} = \frac{2 \times .60}{1 + .60} = \frac{1.20}{1.60} = .75$$

This application of the Spearman-Brown formula makes clear a useful principle of test reliability; the reliability of a test can be increased by lengthening it. This formula shows how much reliability will increase when the length of the test is doubled. Application of the formula, however, assumes that the test is lengthened by adding items like those already in the test.

Another internal-consistency method of estimating reliability is by use of the **Kuder-Richardson Formula 20** (KR-20). Kuder and Richardson developed other formulas but this one is probably the most widely used with standardized tests. It requires a single test administration and a determination of the proportion of individuals passing each item, and the standard deviation of the total set of scores. The formula is not especially helpful in understanding how to interpret the scores, but knowing what the coefficient means if important. Basically, the KR-20 is equivalent to an average of all split-half coefficients when the test is split in all possible ways. Where all items in a test are measuring the same thing (e.g., math reasoning), the result should approximate the split-half reliability estimate. Where the test items are measuring a variety of skills or content areas (i.e., less homogeneous), the KR-20 estimate will be lower than the split-half reliability estimate. Thus, the KR-20 method is useful with homogeneous tests but can be misleading if used with a test designed to measure heterogeneous content.

Internal-consistency methods are used because they require that the test be administered only once. They should not be used with speeded tests, however, because a spuriously high reliability estimate will result. If speed is an important factor in the testing (that is, if the students do not have time to attempt all the items), other methods should be used to estimate reliability.

Standard Error of Measurement

The standard error of measurement is an especially useful way of expressing test reliability because it indicates the amount of error to allow for when interpreting individual test scores. The standard error is derived from a reliability coefficient by means of the following formula:

$$\text{Standard error of measurement} = s\sqrt{1 - r_n}$$

where s = the standard deviation and r_n = the reliability coefficient. In applying this formula to a reliability estimate of .60 obtained for a test where $s = 4.5$, the following results would be obtained.

$$\text{Standard error of measurement} = 4.5 \sqrt{1 - .60}$$
$$= 4.5 \sqrt{.40}$$
$$= 4.5 \times .63$$
$$= 2.8$$

The standard-error of measurement shows how many points we must add to, and subtract from, an individual's test score in order to obtain "reasonable limits" for estimating that individual's true score (that is, a score free of error). In our example, the standard error would be rounded to 3 score points. Thus, if a given student scored 35 on this test, that student's *score band,* for establishing reasonable limits, would range from 32 (35 – 3) to 38 (35 + 3). In other words, we could be reasonably sure that the score band of 32 to 38 included the student's true score (statistically, there are two chances out of three that it does). The standard errors of test scores provide a means of allowing for error during test interpretation. If we view test performance in terms of score bands (also called *confidence bands*), we are not likely to over-interpret small differences between test scores.

For the test user, the standard error of measurement is probably more useful than the reliability coefficient. Although reliability coefficients can be used in evaluating the quality of a test and in comparing the relative merits of different tests, the standard error of measurement is directly applicable to the interpretation of individual test scores.

Reliability of Criterion-Referenced Mastery Tests

As noted earlier, the traditional methods for computing reliability require score variability (that is, a spread of scores) and are therefore useful mainly with norm-referenced tests. When used with criterion-referenced tests, they are likely to provide misleading results. Since criterion-referenced tests are not designed to emphasize differences among individuals, they typically have limited score variability. This restricted spread of scores will result in low correlation estimates of reliability, even if the consistency of our test results is adequate for the use to be made of them.

When a criterion-referenced test is used to determine mastery, our primary concern is with how consistently our test classifies masters and non-masters. If we administered two equivalent forms of a test to the same group of students, for example, we would like the results of both forms to identify the same students as having mastered the material. Such perfect agreement is unrealistic, of course, since some students near the cutoff score are likely to shift from one category to the other on the basis of errors of measurement (due to such factors as lucky guesses or lapses of memory). However, if too many students demonstrated mastery on one form but nonmastery on the other, our decisions concerning who mastered the material would be hopelessly confused. Thus, the reliability of mastery tests can be determined by computing the percentage of consistent mastery-nonmastery decisions over the two forms of the test.

The procedure for comparing test performance on two equivalent forms of a test is relatively simple. After both forms have been administered to a group of students, the resulting data can be placed in a two-by-two table like that shown in Figure 11.3. These data are based on two forms of a 25-item test administered to 40 students. Mastery was set at 80 percent correct (20 items), so all students who scored 20 or higher on both forms of the test were placed in the upper right-hand cell (30 students), and all those who scored below 20 on both forms were placed in the lower left-hand cell (6 students). The remaining students demonstrated mastery on one form and nonmastery on the other (4 students). Since 36 of the 40 students were consistently classified by the two forms of the test, we apparently have reasonably good consistency.

We can compute the percentage of consistency for this procedure with the following formula:

$$\% \text{ Consistency } = \frac{\text{Masters (both forms)} + \text{Nonmaster (both forms)}}{\text{Total number in group}} \times 100$$

$$\% \text{ Consistency } = \frac{30 + 6}{40} \times 100 = 90\%$$

This procedure is simple to use but it has a few limitations. First, two forms of the test are required. This may not be as serious as it seems, however, since in most mastery programs more than one form of the test is needed for retesting those students who fail to demonstrate mastery on the first try. Second, it is difficult to determine what percentage of decision consistency is necessary for a given situation. As with other measures of reliability, the greater the consistency, the more satisfied we will be, but what constitutes a mini-

FORM B

	NONMASTERS	MASTERS
FORM A MASTERS	2	30
FORM A NONMASTERS	6	2

FIGURE 11.3   Classification of 40 Students as Masters or Nonmasters on Two Forms of a Criterion-Referenced Test

---

Factors that Lower the Reliability of Test Scores

1. Test scores are based on too few items. (*Remedy:* Use longer tests or accumulate scores from several short tests.)
2. Range of scores is too limited. (*Remedy:* Adjust item difficulty to obtain larger spread of scores.)
3. Testing conditions are inadequate. (*Remedy:* Arrange opportune time for administration and eliminate interruptions, noise, and other disrupting factors.)
4. Scoring is subjective. (*Remedy:* Prepare scoring keys and follow carefully when scoring essay answers.)

---

mum acceptable level? There is no simple answer to such a question because it depends on the number of items in the test and the consequences of the decision. If a nonmastery decision for a student simply means further study and later retesting, low consistency might be acceptable. However, if the mastery-nonmastery decision concerns whether to give a student a high school certificate, as in some competency testing programs, then a high level of consistency will be demanded. Since there are no clear guidelines for setting minimum levels, we will need to depend on experience in various situations to determine what are reasonable expectations.

More sophisticated techniques have been developed for estimating the reliability of criterion-referenced tests, but the numerous issues and problems involved in their use go beyond the scope of this book. For detailed discussions of these developments, see Berk (1984).

ESTIMATING THE RELIABILITY OF PERFORMANCE ASSESSMENTS

Performance assessments are commonly evaluated by using scoring rubrics that describe a number of levels of performance, ranging from high to low (e.g., outstanding to inadequate). The performance for each student is then judged and placed in the category that best fits the quality of the performance. The reliability of these performance judgments can be determined by obtaining and comparing the scores of two judges who scored the performances independently. The scores of the two judges can be correlated to determine the consistency of the scoring, or the proportion of agreement in scoring can be computed.

Let's assume that a performance task, such as writing sample, was obtained from 32 students and two teachers independently rated the students' performance on a four-point scale where 4 is high and 1 is low. The results of the ratings by the two judges are shown in Table 11.4. The ratings for Judge 1 are presented in the columns and those for Judge 2 are presented in the rows. Thus, Judge 1 assigned a score of 4 to seven students and Judge 2 assigned a score of 4 to eight students. Their ratings agreed on six of the students and disagreed by one score on three of the students. The number of rating agreements can be seen in the boxes on the diagonal from the upper right hand corner to the lower left hand corner. The percentage of agreement can be computed by adding the numbers in these diagonal boxes (6 + 7 + 6 + 5 = 24), dividing by the total number of students in the group (32), and multiplying by 100.

$$\text{Rater agreement} = \frac{24}{32} \times 100 = 75\%$$

By inspection, we can see that all ratings were within one score of each other. The results also indicate that Judge 2 was a more lenient rater than Judge 1 (i.e., gave more high ratings and fewer low ratings). Thus, a table of this nature can be used to determine the consistency of ratings and the extent to which leniency can account for the disagreements.

Although the need for two raters will limit the use of this method, it seems reasonable to expect two teachers in the same area to make periodic checks on the scoring of performance assessments. This will not only provide information on the consistency of the scoring, but will provide the teachers with insight into some of their rating idiosyncrasies.

TABLE 11.4   Classification of Students Based on Performance Ratings by Two Independent Judges

		RATINGS BY JUDGE 1				
	SCORES	1	2	3	4	ROW TOTALS
	4			2	6	8
Ratings by Judge 2	3		3	7	1	11
	2	2	6			8
	1	5				5
COLUMN TOTALS		7	9	9	7	32

Factors that Lower the Reliability of Performance Assessments

1. Insufficient number of tasks. (*Remedy:* Accumulate results from several assessments. For example, several writing samples.)
2. Poorly structured assessment procedures. (*Remedy:* Define carefully the nature of the tasks, the conditions for obtaining the assessment, and the criteria for scoring or judging the results.)
3. Dimensions of performance are specific to the tasks. (*Remedy:* Increase generalizability of performance by selecting tasks that have dimensions like those in similar tasks.)
4. Inadequate scoring guides for judgmental scoring. (*Remedy:* Use scoring rubrics or rating scales that specifically describe the criteria and levels of quality.)
5. Scoring judgments that are influenced by personal bias. (*Remedy:* Check scores or ratings with those of an independent judge. Receive training in judging and rating, if possible.)

The percentage of agreement between the scores assigned by independent judges is a common method of estimating the reliability of performance assessments. It should be noted, however, that this reports on only one type of consistency—*the consistency of the scoring.* It does not indicate the consistency of performance over similar tasks or over different time periods. We can obtain a crude measure of this by examining the performance of students over tasks and time, but a more adequate analysis requires an understanding of **generalizability** theory, which is too technical for treatment here (see Cronbach, 1990).

SUMMARY OF POINTS

1. Validity is the most important quality to consider in assessment and is concerned with the appropriateness, meaningfulness, and usefulness of the specific inferences made from assessment results.
2. Validity is a *unitary concept* based on various forms of evidence (content-related, criterion-related, construct-related and consequences).
3. Content-related evidence of validity refers to how well the sample of tasks represents the domain of tasks to be assessed.
4. Content-related evidence of validity is of major concern in achievement assessment and is "built-in" by following systematic procedures. Validity is lowered by inadequate assessment practices.
5. Criterion-related evidence of validity refers to the degree to which assessment results are related to some other valued measure called a *criterion.*

6. Criterion-related evidence may be based on a predictive study or a concurrent study and is typically expressed by a correlation coefficient or expectancy table.
7. Construct-related evidence of validity refers to how well performance on assessment tasks can be explained in terms of psychological characteristics, or constructs (e.g., mathematical reasoning).
8. The construct-related category of evidence is the most comprehensive. It includes evidence from both content-related and criterion-related studies plus other types of evidence that help clarify the meaning of the assessment results.
9. Consequences of using the assessment is also an important consideration in validity—both positive and negative consequences.
10. Reliability refers to the consistency of scores (i.e., to the degree to which the scores are free from measurement error).
11. Reliability of test scores is typically reported by means of a reliability coefficient or a standard error of measurement.
12. Reliability coefficients can be obtained by a number of different methods (e.g., test-retest, equivalent-forms, internal-consistency) and each one measures a different type of consistency (e.g., over time, over different samples of items, over different parts of the test).
13. Reliability of test scores tends to be lower when the test is short, range of scores is limited, testing conditions are inadequate, and scoring is subjective.
14. The standard error of measurement indicates the amount of error to allow for when interpreting individual test scores.
15. Score bands (or *confidence bands*) take into account the error of measurement and help prevent the over interpretation of small differences between test scores.
16. The reliability of criterion-referenced mastery tests can be obtained by computing the percentage of agreement between two forms of the test in classifying individuals as masters and nonmasters.
17. The reliability of performance-based assessments are commonly determined by the degree of agreement between two or more judges who rate the performance independently.

ADDITIONAL READING

American Psychological Association, *Standards for Educational and Psychological Testing* (Washington, DC: APA, 1985). See the sections on validity (pages 9–18) and reliability (pages 19–23) for descriptions of the concepts and sets of standards. A new edition of *Standards* is scheduled for the late 1990s.

Berk, R. A., ed. *A Guide to Criterion-Referenced Test Construction* (Baltimore, MD: Johns Hopkins University Press, 1984). See Chapter 8 by R. K. Hambleton, "Validating the Test Scores" and Chapter 9 by R. A. Berk, "Selecting the Index of Reliability," for reviews of methods used with criterion-referenced tests.

Cronbach, L. J., *Essentials of Psychological Testing*, 5th ed. (New York: Harper & Row, 1990). Chapters 5 and 6. Describes and illustrates the procedures for determining the validity and reliability of test scores, at a somewhat advanced level.

Ebel, R. L., and Frisbee, D. A., *Essentials of Educational Measurement*, 5th ed. (Englewood Cliffs, NJ: Prentice-Hall, 1991). See Chapter 5, "The Reliability of Test Scores," and Chapter 6, "Validity: Interpretation and Use," for descriptions of the concepts, the methods of determining, and the factors influencing them.

Linn, R. L., and Gronlund, N. E., *Measurement and Assessment in Teaching*, 7th ed. (Englewood Cliffs, NJ: Prentice-Hall, 1995). Chapters 3 and 4. The procedures for determining validity and reliability are described and illustrated, with emphasis on educational assessment. Descriptions of the factors influencing validity and reliability provide guides for the preparation and use of assessment procedures.

Macmillan, J. H., *Classroom Assessment*, (Boston: Allyn & Bacon, 1997). See Chapter 3, "Establishing High-Quality Classroom Assessments," for a brief description of validity and reliability and the other factors to consider when planning classroom assessments.

▶ Glossary

This glossary of assessment terms focuses primarily on the terms used in this book.

Achievement Assessment A procedure that is used to determine the degree to which individuals have achieved the intended learning outcomes of instruction. It includes both paper-and-pencil tests and performance assessments, plus judgments concerning learning progress.

Achievement Test An instrument that typically uses sets of items designed to measure a domain of learning tasks and is administered under specified conditions (e.g., time limits, open or closed book).

Adaptive Testing A procedure whereby the sequence of items presented to each individual is determined by the responses to previous items. A computer is typically used to present the items.

Alternate Forms Two or more forms of a test or assessment that are designed to measure the same abilities (also called equivalent or parallel forms).

Alternative Assessment An assessment procedure that provides an alternative to paper-and-pencil testing.

Analytic Scoring The assignment of scores to individual components of a performance or product (e.g., Evaluate a writing sample by using separate scores for organization, style, mechanics, etc.).

Anecdotal Record A brief description of some significant student behavior, the setting in which it occurred, and an interpretation of its meaning.

Authentic Assessment An assessment procedure that emphasizes the use of tasks and contextual settings like those in the "real world."

Battery of Tests Two or more tests standardized on the same sample of students, so that performance on the different tests can be compared using a common norm group.

Checklist A list of dimensions of a performance or product that is simply checked present or absent.

Correlation Coefficient A statistic indicating the degree of relationship between two sets of test scores or other measures.

Criteria A set of qualities used in judging a performance, a product, or an assessment instrument.

Criterion-Referenced Interpretation   A description of an individual's performance in terms of the tasks he can and cannot perform.

Derived Score   A score that results from converting a raw score to a different score scale (e.g., percentile rank, standard score).

Difficulty Index   Percentage of individuals who obtain the correct answer on a test item or task.

Discrimination Index   The degree to which a test item or task discriminates between high and low scorers on the total test.

Expectancy Table   A two fold chart that shows the relationship between two sets of scores. It can be used to predict the chances of success on one measure (the criterion) for any given score on the other measure (the predictor), and it can be used for obtaining criterion-related evidence of validity.

Generalizability   The extent to which an assessment procedure provides comparable results over different samples of similar tasks, different settings, and different administrations.

Grade Equivalent Score   A derived score that indicates the grade level at which an individual's score matches the average score (e.g., a grade equivalent score of 4.5 indicates the raw score matches the average score of students in the middle of the fourth grade).

Holistic Scoring   The assignment of a score based on an overall impression of a performance or product rather than a consideration of individual elements. The overall judgment is typically guided by descriptions of the various levels of performance or scoring rubrics.

Item Analysis   Traditionally, a method for determining the difficulty and discriminating power of test items. It can also be used to determine the responsiveness of test items to instructional effects.

Kuder-Richardson Formula 20 (KR-20)   A method for estimating reliability based on the internal consistency of a test (i.e., on the extent to which the test items correlate with each other).

Mastery Test   An assessment method used to determine whether an individual has met some predetermined level of performance.

Mean   The arithmetic average that is determined by adding together a set of scores and dividing by the number of scores.

Measurement   A process of obtaining quantitative descriptions of an individual's characteristics or performance (e.g., test scores, numerical ratings of performance).

Median   A counting average that divided a distribution of scores into two equal halves by counting up to the midpoint (the 50th percentile).

Mode   The score that occurs most frequently in a distribution of scores.

Norm-Referenced Interpretation   A description of an individual's performance in terms of how it compares to the performance of others (typically those in a norm group).

Normal Curve   A symmetrical bell-shaped curve based on a precise mathematical equation. It is widely used in interpreting standardized test scores because of its fixed mathematical properties (e.g., when standard deviations are plotted along the baseline of the curve, each portion of the curve contains a fixed percentage of scores).

Normal-Curve Equivalent Score   A normalized standard score that ranges from 1 to 99 with a mean of 50. It is used for reporting performance on standardized achievement tests.

Norms   Data that describe the performance of individuals in some reference group (e.g., national norms, local norms). Norms represent average or typical performance and are not to be interpreted as standards.

Objective Test   A test that can be consistently scored by equally competent scorers (i.e., they obtain the same scores). This contrasts with subjective tests where the scores are influenced by scorer judgment (e.g., essay tests).

Percentage-Correct Score   The percentage of items that an individual answers correctly on a test, or the percentage of tasks an individual performs correctly on a performance assessment.

Percentile Band   A range of percentile ranks that sets reasonable limits within which an individual's true score is likely to fall. It takes into account the inconsistency of obtained scores due to errors of measurement. (Also called an *error* band or *confidence* band.)

Percentile Rank   The percentage of individuals in a group scoring at or below a given score. Not to be confused with the percentage-correct score.

Performance Assessment   A procedure that requires individuals to perform tasks and the process or product of the performance is judged using prespecified criteria.

Portfolio Assessment   A preplanned collection of samples of student work, assessment results, and other data that represent the student's accomplishments. It is viewed by some as a basic type of performance assessment and by others as merely a convenient method for accumulating evidence of student performance.

Range   The difference between the highest score and the lowest score in a distribution of scores.

Rating Scale   A systematic procedure for guiding and recording judgments concerning the degree to which the characteristics of a performance or behavior are present.

Raw Score   The score that is obtained when first scoring a test or performance task (also called an obtained score). The raw score is frequently converted to some type of derived score for interpretation (e.g., percentile rank or standard scores).

Reliability   The degree to which assessment results are consistent from one measurement (or assessment) to another. Reliability estimates typically indicate the consistency of scores or judgments over different forms, different time periods, different parts of the instrument, or different raters. High reliability indicates greater freedom from error.

Scoring Rubric   A set of scoring guidelines that describe the characteristics of the different levels of performance used in scoring or judging a performance.

Standard   A prespecified level of performance that is considered satisfactory for the use to be made of the assessment results (e.g., minimum standards, mastery standards).

Standard Error of Measurement   A method of expressing reliability that estimates the amount of error in test scores. It is the standard deviation of the errors of measurement and is used to compute the error bands (e.g., percentile bands) used in interpreting test scores.

Standard Score   A term used to describe a variety of derived scores that convert raw scores to a standard scale for a more useful interpretation of test results.

Standardized Test   A test constructed to fit detailed specifications, administered under prescribed conditions to selected groups, and scored using definite rules of scoring. Published standardized tests typically include a test manual that contains rules for administration and scoring, norms for interpretation, and validity and reliability data.

Stanine   A standard score that ranges from 1 to 9 with a mean of 5. Each stanine is one half of a standard deviation wide, except 1 and 9 at the ends of the distribution.

T-Score   A standard score with a mean of 50 and standard deviation of 10.

Table of Specifications   A two-way chart that specifies the number or proportion of test items (or assessment tasks) to be designed for each area of content and each type of intended learning outcome when planning a test (or other assessment procedure).

Validity   The extent to which inferences made from assessment results are appropriate, meaningful, and useful in terms of the purpose for the assessment. Validity is a unitary concept that depends on a variety of types of evidence, is expressed by degree (high, low), and refers to the inferences drawn (not the instrument itself).

▶ Index